Tolkien, Philosopher of War

Tolkien, Philosopher of War

Graham James McAleer

The Catholic University of America Press
Washington, D.C.

The paper used in this publication meets the minimum requirements
of American National Standards for Information Science—
Permanence of Paper for Printed Library materials,
ANSI Z39.48-1992.
ISBN 978-0-8132-3866-1 (paperback)
ISBN 978-0-8132-3867-8 (ebook)

Cataloging-in-Publication Data is available from the Library of Congress

Book design by Burt&Burt
Interio typeset in Adobe Jenson Pro and La Parisienne Serif

Dedicated to my wife
Emily Louise McAleer

AND

Our constant companions,
Wally and Ellie

Contents

Abbreviations

CP   *The Concept of the Political* (Carl Schmitt)

PR   *Political Romanticism* (Carl Schmitt)

The Tolkien editions used are Houghton Mifflin unless otherwise stated.

References to the Peter Jackson film versions of Tolkien are marked by a *, e.g., *FR* * 22 points to scene 22 on the scene selection panel of the DVD. *H2* * 12 points to the second *Hobbit* film scene 12.

Preface

This is a tale about a war" (*Letters*, 197 #154), writes Tolkien of *The Lord of the Rings*. At the close of the tale, Frodo's chief anxiety is the possibility of civil war amongst the Hobbits (*Letters*, 255 #195). Returning from the War of the Ring (FR, 14), Frodo, says Tolkien, believes that war is far less effective than most "good men" think. Tolkien's own belief is rather different.[1] It is more metaphysical. Reflecting on Frodo's thinking, Tolkien says: "Actually I am a Christian, and indeed a Roman Catholic, so that I do not expect 'history' to be anything but a 'long defeat'—though it contains (and in a legend may contain more clearly and movingly) some samples or glimpses of final victory" (*Letters*, 255 #195). Tolkien's philosophy of history is a major part of this book. What is history about? Frodo thinks war a matter of utility, that it is to be judged on whether it delivers pragmatic goals. Tolkien thinks history a matter of vanity. Worldly endeavors end in defeat, and it is vanity to think otherwise. *LotR* depicts "a brief episode in History" (*Letters*, 412 #328) and Galadriel explains to Frodo the full implications of the

---

1 Making a survey of early commentary on *LotR*, Janet Croft observes that most commentators believed that Frodo represented Tolkien's own views about war. This led them to propose that *LotR* had a pacifist cast. As she rightly points out, Frodo's experience of the war is only one of many, and Tolkien's work offers a "chorus of voices on war" (Janet Croft, *War and the Works of J. R. R. Tolkien* [New York: Praeger, 2004], 6–8).

war: "Yet if you succeed, then our power is diminished, and Loth-lórien will fade, and the tides of Time will sweep it away" (FR, 356).

Tolkien, Philosopher of War contends that Tolkien thought civilization and war matters of aesthetics, that vanity provokes war and that what strives against vanity, in the very prosecution of war, is a better accounting of beauty. Part of Aquinas's definition of vanity runs: "Now clarity and comeliness imply a certain display: wherefore the word *glory* properly denotes the display of something as regards its seeming comely in the sight of men, whether it be a bodily or a spiritual good" (ST II-II, q. 132, a. 1). Galadriel warns Frodo about the Ring: "The evil that was devised long ago works on in many ways, whether Sauron himself stands or falls." She ponders what would happen should she take the Ring: "'And now at last it comes. You will give me the Ring freely! In place of the Dark Lord you will set up a Queen. And I shall not be dark, but beautiful and terrible as the Morning and the Night.... All shall love me and despair!'" (FR, 356). Adorned with the Ring, why would her worshippers despair? Adding to his definition, Aquinas explains that vanity has a twin structure: it is a vaunting of the self and/or a belittling of others (De malo, q. 9, a. 3). The Ring makes its wearer false and malign, someone who undermines the standing of others. *Tolkien, Philosopher of War* is an inquiry into this undermining of persons and Tolkien's account of a martial beauty able to arrest the subversion. For Tolkien, vanity is a privileged lens through which to look at history.

At stake in "the history of the War of the Ring" is the survival of the West (*Letters*, 179 #144). What did Tolkien think about *our* West and its history? Specifically, what did he think about it as a Catholic? We will begin with a pope and then a Catholic historian whom Tolkien read.

Amongst recent popes, it is Benedict XVI who has thought most about the West. He observes that the founders of the EU—the Christians Adenauer, de Gaulle, and de Gaspari—assumed continuity, that "the great moral impulses of the Enlightenment" seamlessly arose from Europe's Christian heritage. Somewhat agreeing,[2] Benedict nonetheless hesitates, believing that "questions were left open that still await a proper examination."[3] The hesitation stems from the worry that there were two quite different Enlightenments. From Descartes to Leibniz, and even to Adam Smith in the 18th century, philosophy and science engaged with orthodox theology, but this is not true of what Benedict calls the *second* Enlightenment. A discontinuity creeps into the long fermentation of humanism in the West.[4] Nineteenth-century revolutionary thinkers, like Comte and Marx, propounded secular solutions where "man as a product is subject to the control of man."[5] Though the connection between the first and second Enlightenments is what Benedict thinks obscure, the goals of the latter are crystal clear. The tool of the second Enlightenment is technoscience and its humanitarian hope is to make suffering disappear.[6] Famed Italian anarchist Giorgio Agamben agrees with Benedict.[7] The second Enlightenment is a Gnosticism: "at the heart of the redemptive process lies, not the suffering and death of Christ, not the crucifixion, but the 'message concerning the holy path,' the teaching. The illumination comes, not through pain, but through the communication of knowledge."[8] It comes with variations, but the idea of two Enlightenments is an old one in Catholic letters.

Writing in the 1920s, the prominent English Catholic historian Christopher Dawson argued that in England, "the visionary millenarist ideas of the earlier period had been transformed into a rational

---

2 The Enlightenment "contains important values that are essential for us, precisely as Christians, and we do not wish to do without them" (Joseph Ratzinger, *Christianity and the Crisis of Cultures* [San Francisco: Ignatius, 2006], 35, 39).

3 Joseph Ratzinger, *Values in a Time of Upheaval* (New York: Crossroad, 2006), 152.

4 For this history, please see McAleer & Rosenthal, *The Wisdom of Our Ancestors: Conservative Humanism and the Western Tradition* (Notre Dame, IN: University of Notre Dame Press, 2023).

5 Ratzinger, *Values in a Time of Upheaval*, 156–57. Cf. J. Ratzinger, *Christianity and the Crisis of Cultures*, 26–28.

6 "Learning to live also means learning to suffer. This is why reverence for that which is holy is also essential" (*Values in a Time of Upheaval*, 159).

7 Giorgio Agamben, *The Mystery of Evil: Benedict XVI and the End of Days* (Stanford, CA: Stanford University Press, 2017), 15–17.

8 Joseph Ratzinger, *Truth and Tolerance* (San Francisco: Ignatius, 2003), 89. Benedict relies on the definition of Gnosticism given by Hugo Ball. I will be using Voegelin's.

enthusiasm for moral and material progress. Even the economic doctrines of Adam Smith rest on a foundation of religious optimism, which remained a characteristic feature of later British Liberalism."[9] In his 1929 *Progress and Religion*, Dawson isolates two strains in the Enlightenment, one relying on religious optimism and another branch channeling millenarianism:

> The older philosophic theory of Progress, with its dogmatic appeal to Reason, and its reliance on the authority of an enlightened despotism, corresponds to the Christian tradition in its orthodox form, while the doctrine of the revolutionary idealists has even closer affinity with the apocalyptic hopes of the earlier Millenarists and Anabaptists. Indeed it is often difficult to distinguish the descriptions of the social millennium of the revolutionaries from those of a purely religious apocalyptic.[10]

Liberal modernism, Dawson argues, has been a productive *via media* between medieval traditionalism and revolutionary apocalypticism of Left and Right varieties.[11] However, Liberalism is unstable. Though political rights have flourished under bourgeois Progressivism, those gains are vulnerable. Material progress depends on business but "economically [the ordinary worker] lost the control that the craftsman possessed under the old system of hand industry over the conditions of his work, and became a mere cog in the vast machinery of modern industrialism."[12] The division of labor[13] requires ever greater bureaucratic management (Fascism)[14] and its damage to persons

---

9 Christopher Dawson, *Progress and Religion* (London: Sheed & Ward, 1936), 192.

10 Dawson, *Progress and Religion*, 197.

11 Dawson, 203.

12 Dawson, 208.

13 "Manufactures, accordingly, prosper most, where the mind is least consulted, and where the workshop may, without any great effort of imagination, be considered as an engine, the parts of which are men" (Adam Ferguson, *An Essay on the History of Civil Society* [Cambridge: Cambridge University Press, 1995], 174).

14 Ajay Chaudhary & Raphaële Chappe, "The Supermanagerial Reich," Los Angeles Review of Books, November 7, 2016, https://lareviewofbooks.org/article/the-supermanagerial-reich/.

stokes the militancy of trade unions (Bolshevism).[15] The problem is not only economic, but religious, too. Dawson argues that the skepticism inherent in tolerant and bourgeois Liberalism weakened establishment religion, leaving the undernourished religious impulse to mutate into apocalypticism in Left and Right party politics:[16] "The driving force of the Socialist movement, in fact, has always been its belief in a social apocalypse."[17]

Tolkien—the most influential Catholic writer of the modern age[18]—read *Progress and Religion* and quoted Dawson in drafts of *On Fairy-stories*, a lecture Tolkien gave at St. Andrew's in 1939 (*The Hobbit* had appeared in 1937).[19] Noticeable is the lack of a discussion of war in *Progress and Religion*. The argument of Europe's leading Catholic philosopher in the period, Max Scheler, that WW1 was a bourgeois war did not register with Dawson.[20] I will argue that Tolkien took note. Rightly, Philip Mitchell contends that Tolkien did not share Dawson's calibrated confidence in British Liberalism. He points to a poem Tolkien wrote in late 1931:[21]

I will not walk with your progressive apes,
erect and sapient. Before them gapes
the dark abyss to which their progress tends
if by God's mercy progress ever ends.[22]

15 Dawson, *Progress and Religion*, 216. Cf. ISI Archive, "The Lecture: 'Conservatism,' by Christopher Dawson," Part I.2, Intercollegiate Studies Institute, https://isi.org/intercollegiate-review/christopher-dawson-on-conservatism-1932/.

16 Dawson, 218–19, 228–29.

17 Dawson, 198.

18 Wars are now fought using his lexicon: https://unherd.com/2022/09/why-russia-rewrote-lord-of-the-rings/?.

19 For Tolkien's considerable use of Dawson, see the index of the critical edition, J. R. R. Tolkien, *Tolkien on Fairy Stories*, ed. Verlyn Flieger & Douglas Anderson (New York: HarperCollins, 2008).

20 In his 1937 "Essay on War," Dawson cautiously favors the argument that commercial societies are the most peaceable: https://www.catholicculture.org/culture/library/view.cfm?recnum=6369.

21 Philip Irving Mitchell, "'Legend and History Have Met and Fused': The Interlocution of Anthropology, Historiography, and Incarnation in J. R. R. Tolkien's 'On Fairy-stories,'" *Tolkien Studies* 8 (2011): 6.

22 J. R. R. Tolkien, "Philomythus to Misomythus," Mythopoeia, http://vrici.lojban.org/~cowan/mythopoeia.html. This image is very like Pascal, *Pensées* (New York: Penguin, 1995), 59 #199.

An orphan, Tolkien describes his guardian, the Oratorian Francis Xavier Morgan, as "an upper-class Welsh-Spaniard Tory," and: "I first learned charity and forgiveness from him; and in the light of it pierced even the 'liberal' darkness out of which I came, knowing more about 'Bloody Mary' than the Mother of Jesus—who was never mentioned except as an object of wicked worship by the Romanists" (*Letters*, 354 #267).

In popular imagination, Tolkien is a Luddite,[23] but recent scholarship has identified Tolkien's extensive modern sympathies. *Tolkien, Philosopher of War* contributes to this growing literature. Rather than casting Tolkien as a throwback to the Middle Ages, it is better to think of him as an ancestral thinker, embracing ancient, medieval, and modern legacies worthy of affirmation.[24] We find in Tolkien, I propose, a *modern* critique of Enlightenment thinking, specifically those philosophies of history that wrest the initiative from God in divinizing man. His worry is apocalyptic politics, those political movements that take Christ's *Be ye therefore perfect, even as your Father which is in heaven is perfect* (Matt. 5:48) out of the realm of grace and make it a platform for political action. *Tolkien, Philosopher of War* has three core theses: metaphysical, political, and aesthetic. Linking them is the problem of vanity, the animating principle of Dawson's British Liberalism. Put differently, Tolkien had little confidence that the two branches of the Enlightenment identified by Dawson are significantly different. Like Benedict, he worried that the West had lurched towards Gnosticism.

John Garth begins his biographical study, *Tolkien and the Great War*, with a "single observation" in mind: how strange it is that Tolkien wrote a mythology amidst "the crisis of disenchantment" that

---

23 About Tolkien, Ralph Wood declares, "he was a confessed Luddite" (Ralph Wood, "Tolkien and Postmodernism," *Tolkien among the Moderns*, ed. Ralph C. Wood [Notre Dame, IN: University of Notre Dame Press, 2015], 247). Cf. Meredith Veldman, *Fantasy, the Bomb, and the Greening of Britain: Romantic Protest, 1945–1980* (Cambridge: Cambridge University Press, 1994), 89.

24 For the idea of ancestral thinking, please see McAleer & Rosenthal, *The Wisdom of Our Ancestors*, and especially the discussion of Tolkien in Chapter 3.

swept Europe after WW1.[25] This is not quite right. There was no disenchantment—that is the wrong way to think about modernity.[26] Tolkien's myth squares off against the *other myth* gripping Western consciousness: its fascination with Gnostic apocalypticism.[27] It is striking that in 1951—the same year as Tolkien's important letter to the publisher Milton Waldman explaining the core themes of *LotR*—Albert Camus published *The Rebel*, with the same diagnosis of the West as Tolkien.[28]

Garth's starting point is repeated in Janet Croft's *War and the Works of J. R. R. Tolkien.*[29] Her literary study builds on Paul Fussell's classic, *The Great War and Modern Memory.* Fussell argued that Robert Graves's *Goodbye to All That* was typical of the ironizing of WW1 writers, who turned their backs on the false promise of an unworthy established order.[30] Those who did not turn to irony but kept faith with the military enchantments of the Victorian and Edwardian ages—an English thoughtscape of knights in green and pleasant lands—did so as a "cope" in order to master trauma. Croft finds this in Tolkien. "Tolkien's distaste for contemporary war can also be traced to his understanding of the causes and agonies of modern war neuroses." Modern technology generated "Tolkien's dislike of all modern war and preference for earlier models of military conflict."[31] This is not quite right. Like David Jones, Tolkien observed continuity in a soldier's experience between the Middle Ages and

---

25 John Garth, *Tolkien and the Great War: The Threshold of Middle-earth* (Boston: Houghton Mifflin, 2003), xiii, and especially his Postscript.

26 Jason Josephson-Storm, *The Myth of Disenchantment* (Chicago: University of Chicago Press, 2017). Even during the early Enlightenment, generals developed battle plans having consulted astrologers (Anders Engberg-Pedersen, *Martial Aesthetics: How War Became an Art Form* [Stanford, CA: Stanford University Press, 2023], 23–27).

27 Should someone ask: But what about all the post-WW1 disenchantment literature: surely, literary critics cannot be wrong in their assessment of its profusion? No, not at all. As Schmitt points out, such a profusion is completely predictable since all politics aims at the polemical subversion of its opponent (*CP*, 74–76). The Gnostic myth polemically generates an ironizing of the pillars of the old, to-be-dethroned *cosmion* (Voegelin).

28 Please see my discussion of Camus's *The Rebel* ("Camus and the Crisis of the West," Law & Liberty, August 18, 2023, https://lawliberty.org/camus-and-the-crisis-of-the-west/).

29 Croft, *War and the Works of J. R. R. Tolkien*, 14.

30 Garth, *Tolkien and the Great War,* 288.

31 Croft, *War and the Works of J. R. R. Tolkien,* 29, 145–46.

WW1. At stake in modern war is not psychology but metaphysics, the problem of absolute war.

Tolkien seeks to restrain the myth of total war—what Clausewitz calls *absolute war,* when "the God of War himself" visits.[32] Reviewing history, Clausewitz argues that wars in the Middle Ages were micro events, but Napoleon inaugurated absolute war, the total deployment of a nation in combat. In Tolkien's metaphysical hands, absolute war is apocalyptic war brought on by the desire to escape the cosmos. Tolkien proposes that only a myth within a cosmos (Middle-earth!) has the depth of measure and order to restrain "the God of War himself."

It is not right to think of Tolkien's work as escapism.[33] As he says repeatedly, fairy stories have their setting in the cosmos. During WW2, Tolkien served in civil defense and, moaning about going to the victory parade at the end of the war, he corrected himself:

> There is a stand-down parade of Civil Defence in the Parks in the afternoon, to which I shall prob. have to drag myself. But I am afraid it all seems rather a mockery to me, for the War is not over (and the one that is, or the part of it, has largely been lost). But it is of course wrong to fall into such a mood, for Wars are always lost, and The War always goes on; and it is no good growing faint! (*Letters,* 115–16 #101)[34]

What is "the War" that is not yet finished at the close of WW2? Tolkien will not wobble in his resistance to that war, but what is it, exactly? *Tolkien, Philosopher of War* proposes that it is absolute war, a propulsive myth, the Gnostic assault on humans set in a cosmos. It is what Albert Camus called the war of convulsion.

---

32 Carl von Clausewitz, *On War,* ed. Michael Howard & Peter Paret (Princeton, NJ: Princeton University Press, 1984), 583.

33 A common "take" on Tolkien, for example, Veldman, *Fantasy, the Bomb, and the Greening of Britain: Romantic Protest, 1945–1980,* 114.

34 Note that Tolkien uses the idiom of stand-to and stand-down, which David Jones claims was a liturgical moment across the entire Western Front, performed by both sides, at dawn and dusk in anticipation of battle (David Jones, *In Parenthesis* [New York: New York Review Books, 2003], n. 3, 202).

Pace Dawson, Tolkien took note of a tight analytical connection between the vanity driving commercial civilization—which Hume, Smith, and Ferguson all identified—and the vanity driving the Promethean fantasies of apocalyptic politics. War—absolute war—is a predictable outcome of this analytical connection.[35]

The three theses of *Tolkien, Philosopher of War* run: 1) metaphysical: the apocalyptic anxiety of Tolkien's lore is traceable to the Gnostic rejection of the analogy of being, a rejection typical of the philosophies of history that dominated his day; 2) political: in the English context, Tolkien sided with the Tories against Whiggery,[36] defending monarchy as a counterweight to the vanity driving a progressive philosophy of history;[37] 3) aesthetic: Futurism's philosophy of history celebrated the Machine; inverting the value order, the Futurism art movement encoded anti-Christianity, fascist politics, and apocalyptic war.[38] Tolkien's "cosmogonical drama," with its pastoralism and portraits of angels (Gandalf) and gods (Nienna), depicts an aesthetic resistance to Futurism.

Tolkien does not subscribe to Dawson's two Enlightenments theory, therefore. In the pages below, I show that *LotR* is a dissent from who you and I are. We might huff and we might puff about our cultural condition, but it remains true that we are the creatures of a revolution in thought and sensibility crafted by the great eighteenth-century philosophers David Hume and Adam Smith. Of course, they were not alone, but it was especially these two Scottish Whigs who explained the benefits of a commercial civilization. Put briefly, these Whigs argued that trade and industry are better than knights and priests; that the former replacing the latter would enable

---

35 The post-liberal Carl Schmitt linked vanity, commerce, apocalypticism, and total war in his 1942 *Land and Sea* (Candor, NY: Telos, 2015).

36 Cf. Veldman, *Fantasy, the Bomb, and the Greening of Britain*, 92.

37 Though not attracted to the socialism of William Morris, Tolkien read Morris extensively, shared his sensibility in art, and his skepticism of Whiggery. Cf. Raymond Williams, *Culture and Society: 1780–1950* (New York: Columbia University Press, 1983), 148–49.

38 Emilio Gentile, *The Origins of Fascist Ideology, 1918–1925* (New York: Enigma Books, 2005), 86–87.

us to live longer, in better conditions, and so make us happier.[39] They thought that vanity—an attraction to refined complex systems—drives commerce.[40] Every time you graze your hand across your iPad, even if it is to find your HBO app to watch *Game of Thrones*, you concede the Whig point. Condensing a complicated history to make a point vivid, what Dawson perhaps did not see clearly, but which Tolkien did, is that you do not get Marx's apocalyptic politics without Adam Smith. Put differently, Tolkien is post-liberal and defends monarchy as a control on the convulsive vanity of modern mass politics.

Tolkien is a philosopher of war because he saw clearly that ours is an aesthetic problem. *Tolkien, Philosopher of War* explores Tolkien's challenging thesis that aesthetics is the origin of war. The discovery and conquering of the enchanted Elf city of Gondolin is triggered when the brothers, Húrin and Huor—favorites of the Elf King Thingol—appear back amongst their own people (the race of men) unaccountably in "fine raiment" (*S*, 159). Tolkien's thesis has a lineage, and he was not alone in his day in holding it. The idea is basic to Plato (*Republic*, Book 2, 372c–373e), Smith,[41] Ferguson,[42] Hegel,[43] and the contemporary war theorist Engberg-Pedersen links war and poetics, putting it in the register of the map and "techno-aesthetics."[44] Here is von Clausewitz: "Let us consider the campaign that Frederick the Great fought in 1760, famous for its dazzling marches and maneuvers, praised by critics as a work of art—indeed a

---

39 Adam Smith, *Lectures on Jurisprudence* (Indianapolis: Liberty Fund, 1982), 319–20.

40 Adam Smith, *The Theory of Moral Sentiments* (Indianapolis: Liberty Fund, 1994), 179–85; Ferguson, *An Essay on the History of Civil Society*, 14, 174; David Hume, "Of Commerce," in David Hume, *Essays: Moral, Political, and Literary* (Indianapolis: Liberty Fund, 1987), 262–63.

41 Adam Smith, *An Inquiry into the Nature and Causes of the Wealth of Nations*, Vol. 2 (Indianapolis: Liberty Fund, 1982), 622–23, 697; and *The Theory of Moral Sentiments*, 183–85.

42 Ferguson, *An Essay on the History of Civil Society*, 27–29.

43 See Francis Fukuyama, *The End of History and the Last Man* (New York: Free Press, 2006), xvi–xvii.

44 Anders Engberg-Pedersen, *Empire of Chance: The Napoleonic Wars and the Disorder of Things* (Cambridge, MA: Harvard University Press, 2015), 8. The idea of symmetry and balance is basic to Mearsheimer (John Mearsheimer, *The Tragedy of Great Power Politics* [New York: Norton, 2014], 337). See the interesting Soviet war art in Étienne Balibar, "Marxism and War," *Radical Philosophy* 160 (March/April, 2010): 15.

masterpiece."[45] Intriguingly, Tolkien's co-religionist and fellow veteran of the Somme, the modernist Welsh poet David Jones—a reader of Tolkien[46]—argues the same.[47] Jones:

> Nelson, writing to Lady Hamilton before Trafalgar of the feelings shown by the senior officers of the fleet when he disclosed to them his dispositions of battle, says: "Some shed tears, all approved—it was new—it was singular—it was simple." Is this the *splendor formae* of St. Thomas "shining in the proportioned parts" of the art of naval attack?[48]

In one of the last passages Tolkien ever wrote, he explains why the Ñoldor—the rebel Elves—were punished by the gods: they "did hideous deeds of robbery and bloodshed and treachery." What is especially interesting is that Tolkien crossed out the word *wicked*, replacing it with *hideous*.[49] The latter word keeps the moral tone of the former but adds a strong aesthetic mode of aversion. It is the same with the name *Orc*, which, Tolkien says, means grotesque.[50] Aesthetics are pronounced in Tolkien's description of Sauron's works. To uproot the human settlements of Barahir, allies of the Elves, Morgoth cast a "dread and dark enchantment" over the forest, thereafter known as The Forest under Nightshade: "The trees that grew there after the burning were black and grim, and their roots tangled, groping in the dark like claws; and those who strayed among them became lost and blind, and were strangled or pursued to madness by phantoms of terror" (S, 155). I will show in detail that Tolkien shared the outlook of an influential twentieth-century

---

45 Clausewitz, *On War*, Book 3, Chapter 1, 179.

46 Carl Phelpstead, "Tolkien, David Jones, and the God Nodens," 2–3, Academia, accessed March 15, 2024, *https://www.academia.edu/21037405/Tolkien_David_Jones_and_the_God_Nodens*. For the influence of Dawson on Jones, see Kathleen Henderson Staudt, *At the Turn of a Civilization: David Jones and Modern Poetics* (Ann Arbor: The University of Michigan Press, 1994), 124–27.

47 Cf. Barton Friedman, "Tolkien and David Jones: The Great War and the War of the Ring," *CLIO: A Journal of Literature, History, and the Philosophy of History* 11, no. 2 (1982): 117–18.

48 David Jones, "Art in Relation to War," in David Jones, *The Dying Gaul and Other Writings*, ed. Harman Grisewood (New York: Faber & Faber, 1978), 129–30.

49 J. R. R. Tolkien, *The Nature of Middle-earth*, ed. Carl Hostetter (Boston: Houghton Mifflin, 2021), 308.

50 Stuart Lee, "'Tolkien in Oxford' (BBC, 1968): A Reconstruction." *Tolkien Studies* 15 (2018): 146.

Central European conservatism[51]—the representatives of which were mostly Catholics—that modernity's celebration of vanity has twisted and mauled the hierarchy of values.

In Tolkien's day, this twisting was vividly on display in the Futurism art movement. Futurism was a cult of the machine, promoting fascist apocalypticism (chapter 1).[52] The movement began in Italy, but the English variant, Vorticism, had a potent advocate in Ezra Pound ("His gods are violent gods").[53] The antidote Tolkien offers, a loving appreciation of home and flora, is not mere English pastoralism (Fussell):[54] rather an argument that apocalyptic violence is curtailed by deference to our place in the cosmos and obedience to the appeal transcendence makes to us (chapter 2 and chapter 6). This is why Tolkien's "cosmogonical drama" stars the Valar. Legion is the number of articles on Tolkien and environmentalism. This is worthy, but Tolkien's talk of the countryside is an offshoot of his, in fact, cosmological account of war. The reason his is a cosmological account is that the philosophies of history with which he contends are Gnostic.

Recently, King Charles III has written approvingly of the traditionalist vision of persons living in harmony with nature and God. He contends that modernity is an age of fractures, celebrating a fragmentation that breaks with the wisdom of earlier civilizations that believed we are set in a cosmic, divine order.[55] As an example of a traditionalist, the king gives Thomas Aquinas. He could also have name-checked Tolkien. By contrast, Gnostic philosophies of

51 For Roger Scruton's observation that contemporary conservativism owes much to this intellectual tradition, see "Why I became a conservative," *The New Criterion* 21, no. 6 (February 2003): 4.

52 James Leveque, "Futurism's First War: Apocalyptic Space in F. T. Marinetti's Writings from Tripoli," *Romance Notes* 55, no. 3 (2015): 425–37.

53 Pound, as quoted by William Wees, "Ezra Pound as a Vorticist," *Wisconsin Studies in Contemporary Literature* 6, no. 1 (1965): 58.

54 Paul Fussell, *The Great War and Modern Memory* (Oxford: Oxford University Press, 1975), especially 245. Though Fussell does not discuss Tolkien, some Tolkienists are made nervous by his classic, but problematic, book. For example, Janet Croft, "The Great War and Tolkien's Memory: An Examination of World War I Themes in *The Hobbit* and *The Lord of the Rings*," *Mythlore* 23, no. 4 (2002): 9.

55 Charles III, *Harmony: A New Way of Looking at Our World* (New York: HarperCollins, 2010), 148–50.

history are apocalyptic, wanting rid of the cosmos. Dissatisfied with, and intent on correcting, a recalcitrant world, violence is indulged. War is stoked by philosophies of history—communist, fascist, and liberal progressivist—that share the Gnostic complaint against our cosmic standing. For this reason, and in opposition to our convulsive modern mass political movements, Tolkien proposes that a sober civilizational order requires a philosophy of history of incomplete knowledge, restraint, and patience.

Initially, each of the Valar has a unique particular insight into the architecture of Middle-earth. Even once the part that each plays is revealed to all, the Valar still do not know the full trajectory of Eru's plan for Arda. In their diplomacy to the Númenóreans, the Elves stress this incomplete knowledge (S, 264–65), as does Gandalf (chapter 1). Respecting restraint, the Faithful are those Númenóreans who escape the collapse of Númenor into the sea. This collapse is Eru's punishment of the vast majority of Númenóreans who unrestrainedly pursue immortality, casting aside the explicit Ban that they are not to try to set foot on Valinor, land of the gods. Consistently, Gandalf's great counsel is patience.[56] The themes of incomplete knowledge, restraint, and patience capture what Jesuit theologian Erich Przywara calls a "posture of distance."[57] It is the special mark of Catholic spirituality, argues Przywara, that though love of God pushes us to wish intimacy, reverence for God's sovereignty rightly makes us hesitate: *And Joseph said unto them, Fear not: for am I in the place of God?* (Gen. 50:19). Theologically, this spirituality expresses the analogy of being (*analogia entis*). The Fourth Lateran Council stated that "one cannot note any similarity between creator and creature, however great, without being compelled to observe an even greater dissimilarity between them" (*AE*, 73). Catholic liturgical

---

56 Nicholas Polk, "The Holy Fellowship: Holiness in *The Lord of the Rings*," *Mallorn: The Journal of the Tolkien Society* 57 (2016): 29.

57 Erich Przywara, *Analogia Entis* (Grand Rapids, MI: Eerdmans, 2014), 197, 375. Austin Farrer was an Anglican Divine well known to Tolkien. As Irving Mitchell shows, Farrer addressed Przywara's thought at length (Philip Irving Mitchell, *The Shared Witness of C. S. Lewis and Austin Farrer* [Kent, OH: The Kent State University Press, 2021], 73–76). Tolkien sent to Katherine Farrer, Farrer's wife, a copy of *The Silmarillion* (*Letters*, 130 #115), and spoke with her about most of his works. Farrer read a lesson at the funeral of C. S. Lewis (*Letters*, 341 #251).

art seeks to display this insight in a "posture of distance." I contend that Tolkien's lore is a liturgical art,[58] a crafted obedience to the *analogia entis*, to our situation suspended[59] between a providential cosmos (*Letters*, 413 #328) and "darkness of the origin and end (the '*signum mortis*') of the creaturely overshadows any glory of God in the creature" (*AE*, 552). As Tolkien repeatedly explains, it was his belief that there are only fleeting windows into the mercy and joy underwriting the cosmos. For this reason, Gandalf is a protégé of Nienna, the Ainu of sorrow. Critical to the role he plays in *LotR*, Gandalf learnt patience from Nienna (*S*, 31).

Understanding Tolkien's lore as a dramatization of the "posture of distance" helps clarify Tolkien's core commitments. In places, this book relies on the exceptional Tolkien scholarship of Verlyn Flieger. Intriguingly, she speaks of "Tolkien's obliquely orthodox, highly unorthodox, ultra-Christian, extra-Christian exercise in creative imagination."[60] This requires comment. Flieger argues that Tolkien's "is a far darker world than that envisioned by Christianity." In evidence, she notes that, though original sin is often thought to explain Tolkien's pessimism, this is not really possible because corruption enters Arda through Melkor, before humans roam Middle-earth.[61] This is a curious argument,[62] as there is a longstanding Catholic tradition of pessimism. As Philippe Nemo points out, St. Anselm was a critical corrective of the pessimism standard within

---

58 Tolkien speaks of the sweep of his favorite modern poet, the English Catholic Francis Thompson (1859–1907), commenting, "the images drawn from astronomy and geology, and especially those that could be described as Catholic ritual writ large across the universe" (from a speech at Exeter College, Oxford, as quoted by Holly Ordway, *Tolkien's Modern Reading: Middle-earth Beyond the Middle Ages* [n.p.: Word on Fire Academic], 231). *The Silmarillion* has similar ambition.

59 Please see my *Erich Przywara and Postmodern Natural Law* (Notre Dame, IN: University of Notre Dame Press, 2019), 2–3.

60 Verlyn Flieger, *Splintered Light: Logos and Language in Tolkien's World* (Kent, OH: The Kent State University Press, 2002), xii.

61 Verlyn Flieger, *Interrupted Music: The Making of Tolkien's Mythology* (Kent, OH: Kent State University Press, 2005), 140.

62 She is not alone. Michael White's book is a case in point. He ties himself in knots trying to downplay Tolkien's Catholicism, all the while acknowledging that Tolkien's faith suffused the man. For the same reason, note the caution sounded about the *Letters* by Holly Ordway. She relays that Carpenter, the editor of the *Letters*, particularly disliked Christianity (Ordway, *Tolkien's Modern Reading*, 10–19).

the Church that preceded him.[63] In modernity, Christian pessimism runs from Pascal, through Kierkegaard, to Schmitt. Furthermore, in Christianity, corruption begins *and ends* with Lucifer. Aquinas: "We have now to consider the extrinsic principles of acts. Now the extrinsic principle inclining to evil is the devil. . . . But the extrinsic principle moving to good is God."[64] *And he said unto them, I beheld Satan as lightning fall from heaven* (Luke 10:18). In a reflection on consciousness and time, Aquinas wonders whether Satan sinned in the very first moment of his creation.[65] Melkor is a Lucifer figure, a *Diabolus*, as Tolkien likes to name him (*Letters*, 191 #153), one of the Biblical principalities. Indeed, Ephesians 6:11–12 makes a pretty good plot summary of *The Silmarillion*: *Put on the whole armor of God, that ye may be able to stand against the wiles of the devil. For we wrestle not against flesh and blood, but against principalities, against powers, against the rulers of the darkness of this world, against spiritual wickedness in high places.*

In evidence, Flieger also offers that Eru is "a curiously remote and, for the most part, inactive figure, uninvolved." Yet, in Catholic angelology, it is the role of the angels to minister to the needs of earth[66]—just as Tolkien depicts the Valar and *their* ministers, the Eagles (*S*, 110) and the Wizards (*S*, 299).[67] Further evidence of departure from Christianity, Flieger supposes, is that the Valar "have only partial comprehension of the world they have helped make."[68] As we just saw, the incompleteness of the Valar's knowledge is critical to a Christian understanding of the entirety of *created* order

---

63 Philippe Nemo, *What Is the West?* (Pittsburgh: Duquesne University Press, 2005), 46–50.

64 Thomas Aquinas, *Summa Theologica*, I-II, q. 90.

65 Thomas Aquinas, *On Evil* (Oxford: Oxford University Press, 2003), 458–66.

66 Austin Farrer speaks about angels "who are the motive-forces of nature and the controllers of history" (as quoted in Irving Mitchell, *The Shared Witness of C. S. Lewis and Austin Farrer*, 208). Innovatively, Giorgio Agamben has developed an anarchist theory around ministering angels: amongst many works, see Giorgio Agamben, *The Kingdom and the Glory* (Stanford, CA: Stanford University Press, 2011).

67 An authority, Erik Petersen, commenting on the Book of Revelation, puts it thusly: "Yet the eternal ruler is invisible—as is every true ruler—and only his throne and the brilliant shining of his dominion, jewel-like, can be seen" (Erik Petersen, *Theological Tractates* [Stanford, CA: Stanford University Press, 2011], 110).

68 Flieger, *Interrupted Music: The Making of Tolkien's Mythology*, 140.

structured as a *potentia obedientialis*. This is why the human Jesus cautions about the Apocalypse: *But of that day and hour knoweth no man, no, not the angels of heaven, but my Father only* (Matt. 24:36; cf. 2 Thess. 2:3–6). It is not the place of those of us created to accelerate the Apocalypse: *For I would not, brethren, that ye should be ignorant of this mystery, lest ye should be wise in your own conceits* (Rom. 11:25). This is the problem with Gnosticism. As Voegelin quips, Gnostics "want to read from God as they read from a book."[69] Metaphysically, this just is not possible. Tolkien thinks of creation as music, the interplay of sound and silence. God is not remote, but rather, the heard silence of a sounding note, the shimmer or elusive part of the measure of the rhythm of a cosmic music. Przywara explains:

> Only in the sense of such a rhythm and such a measure is analogy a "principle"... it is "principally" the mystery of the primordial music of this rhythm—as with the fugues in Bach's "Art of the Fugue," which, interweaving one another, pass beyond themselves into "great silence." The "resonant analogy" is fulfilled in this "silent analogy." (*AE*, 314)

It is because God is both intimate and elusive or, as is plain from Eru's conversation with Aulë, modest, that Erendis warns Aldarion: "The Edain remain mortal Men, Aldarion, great though they be: and we cannot dwell in the time that is to come, lest we lose our now for a phantom of our own design."[70] Aldarion is impressive: he sees far, has energy, and men gladly follow him. Yet, Aldarion's father, King Meneldur, who is an astronomer, repeatedly cautions his son that he belongs to a place, one vouchsafed by the Valar.[71] Aquinas adds his voice to the caution: "And we sometimes understand vain to mean what lacks solidity or stability."[72] Aldarion is not without fame

---

69 Eric Voegelin, "Christianity's Decisive Difference," an excerpt from "A Letter to Alfred Shutz" (January 1, 1953), *VoegelinView*, January 1, 2015.

70 J. R. R. Tolkien, *Unfinished Tales* (New York: Ballantine, 1980), 192.

71 J. R. R. Tolkien, *Unfinished Tales*, 188–89.

72 Aquinas, *On Evil*, 343.

and an important role in preserving Middle-earth, but, in his own day, his projects failed: "But all Aldarion's labours were swept away. The works that he began again at Vinyalondë were never completed, and the sea gnawed them."[73] Tolkien's lore is one great caution about the phantoms of our own design. His stories are evidence for Eric Voegelin's thesis: "Still, myth not only survives but, in our time, even revives in response to the perversion of immanence in the period of enlightenment and ideology."[74] His art is a commentary on 1 Corinthians 4:9: *For I think that God hath set forth us the apostles last, as it were appointed to death: for we are made a spectacle unto the world, and to angels, and to men.*

Impressive about Tolkien is the scope of his thought. Tolkien's writing depicts a conflict over the hierarchy of value. He not only identified the problem of vanity but proposed a solution: his is a dramatization of the political establishment necessary for checking the lure of Gnostic dissatisfaction with our finitude. Hence, chapter 1 contrasts Tolkien's use of apocalypse in his account of war with the apocalyptic politics of Gnosticism. War is hard-wired into the Enlightenment,[75] contends Tolkien, because its philosophies of history trade on vanity. His critique is ultimately cosmological, and this argument expands in chapter 2, which considers the strategic role of geography and flora in war. Chapter 3 builds on the strategic role of land and explains why the decidedly non-militaristic homebody Hobbits end up fighting for the Shire. This chapter also returns us to the problem of the Whigs and sets up the Tory Tolkien of chapter 4. This chapter, and the last two, explores what war rightly fought protects, which, according to Tolkien, is dignity. Using Schmitt's theory of war, this chapter examines how monarchy contributes to dignity, but also firmly places Tolkien's writing in the tradition of Schelerian value theory, which Schmitt rejected. Chapter 5 continues

---

73 J. R. R. Tolkien, *Unfinished Tales*, 215.

74 Eric Voegelin, "Anxiety and Reason," in *The Collected Works of Eric Voegelin*, vol. 28, *What Is History? and Other Late Unpublished Writings* (Baton Rouge: Louisiana State University Press, 1990), 81.

75 Cf. Schmitt, *Land and Sea*, 55–58.

to explore dignity, engaging Scheler's moral psychology to judge the demonic possession wrought by the Ring and which brought to ruin the old Kings of Men. Basic to Tolkien's art, he explains, is "a study of the ennoblement (or sanctification) of the humble" (*Letters*, 237 #181). Chapter 6 elaborates why value hierarchy is critical to that task. Its focus is Arwen's battle standard since, as Tolkien explains, the relationship between Arwen and Aragorn "is part of the essential story." We shall see that the Standard of Elendil is a lesson in the ennoblement of the humble, Arwen and Aragorn, in fact. Atop the established order of Middle-earth they may be, but they suffer their part in the "cosmogonical drama" of Eru's Arda with steadfast hope. In WW1, Tolkien took "the King's shilling" and never seems to have regretted fighting for king and country. In short, Tolkien's monarchical and military mythology—a post-liberalism—nimbly confirms Eric Voegelin's observation: "There is no alternative to an eschatological extravaganza but to accept the mystery of the cosmos."[76]

---

76 Eric Voegelin, *The Collected Works of Eric Voegelin*, vol. 17, and *Order and History*, vol. 4, *The Ecumenic Age* (Baton Rouge: Louisiana State University Press, 1990), 28.

Acknowledgments

I wrote a preliminary version of chapter 2 for the Western Front Association 2022 Annual Meeting, Baltimore. I am grateful to the audience for feedback, and especially to Mark Deckard (Lancaster Bible College) for reading and commenting on the paper. A version of chapter 1 became a talk I gave in 2022 at the Agathon Institute, Rochester Institute of Technology. I want to thank Alisia Chase for the opportunity to speak at Agathon. Parts of chapter 6 began as the Benedict XVI Memorial Lecture I gave in 2016 at Oscott College, Birmingham, Tolkien's hometown. These opportunities all helped make this book happen.

Thanks are due Brian Smith, John Grove, and Richard Reinsch, editors at the online magazine *Law & Liberty*, who have indulged my wanting to write on Tolkien. Similarly, the anonymous readers at The Catholic University of America Press both gave me confidence that I was on the right track and pushed me to refine the presentation of ideas.

Famously, Tolkien had a friendship circle, and I want to thank my friends for hours of conversation: Christopher Wojtulewicz, Alexander Rosenthal, Paul Seaton, Jim Buckley, Lee Trepanier, and Brian Murray. Especially, I want to thank Fr. John Peck, SJ, for many important hours discussing philosophy and theology drinking beers at De Kliene Duivel, Hampden. Besides those conversations, large parts of this book were written at this Belgian alehouse in Baltimore. Tolkien would have loved the place, but sadly it became a casualty of Covid.

Finally, I am deeply grateful to John Martino and Trevor Lipscombe at The Catholic University of America Press for all the interest they have shown in my work. I am delighted to be counted amongst their authors.

Tolkien, Philosopher of War

Opening Remarks

C hapter 1 of *The Silmarillion* starts: "It is told among the wise that the First War began before Arda was full-shaped. . . ." Likely a nod to Viking myth, in which the creation of earth includes homicide,[1] this opening[2] firmly sets up a core theme of the greatest English writer of the twentieth century:[3] war. An indication is the estimated two million war gamers that use *The Lord of the Rings* motifs for their battles. What are Tolkien's central motifs? The first two pages of Tolkien's magnum opus, *The Silmarillion*—"the history of the War of the Exiled Elves against the Enemy" (*Letters*, 148 #131)—dwell on beauty and vanity, melody and discord, and battle and apocalypse. *The Silmarillion* begins with a pretender to the throne challenging the sovereignty of God in a rap-battle, as it were: "a war of sound" makes beauty falter, and atop "dark waters that made war one upon another," melody founders (*S*, 16).[4] Verlyn Flieger notes, "*The Silmarillion* is almost entirely concerned

---

1 Neil Price, *Children of Ash and Elm: A History of the Vikings* (New York: Basic Books, 2020), 1.

2 It should be noted that the first chapter of *The Silmarillion* is not the start of the story. It is preceded by an Overture, the utterly beautiful description of a musical Creation. *The Music of the Ainur* (*S*, xiv) recalls themes from St. Bonaventure's *A Journey into the Mind of God*, chapter 2: 10.

3 Thomas Shippey, *J. R. R. Tolkien: Author of the Century* (Boston: Houghton Mifflin, 2000), xvii–xxvii.

4 About *The Silmarillion*, John Garth writes, it "arose out of the encounter between an imaginative genius and the war that inaugurated the modern age" (Garth, *Tolkien and the Great War*, 39).

with warfare,"[5] and Janet Croft concurs: "Understanding Tolkien's approach to war is crucial to fully understanding his works, particularly *The Lord of the Rings*, as a whole."[6] And this is unsurprising, for, as John Mearsheimer points out, amongst contending powers, "war is the main strategy states employ to acquire relative power."[7] As Reuven Naveh astutely points out, the musical conflict between God and Melkor[8] at the start of *The Silmarillion* is a struggle for good political order.[9] Tolkien is a philosopher of war because he is an advocate for civilization.

This is a philosophy book. I hope its ideas add depth to the imaginative play of Tolkien wargamers and helps other Tolkien fans think about the moral and political aspects of war. In terms of book sales, Tolkien keeps pace with the Bible and the Koran.[10] This is because he talks about the oldest and deepest matters, the "more elemental" things, as Tolkien puts it. War is one of those things, as is civilization.[11] David Jones observes: "All our tradition is of war, and the hero at his tasks. . . . We have thought very much in terms of war, and the arts have in various ways reflected that thought."[12]

---

5 Flieger, *Interrupted Music*, 14. Cf. Nora Alfaiz, "The Preservation of National Unity," in *Baptism of Fire: The Birth of the Modern British Fantastic in World War 1*, ed. Janet Brennan Croft (n.p.: Mythopoeic Press, 2015), 81.

6 Janet Croft, "War," in *A Companion to J. R. R. Tolkien*, ed. Stuart D. Lee (Hoboken, NJ: Wiley, 2014), 470. Hugh Brogan, "Tolkien's Great War," in *Children and Their Books*, ed. Gillian Avery & Julia Briggs (Oxford: Oxford University Press, 1990), 353–54 points out a striking similarity between a passage in Sassoon and the vaporization of Sauron. He speculates that Tolkien may have modeled his passage on Sassoon's but concedes both could just as well be vividly recording shell-bursts: "And if the Great War could break through so vividly at such an important moment of *The Lord of the Rings*, may it not have manifested itself elsewhere? Here is a concrete problem to investigate."

7 Mearsheimer, *The Tragedy of Great Power Politics*, 138.

8 For comparable ideas about war and the cosmic, see Jones, "Art in Relation to War," 126, 132, and 136.

9 Reuven Naveh, "The Ainulindale and Tolkien's Approach to Modernity," in *The Return of the Ring: Proceedings of the Tolkien Society Conference 2012*, Vol. 2, ed. Lynn Forest-Hill (Edinburgh: Luna Press, 2016), 109–10.

10 Niall Ferguson, "How the World Misunderstood Tolkien, the ultra-Tory," *Daily Telegraph*, December 3, 2021.

11 Cf. "Without the rivalship of nations, and the practice of war, civil society itself could scarcely have found an object, or a form" (Ferguson, *An Essay on the History of Civil Society*, 28).

12 Jones, "Art in Relation to War," 126–27. Cf. Carl Schmitt's discussion of the Jesuit Paul Hoste, who penned the first book of naval tactics. Drawing on a fifty-year history of naval battle, Hoste

War

War touches the things we cherish and fear: life and land, building and belonging, subversion and possession, plunder and justice, and anger and mercy.[13] Arguing that war is the origin of civilization, David Hume says "camps are the true mothers of cities."[14] Canadian historian Margaret McClain observes: "It is another uncomfortable truth about war that it brings both destruction and creation."[15] War touches on the elemental,[16] some of which is terrible, as the Dwarves of Moria learn, digging down deep enough to where Balrogs await. Grimly, Cormac McCarthy begins his classic novel, the bleak Western, *Blood Meridian*, with the observation that a 300,000-year-old hominid skull shows evidence of having been scalped. We are in awe of the hand motifs in Neolithic cave paintings,[17] but studies suggest the art was made with hands with fingers or tips of fingers sliced off.[18] Flieger puts it well: Elves and dragons "provide the surface texture. Below that surface is a substrate of darker, flintier material, stained and spotted by the Age of Anxiety in which Tolkien lived and out of which he wrote."[19]

proposes: "A wholly new tactics for sea battle and for conducting sea war is bound up with this, a new, high art of the 'evolutions,' which before, during, and after the sea battle are necessary" (Schmitt, *Land and Sea*, 32–33). The "evolutions" are the sea maneuvers made possible by the play of a panoply of sails able to be "sailed sideward into the winds."

13 "Every reflection on politics encompasses the reality of war, which is a crucial and permanent aspect of politics" (Pierre Manent, *A World beyond Politics?* [Princeton, NJ: Princeton University Press, 2006], 72–73). Cf. Tom Holland's summary of Rome: "The capacity of the legions to exercise extreme violence was the necessary condition of the Pax Romana" (*Pax: War and Peace in Rome's Golden Age* [New York: Basic Books, 2023], 16).

14 David Hume, *A Treatise of Human Nature* (Oxford: Oxford University Press, 2011), 3.2.8, 346. Cf. Smith, *Lectures on Jurisprudence*, 249.

15 Margaret MacMillan, *War: How Conflict Shaped Us* (New York: Random House, 2020), 26–27. Cf. Ian Morris, *War! What Is It Good For?* (New York: Farrar, Straus and Giroux, 2014).

16 About a fighter in battle, an early Welsh poem runs: "His sword rang in mothers' heads" (Jones, "Art in Relation to War," 130)

17 There are no representational cave paintings at Cheddar Gorge, but Tolkien drew his own cave paintings—see plate 67, Wayne Hammond & Christina Scull, *J. R. R. Tolkien, Artist and Illustrator* (Boston: Houghton Mifflin, 1995), 73.

18 Brea MacCauley, "A Cross-cultural Perspective on Upper Paleolithic Hand Images with Missing Phalanges," *Journal of Paleolithic Archaeology* 1, no. 4 (2018): 314–33, and especially 319.

19 Flieger, *A Question of Time: J. R. R. Tolkien's Road to* Faërie (Kent, OH: The Kent State University Press, 1997), 7.

McCarthy offers this image of the Galton Gang, a historical group of paramilitaries employed by the Mexican government: "In the morning the rain had stopped and they appeared in the streets, tattered, stinking, ornamented with human parts like cannibals."[20] This horrid description captures something curious that Tolkien also believes basic to war: our appetite to adorn.[21] In the burial pit of Cheddar Man—a Neolithic man killed with an axe blow to his head, circa 8300 BC—five skulls were found, their owners scalped and turned into drinking cups.[22] The body was discovered in 1903, and Tolkien visited the caves on his honeymoon and later in 1940 (*Letters*, 321 #407).

What is the origin of war? Tolkien's provocative suggestion is that it is an appetite to decorate. Von Clausewitz observes that all militaries collect battle trophies to display.[23] Even museums do so: you can see Tolkien's war revolver on display at the Imperial War Museum. McCarthy's marauders are decked out in scalps[24] and other bits and bobs.[25] Comparably, Tolkien explains that Melkor "grew hot" with impatience at the "emptiness" of the Void, puzzled why God "took no thought for the Void" (*S*, 16). He wanted to build, and fill the Void, bringing "into Being things of his own." About the creative efforts of his lieutenant, Tolkien writes: "Sauron was become now a sorcerer of dreadful power, master of shadows and of phantoms, foul in wisdom, cruel in strength, misshaping what he touched, twisting

---

20 Cormac McCarthy, *Blood Meridian* (New York: Vintage, 1985), 197.

21 "Ornament is the exuberance of the workman" (Eric Gill, *Work & Property* [London: J. M. Dent, 1937], 124).

22 Ian Morris, *Geography is Destiny. Britain and the World: A 10,000-Year History* (New York: Farrar, Straus and Giroux, 2022), 44.

23 Clausewitz, *On War*, 233–34.

24 See the Brad Pitt scene in *Legends of the Fall*, when he returns from the frontlines in WW1 bedecked in German scalps. In a 2022 Amazon TV thriller, *Terminal-List*, an officer who lost his men swears revenge on the man responsible for the ambush and promises the other survivor of the unit that he'll scalp their enemy. For the inverse phenomenon, the Uskoks of the Adriatic would nail turbans to the heads of Ottoman captives (Robert D. Kaplan, *Adriatic: A Concert of Civilizations and the End of the Modern Age* [New York: Random House, 2022], 192).

25 For the highly regarded description of Comanche raiders, "a legion of horribles," McCarthy: "the breastplate and pauldrons deeply dented with the old blows of mace and saber done in another country by men whose very bones were dust" (*Blood Meridian*, 55).

what he ruled, lord of werewolves; his dominion was torment" (S, 156). At its most elemental, politics, proposes Tolkien, is the raw struggle between sober civilizational order and the horrid lure of primitivism.[26] This is the construction I would put on Churchill's pronouncement: "War is the normal occupation of man. War—and gardening."[27]

For Tolkien, war is really a dispute about beauty:

> And it seemed at last that there were two musics progressing at one time before the seat of Ilúvatar, and they were utterly at variance. The one was deep and wide and beautiful, but slow and blended with an immeasurable sorrow, from which its beauty chiefly came. The other had now achieved a unity of its own; but it was loud, and vain, and endlessly repeated; and it had little harmony, but rather a clamorous unison as of many trumpets braying upon a few notes. (S, 16–17)

Solemnity versus the rapid clacks of a machine.[28] Much is made of Tolkien's environmental dispute with modernity,[29] but behind this important issue is a more metaphysical question: Why is the melodic not enough? God offers ornate harmonies and Melkor—the angel Eru most favored—is not satisfied. What impedes the grip of the beautiful upon us? Is beauty impotent without extra supports aiding

---

26 Jacques Lacan argues that the imagination is the psyche's tool for allowing human desire's most catastrophic fantasies indulgence, without getting caught, so to say. Cultural productions and mores skirt close to what is taboo and allow space for cunning, but ultimately controlled, aggressions: think only of the barely controlled rage of spectators in a European football stadium, the slayings in computer games, as well as the murders at the Opera (Jacques Lacan, "Aggressiveness in Psychoanalysis," in Écrits [New York: Norton, 2006], 82–101, especially 89–92).

27 As cited in Janet Croft's War and the Works of J. R. R. Tolkien, 38.

28 One summary of The Rite of Spring ran: "Against our helpless ears to fling its crash, clash, cling, clang, bing, bang, bing" (Modris Eksteins, Rites of Spring: The Great War and the Birth of the Modern Age [New York: Anchor Books, 1990], 9). The seminal Russian ballet was inspired by a tribal war-game (Robert Craft, "The Rite of Spring: Genesis of a Masterpiece," Perspectives of New Music 5, no. 1 [1966]: 29). Seeing the ballet in 1921, T. S. Eliot: "Whether Strawinsky's music be permanent or ephemeral I do not know; but it did seem to transform the rhythm of the steppes into the scream of the motor horn, the rattle of machinery, the grind of wheels, the beating of iron and steel, the roar of the underground railway, and the other barbaric cries of modern life; and to transform these despairing noises into music" (T. S. Eliot, London Letter, 1921, https://theworld.com/~raparker/exploring/tseliot/works/london-letters/london-letter-1921-10.html).

29 From amongst a vast literature, see Patrick Curry, Defending Middle-earth: Tolkien, Myth and Modernity (London: St. Martin's Press, 1997).

it to counsel our "hot" desire? Tolkien frequently expresses his belief that people are never long satisfied with the good (*Letters*, 344 #256). Why do some turn to horrible adornment?

The aesthetic problem is also moral and metaphysical. War stems from our painful experience of time (*Letters*, 246 #186),[30] which explains why Tolkien's metaphysical frame is music; a handy way to speak about the Gnostic refusal to tolerate the intervals of the *analogia entis*. Gandalf: "All that we have to decide is what to do with the time that is given us" (*FR*, 50). Respectively, I take the ideas of Gnosticism and analogy of being from Voegelin and Przywara. Detailed in chapter 1, Gnostic politics is a frenzied effort to bring history to a perfect close. By contrast, Przywara argues that the intervals of history reflect our metaphysical situation: we are suspended between our station in the cosmos and our (incomplete) intimacy with God. Turning to "creative" violence to speed things up, Gnostic politics wants to close the gap of the *analogia entis* and usher in unity at the apocalyptic end of days.[31] For a taste, note the vivid way Karl Marx paints a revolutionary assault on Rome. About the pope, Marx says, how surprised he will be "when the reflection of burning cities in the sky will mark the dawn," when the celestial harmonies are replaced by revolutionary songs, "with the guillotine beating time."[32] Voegelin characterizes this fantasy as a *Blutrausch*, a "blood-intoxication," whereby a superman—a Gnostic hero—will emerge from human sacrifice.[33] In this light, chapter 1 discusses the late Númenórean religious practice of human sacrifice, a precursor to their war on the gods. Apocalyptic politics are intolerant and jacked-up because totality depends on closing all shortfalls: "anybody who wants to lead his own way of life, unmolested by the idealist, is a criminal."[34] Instead

---

30 Cf. Aquinas on time and vanity (*On Evil*, 343).

31 Cf. Dawson, *Progress and Religion*, 229.

32 As quoted by Walter Benjamin, *Arcades Project* (Cambridge, MA: Harvard University Press, 2002), 652.

33 Voegelin, *The Ecumenic Age*, 253–54.

34 Eric Voegelin, *The Collected Works of Eric Voegelin*, vol. 22, and *History of Political Ideas, Volume IV: Renaissance and Reformation* (Columbia: University of Missouri Press, 1998), 129. For the same idea in Camus, see his portrait of Saint-Just in *The Rebel* (New York: Vintage, 1991), 121–32.

of alienation, anxiety, and *agita*, Tolkien counsels patience, for, he contends, there can be no rushing across the interval (*AE*, 314) that makes us incomplete and confused parts[35] of a serene unity:[36]

> And many other things Ilúvatar spoke to the Ainur at that time, and because of their memory of his words, and the knowledge that each has of the music that he himself made, the Ainur know much of what was, and is, and is to come, and few things are unseen by them. Yet some things there are that they cannot see, neither alone nor taking counsel together; for to none but himself has Ilúvatar revealed all that he has in store, and in every age there come forth things that are new and have no foretelling, for they do not proceed from the past. (*S*, 17–18)

Profound reasons move war to the center of Tolkien's thinking, therefore. He was neither a warmonger, nor someone, like Fichte, who thought war distilled the essence of a nation.[37] Appreciating the scope of the problem of war for Tolkien helps us better see the value he placed on some other things. For example, in chapter 3 I discuss moral order, chapter 5 liberty, and chapter 6 establishment. For now, consider the connection between war and gardens.

---

35 Reflecting on what she calls the "dual presentation of Time and Timelessness" in Tolkien, Flieger aptly points to a discussion between Gimli and Legolas (*RK*, 855): "'Yet seldom do they fail of their seed,' said Legolas. 'And that will lie in the dust and rot to spring up again in times and places unlooked for. The deeds of men will outlast us, Gimli.'" This passage captures nicely the human positioned in the *analogia entis*. For Flieger's observation, *A Question of Time*, 113.

36 In a fascinating article on Russian fan fiction critical of Tolkien, Jim Clarke discusses a re-writing of *LotR* by Kyrill Yeskov. In Yeskov's re-telling, Mordor is championed as a bastion of Enlightenment technology and industrialism. Tolkien's pastoralism is presented as a regression and primitivization. Yeskov is likely great reading, but I think he and Clarke miss Tolkien's target: Gnostic philosophies of history are rupturing and malforming, necessarily committed to twisting out of shape our given cosmic nature. Hence, Melkor's evil is the twisting of captured Elves into Orcs. See Jim Clarke, "Tolkien, the Russians and Industrialisation," in *The Return of the Ring: Proceedings of the Tolkien Society Conference 2012*, vol. 2, 111–22, and especially 121–22.

37 Fichte thought the Prussian fight against Napoleon would "create the apocalyptic community of the whole" (Jürgen Gebhardt, "Political Eschatology and Soteriological Nationalism in Nineteenth Century Germany," in *The Promise of History: Essays in Political Philosophy*, ed. Athanasios Moulakis [Berlin: De Gruyter, 1985], 65).

Civilization

The First War concludes when Melkor flees before the wrath of the Vala, Tulkas (the first paragraph of chapter 1 of *The Silmarillion*). We will want to examine the role of the gods in war, as well as the visits of angels—like Gandalf (*Letters*, 202 #156)—but for now, consider Tolkien's clear preference for plants over machines. Tolkien's is not a simple "green is good" message. For example, Hobbits have a long-standing conflict with trees at the Hedge:

> They do say the trees do actually move, and can surround strangers and hem them in. In fact long ago they attacked the Hedge: they came and planted themselves right by it, and leaned over it. But the hobbits came and cut down hundreds of trees, and made a great bonfire in the Forest, and burned all the ground in a long strip east of the Hedge." (*FR*, 108)

This is interesting because the fight over the Hedge pits two of Tolkien's favorite things against one another: he both thought of himself as a gardening Hobbit and had a profound love of trees. The example shows that flora have strategic value in Tolkien (chapter 2), that they are a safeguard of civilization (chapter 3).

Fleeing from Tulkas, Melkor takes sanctuary outside Arda (Middle-earth) altogether (*S*, 35). In military manuals, sanctuary is a time of respite from operations.[38] In that time of relief from war, "the seeds that Yavanna had sown began swiftly to sprout and to burgeon, and there arose a multitude of growing things great and small" (*S*, 35). However, Melkor returns, and then hatred poisoning the land, "green things fell sick and rotted, and rivers were choked with weeds and slime, and fens were made, rank and poisonous, the breeding place of flies" (*S*, 36). By the time we hit the second page of chapter 1 of *The Silmarillion*, Melkor "came forth suddenly to war" again (*S*, 36). In his renewed assault on Arda, he strikes down the lamps that light the world. The third page tells how the Valar contain Melkor but must

---

38 David Petraeus, *The U.S. Army/Marine Corps Counterinsurgency Field Manual: U.S. Army Field Manual* (Chicago: The University of Chicago Press, 2007), 28–29.

make a strategic retreat, moving to "the westernmost of all lands upon the borders of the world." There, the "Valar fortified their dwelling" (*S*, 37) by raising a mountain range, the Pelóri. Melkor had already built "a vast fortress, deep under Earth, beneath dark mountains" where, without light, green things could not grow. By contrast:

> Behind the walls of the Pelóri the Valar established their domain in that region which is called Valinor; and there were their houses, their gardens, and their towers. In that guarded land the Valar gathered great store of light and all the fairest things that were saved from the ruin; and many others yet fairer they made anew, and Valinor became more blessed even than Middle-earth in the Spring of Arda. (*S*, 37)

This passage shows Tolkien's concern with the grandest themes: space and time, geography and history, building and adornment, and gardens and civilization. As his son and editor, Christopher, relays:

> Moreover the old legends ("old" now not only in their derivation from the remote First Age, but also in terms of my father's life) became the vehicle and depository of his profoundest reflections. In his later writing mythology and poetry sank down behind his theological and philosophical preoccupations. . . . (*S*, vii)

He also spoke of his father's dislike of modern things,[39] but this needs to be understood properly.

In a BBC interview towards the end of his life, Tolkien is asked about motor cars. He replies: "Love them. Love riding them, like driving them."[40] The interviewer is perplexed and asks Tolkien what he thinks of the noise they create around Oxford. He replies that medieval Oxford was an "extraordinarily deafeningly noisy place;" in part because of the noise of "enormous wains" with steel wheels on

---

39 Michael White, *J. R. R. Tolkien* (Indianapolis, IN: Alpha, 2002), 216.

40 Darryl Jones relays the amusing story that on Tolkien's visit to Ireland he had his academic host pop in the car and drive them around to all the best pubs in the area ("Foreword," in *Tolkien: The Forest and the City*, ed. Helen Conrad-O'Briain & Gerard Hynes [Dublin: Four Courts Press, 2013], 6).

the cobbles.[41] Tolkien was not straightforwardly anti-modern—he enjoyed taking the family for a "car-ride." Hardly commonplace, he owned a car as early as 1937, at least.[42] However, he came of age when Futurism was all the rage,[43] and he reacted horribly to its cult of the machine.[44] For deep reasons, he thought this cult idolatrous[45] and hoped that those suffering "industrialized and militarized agriculture" might become "a little more anarchic" (*Letters*, 179 #144). He thought of himself as a resistance writer.[46] His calibrated dislike of modern things can be resolved into two intimates of war: vanity and reprimitivism.[47]

Tolkien, Symbolist

Tolkien was intent on avoiding both Whiggery and apocalypticism. Astutely, he saw they are connected. This can be seen in the most consequential book of the last thirty years, Francis Fukuyama's *The End of History and the Last Man*. This book shaped the ideal of globalization that dominated policy circles until the presidency of Donald Trump and the 2022 Russo-Ukraine War. Fukuyama

---

41 Lee, "Tolkien in Oxford," 150.

42 J. R. R. Tolkien, *The Letters of J. R. R. Tolkien: Revised and Expanded Edition* (New York: HarperCollins, 2023), 27 #15b.

43 Ezra Pound: "Marinetti and Futurism gave a great fillip to all European literature. The movement which I, Eliot, Joyce and others started in London would not have existed but for Futurism" (as cited in *International Futurism in Arts and Literature*, ed. Günter Berghaus. [Berlin: De Gruyter, 2000], 100). Cf. David Jones, "Notes on the 1930s," in *The Dying Gaul and Other Writings*, 42.

44 "And the Italian futurist Umberto Boccioni, reflecting the widespread preoccupation with machines and change, declared, 'There is no such thing as a nonmoving object in our modern perception of life.' Diaghilev was attuned to these developments, which hailed a will to constant metamorphosis and praised the beauty of transitoriness" (Eksteins, *Rites of Spring*, 31).

45 See Giacomo Balla's planned triptych based on the motor car, *Abstract Speed + Sound* (1913–14).

46 Replying to the charge that fairy stories are just escapism, Tolkien argues they are a resistance literature: "In the same way these critics, to make confusion worse, and so to bring into contempt their opponents, stick their label of scorn not only on to Desertion, but on to real Escape, and what are often its companions, Disgust, Anger, Condemnation, and Revolt. Not only do they confound the escape of the prisoner with the flight of the deserter; but they would seem to prefer the acquiescence of the 'quisling' to the resistance of the patriot. To such thinking you have only to say 'the land you loved is doomed' to excuse any treachery, indeed to glorify it" (https://coolcalvary.files.wordpress.com/2018/10/on-fairy-stories1.pdf, 30).

47 For treatment of this idea, please see McAleer & Rosenthal, *The Wisdom of Our Ancestors*, chapter 8.

twinned the Whig theory of history with Hegel's philosophy of history. He linked what he called "the Mechanism"—the techniques of contemporary business management and government administration—with Hegel's idea that modernity offers the social recognition of all. Liberal democratic commercial civilizational is thus the culminating "end-point" of history. In short, the hybrid of bourgeois Liberalism and the Hegelian democratic state *supersedes* earlier and ostensibly more primitive epochs and discourses. As Stefan Rossbach insightfully notes, Fukuyama's thesis trades upon the apocalyptic strain in the West's political thinking:[48] Liberalism is nothing short of a *renovatio mundi*.[49] As John Mearsheimer wryly points out, this triumphant philosophy of history has, on average, meant an Anglo-American-led war for two of every three years since the publication of *The End of History*.[50]

How to avoid the weird hybrid of progressive apocalypticism? Tolkien did not propose a return to the Middle Ages. His is not a paleo-conservatism (like T. S. Eliot's, perhaps). He certainly wanted to reconnect with what was lost in the Whig revolution, but there was—and is—a different live option, affirming the core holdings of Toryism. *LotR* is not nostalgia, but a modern criticism and, implicitly, an aesthetic proposal. Tolkien is what Voegelin calls a symbolist.[51]

Voegelin contends that different politics express symbols[52]—*cosmions* or "little worlds"—thus each political myth has its symbolist.[53] A symbolist is someone who displays hyper-condensed emblems of

---

48 Stefan Rossbach, *Gnostic Wars: The Cold War in the Context of a History of Western Spirituality* (Edinburgh: Edinburgh University Press, 1999), 224.

49 Voegelin argues that modernity retains an "eschatological tension left over from the Puritan Revolution," itself dating to Israel, which endows liberalism with a sense of finality (Voegelin, "Industrial Society in Search of Reason," in *World Technology and Human Destiny*, ed. Raymond Aron, 37, 170). Cf. Schmitt, *Land and Sea*, 68–69.

50 For Mearsheimer on the wars of globalization, see his debate with Fukuyama: https://www.youtube.com/watch?v=lzqkXhdo0qc.

51 Voegelin, *The Ecumenic Age*, 59.

52 Studying the symbols generates "sequences of order in the historical revelation of the spirit; and finally it can in this way produce in fact a philosophy of history" (Voegelin, *Anamnesis*, 32).

53 Voegelin, *The Ecumenic Age*, 59. Comte is the symbolist of positivism, proffering the symbol of the "industrial manager-positivist" (Voegelin, "Industrial Society in Search of Reason," 36).

a style of consciousness, offering a portrait of a manner of existence. Tolkien's writings, maps, and drawings can be viewed as such. A symbol conveys a philosophy of history: examples include Comte's progressivism, Marx's communism, Sorel's anarchist General Strike, Futurism's fascism, and Tolkien's divine and monarchical Middle-earth.[54] As we will see, Tolkien's is the better symbol because it does not trade on apocalyptic politics.

Tolkien writes an icon.[55] Part prayer, part proposition,[56] his lore is the symbol of a way of being in the world that conveys a community loyal to place, with family property that supports craft, an exemplar of a deeply held identity decorating and nourishing persons. This proposal is, in social philosophy, known as Distributism,[57] and, more broadly, a variant of post-liberalism (chapter 3). For depicting conflict between industrialism and pastoralism, Tolkien has been accused of having a "simplifying mind."[58] Such criticism mistakes two things. Firstly, Tolkien's great theme of gardens against machines is a rivalry of two symbols, one cosmological and obediential (conservative), the other Gnostic (revolutionary). These ways of being in the world are in conflict. Secondly, symbols need unpacking. Far from being

---

54 For Voegelin, a symbol is what he calls a *cosmion*, "a whole little world" wherein clear to consciousness is a pattern of life, an essence transcending the persons instantiating it. It sets a style of life and sometimes has significant theoretical weight, e.g., the social contract theory of government is a symbol for those strongly believing—even in the face of contrary evidence—that they participate in a government that only rules by their leave (Eric Voegelin, "Immortality: Experience and Symbol," in *The Collected Works of Eric Voegelin*, vol. 12 [Baton Rouge: Louisiana State University Press, 1990], 52–53).

55 "The Church's act of praise is expressed together with the praise of the cosmos, every meditation on the role of music in the cultus of the Church must also therefore take notice of the kind of praise of the sun, moon, and stars" (Petersen, *Theological Tractates*, 126).

56 Fleiger has taken note of Tolkien's testimony of the influence of philosopher and fellow-Inkling, Owen Barfield (Flieger, *Splintered Light*, 60). In *Poetic Diction*, first published in 1928, Barfield quotes Emerson: "Because of this radical correspondence between visible things and human thoughts, savages, who have only what is necessary, converse in figures. As we go back in history, language becomes more picturesque, until its infancy, when it is all poetry; or all spiritual facts are represented by natural symbols" (Owen Barfield, *Poetic Diction* [New York: Faber and Faber, 1952], 92).

57 Matthew Akers, "Distributism in the Shire," *St. Austin Review* (November 7, 2014): 2. An English Christian social movement, the framework of the Catholic variant of Distributism is found in papal encyclical letters on social, moral, and political matters published during Tolkien's life.

58 G. R. Brown, "Pastoralism and Industrialism in *The Lord of the Rings*," *English Studies in Africa* 19, no. 2 (1976): 88.

simplistic, they contain a host of sub-theses requiring development through application of the arts and sciences. This is why Tolkien spent so much time on linguistics, cartography, geology, botany, and astronomy. In the following chapters, I relay the intellectual heft of Tolkien's symbol—for example, its geopolitical intelligence and worthy political economy—and therewith its plausibility, and how Arda may yet leave its stamp on our earth.

Twentieth Century Thought

Consider Tolkien's claim that modern railway stations would be much better designed if the architects and engineers were nourished more by fantasy.[59] I agree with Patchen Mortimer that it makes no sense to separate Tolkien from his times and to think he emerged from an "aesthetic vacuum."[60] Of course, studies abound in which Tolkien's thought is related back to the Middle Ages[61] and to the neo-medievalism of the likes of Pugin and Ruskin,[62] and this is unquestionably relevant.[63] Rather beautifully, one early reviewer of *LotR* called it, "the last literary masterpiece of the Middle Ages."[64] Does it go too far, though, to speak of "Tolkien's disdain for

---

59 In *On Fairy Stories*, he suggests that architects exposed to more fairy tales would make better modern buildings: "For my part, I cannot convince myself that the roof of Bletchley station is more 'real' than the clouds. And as an artefact I find it less inspiring than the legendary dome of heaven. The bridge to platform 4 is to me less interesting than Bifröst guarded by Heimdall with the Gjallarhorn. From the wildness of my heart I cannot exclude the question whether railway-engineers, if they had been brought up on more fantasy, might not have done better with all their abundant means than they commonly do. Fairy-stories might be, I guess, better Masters of Arts than the academic person I have referred to" (https://coolcalvary.files.wordpress.com/2018/10/on-fairy-stories1.pdf, 31).

60 Mortimer, "Tolkien and Modernism," *Tolkien Studies*, 2 (2005): 114. Cf. Aaron Jackson, "Authoring the Century: J. R. R. Tolkien, the Great War and Modernism," *English* 59, no. 224 (2010): 44–69; and Flieger, *Interrupted Music*, 13.

61 From a huge strain of Tolkien commentary, see John Holmes, "'Inside a Song:' Tolkien's Phonaesthetics," in *Middle-earth Minstrel: Essays on Music in Tolkien*, ed. B. Lee Eden (Jefferson, NC: McFarland & Co., 2010), 38–39.

62 Brogan, "Tolkien's Great War," in *Children and Their Books*, 356–57.

63 Bradford Lee Eden, "Strains of Elvish Song and Voices: Victorian Medievalism, Music, and Tolkien," in *Middle-earth Minstrel: Essays on Music in Tolkien*, 98–99.

64 William Blissett in 1959 as quoted in G. Boswell, "Tolkien as Littérateur," *The South Central Bulletin* 32, no. 4 (1972): 188, n. 11.

modernity"?[65] If we mean the cult of the machine in Futurism, no (chapter 1).[66] However, it would be too easy to say that his dislike of modernity follows from his having been on the receiving end of mechanized war as an infantryman in WW1. For example, like Wittgenstein—another WW1 combat veteran—Tolkien loved detective stories,[67] a thoroughly modern kind of fiction.[68]

Tom Shippey notes that Tolkien saw no great break between Old English and modern English,[69] and that, like Robert Graves, he found *Beowulf* an accurate summation of his own infantry experience.[70] David Jones concurs.[71] Modern life,[72] in its heightened form of industrial war even, was not alien from life in the so-called Dark Ages: "We [veterans of war] can guess, better than our immediate forebears, something of what a paid foot-soldier at Crécy *felt* about a damp bow-string and the heavy Picardy mud, and the relationship between these immediate, intimate, bodily-known things...."[73] Shippey observes that the battle scene between Bard and Smaug in

---

65 Naveh, "The Ainulindale and Tolkien's Approach to Modernity," in *The Return of the Ring: Proceedings of the Tolkien Society Conference 2012*, vol. 2, 102. Cf. Patrick Curry, *Defending Middle-earth*, 25.

66 John Ellison points out that Tolkien's late painting and graphics is almost exclusively plant forms (John Ellison, "Tolkien's Art," *Mallorn* 30 [1993]: 26).

67 Ordway, *Tolkien's Modern Reading*, 150–51.

68 In *Meditation on the Common Concept of Justice*, Leibniz expressed his belief that at the time there were not even ten thinkers throughout Europe looking through microscopes. He argued that princes could do no better for their kingdoms than proliferate the use of microscopes (G. W. Leibniz, *Political Writings* [Cambridge: Cambridge University Press, 1996], 51–53). Ernest Bloch astutely observes that detective fiction is micrological (E. Bloch et al., "A Philosophical View of the Detective Novel," *Discourse* 2 [Summer 1980]: 40).

69 His is an important point. Tolkien seems to have subscribed to Churchill's "our long island story," whereas modernists thought in terms of rupture and crisis. Elizabeth Ward, *David Jones, Mythmaker* (Manchester: Manchester University Press, 1983), 126–27; Michael North, *The Political Aesthetic of Yeats, Eliot, and Pound* (Cambridge: Cambridge University Press, 1991), 15.

70 Shippey, *J. R. R. Tolkien: Author of the Century*, xxviii–xxix.

71 Henderson Staudt, *At the Turn of a Civilization: David Jones and Modern Poetics* (Ann Arbor: The University of Michigan Press, 1994), 14–19.

72 Witt and Richards make the point that Hobbit life revolves around household objects and practices dating to sixty-odd years after the Industrial Revolution. At one point Bilbo fusses, looking for his matches to light his pipe: friction matches were invented in 1827 (Jonathan Witt & Jay Richards, *The Hobbit Party* [San Francisco: Ignatius, 2014], 24–26).

73 Jones, "Art in Relation to War," 128. Jones had read *The Hobbit* and Tolkien's medieval scholarship, but not the trilogy (William Blissett, *The Long Conversation: A Memoir of David Jones* [Oxford: Oxford University Press, 1981], 16).

The Hobbit is shaped by ideals of modern military discipline.[74] In chapter 2, I argue that Tolkien's interest in the strategic importance of geography parallels that of the Edwardian founder of geopolitics, Sir Halford Mackinder. Interestingly, the legal framework of *The Hobbit* is modern and is almost certainly influenced by legalities connected with post-Great War reparations.[75] Furthermore, some have pointed out that Tolkien and the modernists share an interest in myth.[76] Others have observed that Tolkien found a way to think about national and regional belonging through the psychoanalysis of C. G. Jung.[77] Flieger has noted the influence of Barfield on Tolkien. Barfield's is a contemporary, speculative philosophy of language—really, a metaphysical aesthetics—and he literally thought language rooted;[78] and, as Ross Smith points out, so did Tolkien. Smith points to Treebeard: "My name is growing all the time.... Real names tell you the story of the things they belong to in my language" (*TT*, 454).[79] This might explain Tolkien's fondness for the Catholic

---

74 Shippey, *J. R. R. Tolkien: Author of the Century*, 40–41.

75 Murray Smith, "Legal Bother: Law and Related Matters in The Hobbit," in *The Return of the Ring: Proceedings of the Tolkien Society Conference 2012*, vol. 2, 123–42, and especially 128–31.

76 Cf. Margaret Hiley, "Stolen Language, Cosmic Models: Myth and Mythology in Tolkien," *Modern Fiction Studies* 50, no. 4 (2004): 839.

77 "Now it would be English not simply because it was *about* England or because it happened *in* England, but because it was *ingrained in the memory* of countless generations of Englishmen, memory revived, re-experienced, and re-possessed by Lowdham (and presumably also by Jeremy, Guildford, and Ramer), through the genetic re-collections of their ancestors. This is, to say the least, a mode predicated not on Wellsian time-machinery but on Jungian psychology and the theory of the collective unconscious, plus something as close to reincarnation as makes no matter" (Verlyn Flieger, "'Do the Atlantis story and abandon Eriol-Saga.'" *Tolkien Studies* 1 [2004]: 53). Cf. Nancy Bunting, "Tolkien's Jungian Views on Language," *Mallorn: The Journal of the Tolkien Society* 57 (Winter 2016): 17–20.

78 At least since Suárez, the being of a metaphor has been a concern of philosophy (Francisco Suárez, *On Real Relation: Disputatio Metaphysica XLVII* [Milwaukee, WI: Marquette University Press, 2006], 81–84). Barfield: "It is these 'footsteps of nature' whose noise we hear alike in primitive language and in the finest metaphors of poets. Men do not invent those mysterious relations between separate external objects..." (Barfield, *Poetic Diction*, 86–89, 94–95, 163). Cf. Owen Barfield, *Saving the Appearances: A Study in Idolatry* (New York: Faber & Faber, 1957), 59.

79 Ross Smith also points to a passage where Legolas comments on Aragorn's singing: "That, I guess, is the language of the Rohirrim ... for it is like to this land itself; rich and rolling in part, and else hard and stern as the mountains. But I cannot guess what it means, save that it is laden with the sadness of Mortal Men" (*TT*, 496). See R. Smith, "Fitting Sense to Sound: Linguistic Aesthetics and Phonosemantics in the Work of J. R. R. Tolkien," *Tolkien Studies* 3 (2006): 15–16.

Romantic composer Carl Maria von Weber.[80] Of landscape music, Weber:

> If I stand absolutely still and look steadily towards the horizon, the image I obtain may be compared to something similar in the related mental world of my musical imagination, and I may well be able to take it to my heart, retain its contours and develop it. But heavens above! What a mad succession of funeral marches, rondos, furiosos and pastorals somersaults through my eyes! I become more and more silent as I struggle with the all too vivid demands of my brain. I cannot remove my gaze from the shining spectacle provided by nature.[81]

The ideas of morals, politics, and war discussed here are principally concepts shared by Tory philosophers alive when Tolkien wrote. Like all great artists, he was gifted with, and burdened by, remarkable intuitions about human beings and their longings, but he was also a great man for ideas, and there were many striking formulations floating in the air around him. In a letter to Christopher, Tolkien mentions a two-hour conversation with C. S. Lewis about "morals and theology" and Tolkien was so agile around political theory he could rather insightfully "joke," "Beware! All leftists are anti-philology!"[82] His pastoralism owed a debt to Ruskin, Morris, and Beatrix Potter (he owned their books), his engagement with modernity[83] Cardinal Newman (through his close personal connec-

---

80 Lee, "Tolkien in Oxford," 156.

81 As quoted in Joseph Morgan, "Nature, Weber, and a Revision of the French Sublime," in *Sineri Revista de Musicología* 15 (2014): 31, http://www.sineris.es/weber.pdf.

82 J. R. R. Tolkien, *The Letters of J. R. R. Tolkien: Revised and Expanded Edition*, 145 #89a and 367 #194a.

83 Though some fret about how much philosophy Tolkien knew, I do not. Not only was the man a sponge—the range of interests and concerns in his letters is *astonishing*—he also consorted with philosophers. Not only Barfield, but the Oxford Jesuit Martin d'Arcy, and Tolkien identifies philosophical inconsistency in C. S. Lewis, who was learned in philosophy. Just one example. Tolkien and d'Arcy knew one another well enough that when Ignatius "Roy" Campbell came to Oxford to chat with Tolkien, d'Arcy sent him down to the pub where he knew Tolkien would be at that time of day. Tolkien mentions d'Arcy in his *Letters*. His *The Mind and Heart of Love* (New York: Faber and Faber, 1945) went through four impressions and a second edition published: the book includes various discussions of Scheler. Interestingly, he also discusses Wyndham Lewis, the Futurist.

tion with the Birmingham Oratory),[84] and his thinking on death Simone de Beauvoir (from the newspaper, it seems).[85] Contemporary engagement is also found in the emphasis Tolkien places on fellow-ship, alliances, and communal fates. The Patristic idea of a collec-tive eschatology—interpersonal salvation—received fresh, subtle articulation at the time of the First World War in the personalism of Max Scheler (chapter 3 and chapter 5).[86] Tolkien, I argue, is best understood as one of a group of modern conservative thinkers who offer an alternative social philosophy to that of the Whigs. Tolkien's is a contribution to a twentieth-century contest about the character of our civilization.

This alternative to the Whigs is a proposal about land, property, work, adornment,[87] law, the sacred, morals, and monarchy. It is easy to think of Tolkien as a fabulist, a man living in a make-believe world because he had abandoned his own.[88] His is a fairy tale, right?[89] To the contrary, Tolkien himself explains that his is a resistance

---

84 Newman was critical to Przywara's updating of Aquinas's analogy of being. Tolkien served as an altar boy at the Birmingham Oratory, and in his *Letters* he remarks he was "virtually a junior inmate of the Oratory house" (*Letters*, 395 #306). H. Ordway, *Tolkien's Modern Reading*, 1–3.

85 Lee, "Tolkien in Oxford," 156.

86 Christopher Garbowski has noted that Tolkien's aversion to dualism (*Letters*, 371 #291) shows the influence of twentieth-century Catholic personalism (C. Garbowski, *Recovery and Transcendence for the Contemporary Mythmaker: The Spiritual Dimension in the Works of J. R. R. Tolkien* [Zollikofen, Bern: Walking Tree Publications, 2004], 168).

87 Witt and Richards read Tolkien as an Ancap (anarcho-capitalist). I see where they are coming from, but theirs is an odd claim, all the same. I critique their argument in chapter 3, but, in my opinion, they slide too easily from the fact that Bilbo likes doilies and pocket squares to the idea that the Shire is a "tech hub," full of the "innovative conveniences" of modern commercial civilization (Witt & Richards, *The Hobbit Party*, 25–26, 58). You can like ornamental waistcoats—as Bilbo, and Tolkien himself, sported—and be a Tory committed to business *patterned on* craft manufacture well able to support fashion, modern architecture, and the division of labor *inside* a political economy. At one point, Tolkien plays with the idea of having derived *Hobbit* from *rabbit*, an homage to Beatrix Potter, whom he loved. Amongst many accomplishments, she was an extremely successful farmer. Fancy waistcoats—and Tolkien was fascinated by the latter word—figure in her depictions of Jeremy Fisher and in her *The Tailor of Gloucester*, a charming Christmas tale Tolkien owned.

88 The position of Harold Bloom, for example. See his introduction to *Modern Critical Interpretations: J. R. R. Tolkien's The Lord of the Rings*, ed. Harold Bloom (New York: Chelsea House Publications, 2000).

89 On the underselling of the significance of fairy tales, see Bruno Bettelheim's classic volume on the hard psychological work children do listening to and reading fairy tales (*The Uses of Enchantment: The Meaning and Importance of Fairy Tales* [New York: Vintage, 1977]).

literature.[90] The remarkable continuity between his ideas and conservative contemporaries shows that he was part of a reaction to cultural transformations that he disapproved of morally and politically.[91] Tolkien (1892–1973) is an ally of well-known English Catholic writers like G. K. Chesterton (1874–1936) and Evelyn Waugh (1903–1966), British Tories like Mackinder (1861–1947) and Belloc (1870–1953), and, what I want to show especially, an ally of Central European Tory philosophers like Max Scheler (1874–1928), Carl Schmitt (1888–1985), Erich Przywara (1889–1972), Aurel Kolnai (1900–1973), and Eric Voegelin (1901–1985).

Monarchy

In every community, the great themes of war, friendship, treachery, decency, property, land, tyranny, legitimacy, evil, and the gods are the stuff of fascination (consider Plato's *Laws*, for example). How did Tolkien refine his own sense of these themes? This book defends the claim that Tolkien is a fellow traveler with the thinkers above, his art a dramatization that war is connected to the attachment to land, the boundaries of which depend on a sacred love,[92] and express the values of civilization. *When he gave to the sea his decree, That the waters should not pass his commandment: When he appointed the foundations of the earth* (Prov. 8:29). Our Tory thinkers held that civilization is inseparable from distinction, grace, privilege, hierarchy, moral order, political economy, and a retributive attitude willing to defend these things (*Letters*, 179 #144). Like them, Tolkien believes the Whig's valorization of vanity misshapes these themes, provoking

---

90 "The electric street-lamp may indeed be ignored, simply because it is so insignificant and transient. Fairy-stories, at any rate, have many more permanent and fundamental things to talk about. Lightning, for example. The escapist is not so subservient to the whims of evanescent fashion as these opponents. He does not make things (which it may be quite rational to regard as bad) his masters or his gods by worshipping them as inevitable, even 'inexorable.' And his opponents, so easily contemptuous, have no guarantee that he will stop there: he might rouse men to pull down the street-lamps. Escapism has another and even wickeder face: Reaction" (https://coolcalvary.files.wordpress.com/2018/10/on-fairy-stories1.pdf, 30).

91 Tolkien's daily newspapers were the conservative broadsheets, *The Times* and *The Daily Telegraph* (*Letters*, 367 #284). Both then were more conservative than they are today.

92 Shippey, *The Road to Middle-earth* (Houghton Mifflin, 1983), 214.

an apocalyptic return to primitivism. His contribution is to have seen that war stems from vanity's lack of patience. It is because of the link between beauty and patience that monarchy figures so prominently in his writing.

When it was decided that *LotR* should appear as three volumes, a tussle between Tolkien and his publisher broke out. A sticking point was the title of the third volume, *The Return of the King*. Though Tolkien considered dedicating *LotR* to Queen Elizabeth II—he was "deeply moved" when he met her later in life (*Letters*, 418 #334)—this is the title set by the publisher, not Tolkien. He preferred *The War of the Ring*.[93] When pondering the military trappings of monarchy, we see that both titles are intimately connected.[94] War, thinks Tolkien, is sometimes necessary to preserve civilization. Though monarchy is not identical with civilization, monarchy does elevate it. Interestingly, this point unites Whigs and Tories: Hume, Smith, and Kolnai all argue that monarchy is tone-setting, that the institution accentuates the beautiful in establishment. Hume:

> The only difference is, that, in a republic, the candidates for office must look downwards, to gain the suffrages of the people; in a monarchy, they must turn their attention upwards, to court the good graces and favor of the great. To be successful in the former way, it is necessary for a man to make himself *useful*, by his industry, capacity, or knowledge: To be prosperous in the latter way, it is requisite for him to render himself *agreeable*, by his wit, complaisance, or civility. A strong genius succeeds best in republics: A refined taste in monarchies.[95]

The Standard of Elendil, Aragorn's battle standard unfurled at the Battle of the Pelennor Fields on his return to his ancestral city, says much. It displays stars, the White Tree (Nimloth), and the crown of the kings of Gondor (*RK*, 829). The battle standard places the

---

93 White, *J. R. R. Tolkien*, 203.

94 As Joseph Pearce points out, two of Tolkien's books—*LotR* and *The Hobbit*—are about the restoration of monarchs (*Frodo's Journey: Discover the Hidden Meaning of the Lord of the Rings* [Charlotte, NC: St. Benedict Press, 2015], chapter 13 [ebook]).

95 David Hume, "The Rise of the Arts and Sciences," *Essays: Moral, Political, and Literary*, 126.

Crown in a cosmic setting, harmonious with flora and the stars. Monarchy holds its legitimacy when it forces our "attention upwards" (Hume), making us look up at the trees and stars. The time signature of trees and stars is, to us, educative: they are steadfast, and they teach us how to be, also. The word *patience* comes from the Latin *patientia*, the root being *patiens*, which means to endure or wait, itself derived from the verb, *patior*, meaning to suffer. Ultimately, monarchy, contends Tolkien, is a lesson in patience, an institution of time, proposing endurance amidst suffering. It is an anti-Gnostic institution.

Kolnai speaks of "the timeless moral order which genuine Conservative statecraft recognizes as the irremovable measure of its designs and acts" (*PL*, 115). Monarchy alerts us to this timeless moral order because its ornate rituals make vivid gradation, difference, height, offices, honors, style, manners, law, all of which express transcendence and harmony. Monarchy holds its legitimacy from the support it lends to the higher aesthetic and moral properties of establishment. In our world, think of the governmental institutions supporting value clusters, e.g., a nation's Foreign Office and the elegant science of strategy. In Arda, consider Tolkien's description of the Guards of the Citadel, who wear the livery of Elendil—the symbols on Aragorn's battle standard. Their watch is atop the Tower of Ecthelion: at the sight of which, when he first saw it, Pippin "cried aloud." Tolkien's description:

> ... standing high within the topmost wall, shone out against the sky, glimmering like a spike of pearl and silver, tall and fair and shapely, and its pinnacle glittered as if it were wrought of crystals; and white banners broke and fluttered from the battlements in the morning breeze, and high and far he heard a clear ringing as of silver trumpets. (*RK*, 734–35)

Pippin looks upwards, to a height where not only do stars and monarchy combine, but a value order reigns, celestial patience. For the tower is a platform for Nimloth, for a garden:

A sweet fountain played there in the morning sun, and a sward of bright green lay about it; but in the midst, drooping over the pool, stood a dead tree, and the falling drops dripped sadly from its barren and broken branches back into the clear water. Pippin glanced at it as he hurried after Gandalf. It looked mournful, he thought, and he wondered why the dead tree was left in this place where everything else was well tended. (*RK*, 736–37)

Nimloth traces its lineage back to Yavanna, who is aratar, one of the Queens of the Valar (*S*, 27): "Some there are who have seen her standing like a tree under heaven." We will see the full significance of why flora sits at the heart of good political order in chapter 2. For now, note Yavanna is a figure of patience. She sows seeds and "swiftly" "there arose a multitude of growing things great and small," but, importantly, "as yet no flower had bloomed nor any bird had sung, for these things waited still their time in the bosom of Yavanna; but wealth there was in her imagining" (*S*, 35). Nimloth is part of the heraldry of Númenórean sacral-kingship (*Letters*, 206 #156).[96] Right governance and monarchy are paired because monarchy gets aesthetics right. Its time signature is like that of trees and stars, where time is slow and sober. Its "posture of distance," its aloof rites, have a restraining function, holding off the apocalyptic.

This posture is absent in the false kingship of the Enemy, who lowers and primitivizes. Melkor makes the boast to Húrin: "I am the Elder King: Melkor, first and mightiest of all the Valar, who was before the world, and made it."[97] Tolkien writes that Melkor "grew hot" with impatience at the "emptiness" of the Void. To him, the restraint of Yavanna is utterly irksome, and he will destroy her greatest creative act, the Two Trees that light Middle-earth. Sauron, and his master, Melkor, hate civilization—"undying hatred" (*S*, xxii). The armies of Sauron and Saruman are masses of orcs: crude, ill-spoken, grotesque cannibals. They represent the spirit of Melkor, who desires

---

96 Cf. Michael Cunningham, "In the Shadow of the Tree: A Study of the Motif of the White Tree in the Context of JRR Tolkien's Middle-Earth," *Mallorn* 44 (2006): 4.

97 J. R. R. Tolkien, *The Tale of the Children of Húrin* (Boston: Houghton Mifflin, 2007), 64.

to exercise power unreservedly (*Letters*, 145 #131) over a docile, undifferentiated (Voegelin) horde, lacking style, manners, and status: "And hobbits as miserable slaves would please him far more than hobbits happy and free. There is such a thing as malice and revenge" (*FR*, 48). The Ring reprimitivizes: it subverts human dignity by suspending personal determination. Akin to demonic possession, it works by hypnosis, freezing higher functioning (chapter 5). This idea is vividly portrayed by Sauron's mastery of the hollowed-out nine kings, the Ringwraiths.

In a rich article on the Music of the Ainur, Reuven Naveh notes that in tonal music the tonic is the position of stability, unstable moments in the movement resolving at the tonic. He observes that the tonic has been compared to a monarch.[98] By way of confirmation, and in an interesting formulation, Schoenberg argues that it is only atonal music that does not lead to Rome.[99] As we will see, Tolkien proposes that a sober civilizational order requires a philosophy of history of incomplete knowledge, restraint, and patience (*Letters*, 348–49 #257). Tolkien explains that the gods were astonished, caught by surprise at the arrival of the Children of Ilúvatar in Middle-earth: "they perceived that they themselves in the labour of their music had been busy with the preparation of this dwelling, and yet knew not that it had any purpose beyond its own beauty" (*S*, 18). Manwë, "dearest to Ilúvatar and understands most clearly his purposes" has limited knowledge, for he sees and hears more when his Queen sits with him, Varda, Lady of the Stars. It is on account of her gift of perception that Melkor "hated her, and feared her more than all others whom Eru made" (*S*, 26). Melkor hates the restraint she represents.

The deeper meaning of Aragorn's battle standard is that monarchy is keyed to cosmos and therewith is a restraint, a block on apocalypse. The Gnostic invokes apocalypse because tiring of suffering. Monarchy counsels patience. For some evidence, consider

---

98 Naveh, "The Ainulindale and Tolkien's Approach to Modernity," 101, 110.
99 Theodor Adorno, *Philosophy of Modern Music* (London: Continuum, 2004), 3.

the British monarchy. At the time of her death, the word frequently attached to Elizabeth II was the word *steadfast*. Charles III's passion for gardening is another illustration. He has written:

> I suppose, when I think about it, I have gardened to a certain extent from a painter's perspective. Each part of the garden is a separate "painting" and the result of ceaseless walking, ruminating and observing. . . . I think I learnt quite quickly that placing anything in a garden can easily go wrong if you rush at it, so I have tried never to force a plan or design.[100]

As Adam Smith points out, Whiggery appeals to "the bustling, spirited, active folks," but Toryism appeals to "the calm, contented folks of no great spirit and abundant fortunes which they want to enjoy at their own ease, and don't want to be disturbed nor to disturb others."[101] Tolkien would have been thrilled to see a gardener become king—best to have a monarch preoccupied by the aphids on his roses—and would hardly be surprised.

Restraint was not a trademark of Futurism. The leader of English Vorticism was Wyndham Lewis. He wrote a play, *The Enemy of the Stars*, which appeared in the first issue of the movement's magazine, *Blast*. At the bottom of the front cover, in all-caps, were the words: THE END OF THE CHRISTIAN ERA. In his play, Wyndham Lewis casts the cosmos as a machine—"Throats iron eternities, drinking heavy radiance, limbs towers of blatant light, the stars poised, immensely distant, with their metal sides, pantheistic machines,"—a machine, hostile to humans—"The stars shone madly in the archaic blank wilderness of the universe, machines of prey. . . . He rose before this cliff of cadaverous beaming force, imprisoned in a messed socket of existence."[102] This ethos could not contrast more with Tolkien's metaphysical aesthetics, a summation of which is found in the domestic life of Goldberry and Tom Bombadil. From the east window of their thatched cottage, you look out onto their

---

100 Charles III, "Introduction," *Highgrove* (n.p.: Rizzoli, n.d.).
101 Smith, *Lectures on Jurisprudence*, 320.
102 *Blast 1*, 64.

kitchen-garden, and from the west window, their flower-garden. Day-long they sing with "glad voice." Goldberry's voice is "as young and as ancient as Spring" and to Frodo's eyes she appears as "a fair young elf-queen clad in living flowers." Singing a song of hope, Tom gives assurance to the Hobbits: "Waiting on the doorstep for the cold starlight/There my pretty lady is, River-woman's daughter." Beauty has its proper setting amidst the harmony of gardens and beneath the stars. To hold this near, Aragorn's battle standard shows, is worth suffering the fight.

1

History and the Last Battle

> "I am historically minded."
>
> J. R. R. Tolkien (*Letters*, 239 #183)[1]

Tolkien's fairy stories are beloved. Ideals of home, quest, and sacrifice counter war, evil, and catastrophic threat. An indication that Tolkien's apocalyptic anxiety retains its place in our cultural imagination is the one billion dollars Amazon spent on their 2022 television version of *The Lord of the Rings: The Rings of Power*.

Tolkien's letters show that his art consciously attacked the Machine: by Machine, "I intend all use of external plans or devices (apparatus) instead of developments of the inherent inner powers or talents ... bull-dozing the real world, or coercing other wills. The Machine is our more obvious form though more closely related to Magic than is usually recognized" (*S*, xiii). Emblematic of the Futurism movement that dominated art in the first half of the twentieth century, the Machine encoded anti-Christianity, fascist politics,[2] and

---

1 Hammond and Scull argue that Tolkien "had an archivist's soul" (Wayne G. Hammond and Christina Scull, *J. R. R. Tolkien, Artist and Illustrator* [New York: Houghton Mifflin, 1995], 7). Cf. Shandi Stevenson, "Beyond the Circles of this World: The Great War, Time, History, and Eternity in the Fantasy of J. R. R. Tolkien and C. S. Lewis," in *Baptism of Fire*, 110–30.

2 The movement published all manner of manifestoes and magazines. Under the masthead of early editions of a leading magazine, *Futurismo*, ran *Futurism is the spiritual heritage of Fascism* (Susan

apocalyptic war.[3] This chapter documents that Tolkien thought war an aesthetic phenomenon. Aware of the great art movements of his time,[4] Tolkien's account of war contends against Futurism's philosophy of history,[5] the latter of which is an example of what Voegelin calls an "immanentist apocalypse."[6]

The movement imagined a Promethean remaking of humanity—example: Umberto Boccioni's 1913 sculpture, *Unique Forms of Continuity in Space.* In sharp contrast, Tolkien's "cosmogonical drama" proposes a philosophy of history of incomplete knowledge, sobriety, and patience.[7] The Valar, for example, have limited foreknowledge.[8] Tolkien's pastoralism and portraits of angels (Gandalf), Elves (Elrond), and gods (Mandos) dramatize a metaphysical aesthetics countering Futurism's vanity, the movement's Gnostic

---

Thompson, "Futurism, Fascism, and Mino Somenzi's Journals of the 1930s: *Futurismo, Sant'Elia,* and *Artecrazia,*" in *Italian Futurism 1909–1944: Reconstructing the Universe,* ed. Vivien Greene [New York: Guggenheim, 2014], 256).

3 Emilio Gentile: "The Futurists welcomed that cataclysm [WW1] with enthusiasm, viewing it as a propitious opportunity for '"tearing out and scorching the deepest roots' that the ideal of a pacific and loving humanity had embedded in the consciousness of modern man" ("The Reign of the Man Whose Roots Are Cut: Dehumanism and Anti-Christianity in the Futurist Revolution" in *Italian Futurism 1909–1944,* 172).

4 About Tolkien's exposure to modern art, Hammond and Scull: "He could not have escaped hearing about it: exhibitions such as Roger Fry's Post-Impressionist show in 1910 and the International Surrealist Exhibition of 1936 sent shock waves throughout Britain and led to rousing debates" (Hammond and Scull, *J. R. R. Tolkien, Artist and Illustrator,* 11). Cf. Fleiger, *Interrupted Music,* 13. About those "shock waves," Virginia Woolf famously observed: "On or about December 1910 human character changed." One of the first fruits of that date was Vorticism, the English variant of Futurism (Wees, *Vorticism and the English Avant-Garde,* 12––13).

5 A 1910 manifesto of Futurism runs: "That all subjects previously used must be swept aside in order to express our whirling life of steel, of pride, of fever and of speed" (as quoted in Wees, *Vorticism and the English Avant-Garde,* 12). Contrast Tolkien: "A curious disturbance of the mind is often set up by the very act of drawing things of this kind, a state similar in quality and consciousness of morbidity to the sensations in a high fever, when the mind develops a distressing fecundity and facility in figure-making, seeing forms sinister or grotesque in all visible objects about it" (https:// coolcalvary.files.wordpress.com/2018/10/on-fairy-stories1.pdf, 38).

6 Voegelin, "Anxiety and Reason," 82. Voegelin contends that the politics of modernity—positivism, Marxism, communism, fascism, and National Socialism—all stem from philosophies of history that transmute Biblical apocalypticism (Eric Voegelin, "Ersatz Religion," in *Science, Politics and Gnosticism* [Wilmington, DE: Intercollegiate Studies Institute, 2004], 61).

7 For the scope of Tolkien's reflections on the Elves' "mytho-astronomical" picture of the world, including sketches he made, see J. R. R. Tolkien, *The Nature of Middle-earth,* ed. Carl Hostetter (Boston: Houghton Mifflin, 2021), 279–85.

8 J. R. R. Tolkien, *The Nature of Middle-earth,* 307.

rejection of the *analogia entis*.[9] This chapter holds that Tolkien shared with Voegelin and Erich Przywara the conviction that good politics requires situating humanity between geography and history, or cosmos and Revelation. Strikingly, the Númenóreans reject this.

Insufficient Beauty

Though not in the books, the film version of *LotR* includes an amusing scene that delivers a probing point. Éowyn—King Théoden's niece—has a crush on Aragorn and brings him stew she has made. The stew is awful but, ever-gracious, Aragorn eats heroically. Éowyn is puzzled by his looks. She has learnt that Aragorn fought with her grandfather, yet he looks to be a man in his prime, or even younger. Quizzing him, it dawns on her that he is no mere man, but Dúnedain. Aragorn is a descendant of one of the Faithful, a remnant of the Númenóreans who escaped extinction in an apocalypse. The Faithful obeyed the edict of the gods not to trespass upon the lands of the Valar. From vanity, the vast majority of the Númenóreans joined the invasion of Valinor and God sweeps their civilization away in an apocalypse. Though not literally the end of days for Middle-earth, of that event Tolkien says: "It is a foretaste of the End of Arda."[10]

Éowyn's crush poses an intellectual puzzle: blessed with intelligence and grace,[11] how was the beauty of the Númenóreans not enough? Why, despite their divine favor, were they not contented? Why did they wage war against the gods who had so favored them? There might be a hint in Aquinas.

---

9 "In their program to reconstruct the universe, Balla and Depero voiced a desire to create bones and flesh from the invisible, the impalpable, the imponderable, and the imperceptible" (Lisa Panzera, "Celestial Futurism and the 'Parasurreal,'" in *Italian Futurism 1909–1944*, 326). For a good discussion of the cosmic ambitions of modernist apocalypticism, see Roger Griffin, *Modernism and Fascism* (London: Palgrave, 2007), 95–99.

10 This sentence comes from Tolkien's last writings and, interestingly, the sentence is italicized in the text: J. R. R Tolkien, *The Nature of Middle-earth*, 344.

11 Tolkien explains that, on account of their long lives, Númenóreans spent more time on learning lore and crafts and far excelled regular men in sophistication. Furthermore, in a case of divine predilection, by the grace of the Valar they had particularly blessed lives (J. R. R Tolkien, *The Nature of Middle-earth*, 318).

In Aquinas, beauty is not a transcendental.[12] He proposes that the most elementary properties of things are unity, truth, and goodness. These are the transcendentals, and they are convertible: that is, whatever exists, is also one, true, and good. Evil is a privation: a negation, it reduces one of the three properties, and therewith, in proportion, the other two. The core metaphysical attributes of everything are three because of cosmic harmony: everything participates in the Trinity: Father (one), Son (truth), Holy Ghost (goodness). What is missing is beauty. It is as though beauty cannot be quite trusted (chapter 3). Why?

About the *LotR*, Tolkien says: "The story is cast in terms of a good side, and a bad side, beauty against ruthless ugliness, tyranny against kingship ..." (*Letters*, 178 #144). At times, this is plain to see. For example, in the encounter between Wormtongue and Gandalf. In the film version, Wormtongue is presented as a sweaty creeper and Gandalf a pope. Gandalf performs an exorcism, casting out Saruman from Théoden, who transforms from a croaking, twisted, shrunken man to a king in his prime. Here, Gandalf's beauty is quite literally soteriological. However, matters are altogether more complicated with Denethor. Denethor is not straightforwardly evil, but he fails morally. Pippin finds Denethor impressive, but ...: "Denethor looked indeed much more like a great wizard than Gandalf did, more kingly, beautiful, and powerful; and older. Yet by a sense other than sight Pippin perceived that Gandalf had the greater power and the deeper wisdom, and a majesty that was veiled" (*RK*, 740). The problem of beauty is even more stark with Boromir: a valiant knight, but not what you'd call strategically-minded, and, for this reason, he falls for the power of the Ring. Inversely, the Ents, though magnificent, are not conventionally beautiful, nor is Bombadil, who at least plays the part of a jolly, bumbling, playful giant character. Who, or what, is Bombadil is unclear: even Elrond is not sure (*FR*, 258); Tolkien

---

12 For an insightful treatment, see the classic article by Jan Artsen, "Beauty in the Middle Ages: A Forgotten Transcendental?" and listen to the lecture delivered at Catholic University of Leuven (1990): https://ecommons.cornell.edu/bitstream/handle/1813/56590/MPAT_1__1159539705_68_97_pdf.pdf?sequence=1&isAllowed=y.

at one point suggests he is more a what, than a who, the principle of botany (*Letters*, 192 #153).

Tolkien, sometimes, conventionally presents beauty—Galadriel, "a slender elf-woman, clad in simple white, whose gentle voice was soft and sad" (*FR*, 356). Arwen and Aragorn would be examples, Lúthien, another.[13] Sometimes, though, beauty is vanity, a lure, a false friend. Examples include the Arkenstone, the Ring, and, catastrophically for the Elves, the Silmarils. Beauty is a potential lure because it is always adjacent to vanity. Pascal: "There is no better proof of human vanity than to consider the causes and effects of love, because the whole universe can be changed by it. Cleopatra's nose."[14] The history of war and civilizations turns upon the millimeters of a nose. Pascal's comment is one of the truly great condensations of the problem of vanity. Three men—Cesar, Anthony, and Augustus—contended with those few millimeters. The one who resisted the lure bequeathed us our civilization.[15]

Tolkien reports a conversation where he and Lewis decided to write stories: Lewis would take up the theme of space and Tolkien time.[16] Vanity is entwinned in the tension between beauty and history (Eccles. 12:1–8), the tension that makes beauty too slippery for the transcendentals. Tolkien's lore is a philosophy of history alert to Pascal's observation.

Tolkien came of age at a time of intense interest in the philosophy of history.[17] Philosophies of history,[18] sometimes called

---

13 J. R. R. Tolkien, *Lúthien and Beren* (Boston: Houghton Mifflin, 2018), 42.

14 Pascal, *Pensées*, 58–59 #197.

15 Cf. Dawson, *Progress and Religion*, 216.

16 J. R. R. Tolkien, *The Lost Road and Other Writings*, ed. Christopher Tolkien (Boston: Houghton Mifflin, 1987), 7.

17 Michael Potts, "'Evening-Lands': Spenglerian Tropes in *Lord of the Rings*," *Tolkien Studies* 13 (2016): 149–53. Cf. Northrop Frye, *Spiritus Mundi: Essays on Literature, Myth, and Society* (Bloomington: Indiana University Press, 1976), 179–98.

18 As one of the best commentators on Tolkien observes, his own mind seemed to work historically: "As Tolkien developed these scenes, he was summoning to his imagination whole tranches of European culture from centuries past. . . . And really this is what we should expect from a man with such a historical sweep to his thought, with such strong opinions about the course of Western civilization, and who was so keen to install a sense of diuturnity in his sub-created world" (Ordway, *Tolkien's Modern Reading*, 181–82).

speculative histories, are variations on Leibniz's *Theodicy* and Adam Smith's *An Inquiry into the Nature and Causes of the Wealth of Nations*, portraits of the universal drivers of world events. In Tolkien's day,[19] they comprised the dominant systems of thought. The West was in the grip of Comtean positivism,[20] a liberal progressive theory of history—Whiggery—whilst the East was beholden to Hegelian Marxism. We are similarly placed. More or less till the Russo-Ukraine War of 2022, it was broadly held by policy makers at the world's leading institutions that we lived in a globalized world. As already noted, a key architect of globalization was Francis Fukuyama, and his brilliant philosophy of history in *The End of History*. Tolkien is at the other end of the spectrum from Fukuyama's progressivism. Tolkien in 1944: "A small knowledge of history depresses one with a sense of the everlasting mass and weight of human iniquity: old, old, dreary, endless repetitive unchanging incurable wickedness. All towns, all villages, all habitations of men—sinks!" (*Letters*, 80 #69).

Tolkien frames his lore, thusly: "*The Silmarillion* is the history of the War of the Exiled Elves against the Enemy" (*Letters*, 148 #131). Bilbo is a chronicler (*FR*, 1), Elrond a walking history book (*FR*, 244), and Sam tells Frodo they are future history, that their adventure will figure in the stories retold in the Shire (*TT*, 697). Indeed, there are places in the myth where the actors themselves are aware of the mythic times of their own history.[21] For Tolkien, time and war are twins. The reason for this is vanity. Pascal punctured our vanity by pointing out that we are suspended between two abysses: the abyss of nothingness and the abyss of the infinite.[22] He argues we foolishly challenge this reality with our innovations (diversions). Time reveals the abysses, nonetheless, and we are affronted. In his BBC interview,

---

19 Tolkien and Collingwood were both faculty at Pembroke College. Collingwood consulted with Tolkien on his *Roman Britain* and was working on his philosophy of history. *The Idea of History* appeared in 1946, but Dawson criticizes Collingwood's early stabs at the philosophy of history (Dawson, *Progress and Religion*, 44–45).

20 Dawson, *Progress and Religion*, 15.

21 Lionel Basney, "Myth, History, and Time in *The Lord of the Rings*," *Understanding* The Lord of the Rings, ed. Rose A. Zimbardo and Neil D. Isaacs (Boston: Houghton Mifflin, 2004), 183–94.

22 Pascal, *Pensées*, 61 #199.

Tolkien pulls from his pocket a news clipping and reads Simone de Beauvoir contending that death is seen by man as an "unjustifiable violation." Tolkien comments that her insight is the kernel of *LotR*, a tale "about Death and the desire for deathlessness" (*Letters*, 262 #203).[23] It is this vanity that is the engine of war. Against the caution of St. Paul,[24] war would wrest the Apocalypse from God's initiative.

The Last Battle

War begins before earth is full created. Arda and the history of war on Arda begin at the same time. Melkor starts the war, and it and Middle-earth end together. In the original plotting of *The Silmarillion*, Tolkien outlined an apocalyptic Last Battle—"the Last Battle and the Day of Doom" (*S*, 279)—or the Dagor Dagorath—Battle of all Battles—as Gandalf calls it.[25] Rudimentary parts of Tolkien's lore date to the start of WW1[26] and, he tells us, "I wrote a lot else in hospitals before the end of the First Great War" (*Letters*, 215 #163). Nonetheless, *The Silmarillion* was still unfinished at his death in 1973.

It is a matter of some controversy that the Last Battle is not in the final version, a decision made by Christopher Tolkien, seemingly contrary to his father's intentions.[27] The Last Battle is the close of history, what Tolkien also called the Long Battle, because it would last 50 years. In Tolkien's outline, the battle figures in a prophecy made by the Vala of judgement, Mandos (hence, Fëanor dismisses Melkor, "jail-crow of Mandos" [*S*, 72]). The outline varied over the years, and what follows is a composite.

According to the prophecy, at the end of days, Fionwë finally defeats Morgoth. Sallying forth "when the world is old and the

---

23 Lee, "Tolkien in Oxford," 156.

24 "That ye be not soon shaken in mind, or be troubled, neither by spirit, nor by word, nor by letter as from us, as that the day of Christ is at hand. . . . Let no man deceive you by any means: for that day shall not come, except there come a falling away first, and that man of sin be revealed, the son of perdition" (2 Thess. 2: 2–3).

25 J. R. R. Tolkien, *Unfinished Tales*, 395.

26 And before, maybe: Tolkien relayed to Clyde Kilby that some themes were clear to his mind as early as 1906. Clyde Kilby, *Tolkien & The Silmarillion* (Carol Stream, IL: Harold Shaw, 1976), 47.

27 Douglas Kane, *Arda Reconstructed* (Bethlehem, PA: Lehigh University Press, 2009), 236–39.

Powers grow weary,"[28] Morgoth attacks, but Eärendil, returning from the heavens, strikes a first, disorienting blow. Then begins the Last Battle with Tulkas (Vala), Fionwë (Maia), and Túrin (man) leading the line against Melkor. It is Tulkas right at the start of the history of Middle-earth who delivers Melkor's first battlefield reversal, and he represents the gods in battle at the end of history, too. "The black sword of Túrin shall deal unto Morgoth his death," and the apocalypse begins to change geography: Middle-earth is broken and remade, the Silmarils cracked open to rekindle the Two Trees slain by Melkor, and the Mountains of Valinor—a fortification of the gods—levelled, so that the light of the trees illumine the entire world. And there is a resurrection, too: "In that light the Gods will grow young again, and the Elves awake and all their dead arise, and the purpose of Ilúvatar be fulfilled concerning them."[29] This last element dates to the '20s and '30s, part of "the earliest Silmarillion."[30]

The Last Battle is what you might call orthodox apocalypse, apocalypse at the initiative of God. Ultimately, our concern is with the unorthodox Gnostic variety, "immanentist apocalypse."

Though the Second Prophecy of Mandos drops out of the book, apocalyptic war of the first type still figures in the published version. For example: Elves believe that when Dwarves die, they return to the stone from whence they were created by one of the Valar, Aulë. About the Dwarves themselves, Tolkien writes, "yet that is not their own belief." Dwarves claim that Aulë "declared to their Fathers of old that Ilúvatar will hallow them and give them a place among the Children in the End. Then their part shall be to serve Aulë and to aid him in the remaking of Arda after the Last Battle" (S, 44). Dwarves are craftsmen, stone masons, and engineers, capable of great feats of building, exemplified by the awesome halls of Khazad-dûm. An apocalyptic last battle will be followed by a blessed rebuilding.

---

28 J. R. R. Tolkien, *The Peoples of Middle-earth*, ed. Christopher Tolkien (Boston: Houghton Mifflin, 1996), 405.

29 J. R. R. Tolkien, *The Lost Road and Other Writings*, ed. Christopher Tolkien (Boston: Houghton Mifflin, 1987), 333.

30 J. R. R Tolkien, *The Peoples of Middle-earth*, 374–75.

In the manuscript version, the final Númenórean battle ending in the apocalyptic destruction of the Númenóreans is described as a "foretaste" of the end of days. At the end of the battle, "the Elves of Tol-eressëa passed through the gates of death, and were gathered to their kindred in the land of the Gods, and became as they; and the Lonely Isle remained only as a shape of the past."[31] Before this divinization of the Elves, and remaking of geography, God had intervened in the war. So vast was the Númenórean fleet it cut off light from Valinor and the Elves sickened. As the first Númenóreans stormed the beach of the land of the gods, God opens an abyss before Aman and the Lonely Isle and both the sea and ships upon it are sucked into the void, with the troops who had landed buried by hills falling.

I'll say more about this below, but the manuscript version has the Númenóreans inspired by "a message of deliverance," preached to them by a demon. For, though long-lived, the Númenóreans are still mortal and, discontented with their lot, "their masters of lore sought unceasingly for the secrets that should prolong their lives."[32] This is de Beauvoir's point that Tolkien stresses. As we'll see, the problem of time and masters of salvific lore are Gnostic themes.

In *The Silmarillion* as published, the end of history is introduced on the first page, in a passage known as the Second Music of the Ainur:

> Never since have the Ainur made any music like to this music, though it has been said a greater still shall be made before Ilúvatar by the choirs of the Ainur and the Children of Ilúvatar after the end of days. Then the themes of Ilúvatar shall be played aright, and take Being in the moment of their utterance, for all shall then understand fully his intent in their part, and each shall know the comprehension of each, and Ilúvatar shall give to their thoughts the secret fire, being well pleased. (S, 15–16)

---

31 J. R. R. Tolkien, *The Lost Road and Other Writings*, 16.

32 J. R. R. Tolkien, *The Lost Road and Other Writings*, 15.

The cosmological music of God[33] is not presently "played aright" because Melkor has woven his own novel strains into it. Bringing with it war, this new variation in history stems from vanity: "for desire grew hot within him to bring into Being things of his own." Aquinas identifies novelty as the leading characteristic of vanity[34] and that is why time and history figure so prominently in Tolkien. About Melkor, Tolkien says, "it seemed to him that Ilúvatar took no thought for the Void, and he was impatient of its emptiness" (S, 16). The metaphysics of war is keyed to acceleration.

Futurism

Voegelin observes that apocalypse is a recurring symbol of Western political experience.[35] Tolkien is an example and so, too, like a reverse image of him, is the Futurism art movement.

In a letter critical to Tolkien studies—a letter Tolkien wrote to the publisher Milton Waldman in 1951 once *LotR* was completed— Tolkien explains much of his work as "linguistic aesthetics." The letter is included by Christopher Tolkien at the start of *The Silmarillion* to introduce the underlying ideas of the book (it is #131 in the *Letters*). In the Ur-text of his lore, Tolkien explains, beauty is contrasted with the Machine, designed "for making the will more quickly effective" (S, xiii).[36] The English version of Futurism was dubbed Vorticism. Ezra Pound explains why: "It represents, in mechanics, the greatest efficiency."[37] Though the English variant, like the Italian,

---

33 Bradford Lee Eden, "The 'Music of the Spheres': Relationships between Tolkien's *The Silmarillion* and Medieval Cosmological and Religious Theory," in *Tolkien the Medievalist*, ed. Jane Chance [London: Routledge, 2003], 184–86.

34 Aquinas, *On Evil*, 349.

35 E. Voegelin, *What Is History? and Other Late Unpublished Writings*, Collected Works, vol. 28 (Baton Rouge: Louisiana State University Press, 1990), 15–16.

36 "Modern Urban civilization no longer has any contact with the soil or the instinctive life of nature. The whole population lives in a high state of nervous tension, even where it has not reached the frenzied activity of American city life. Everywhere the conditions of life are becoming more and more artificial, and make an increasing demand on men's nervous energies. The rhythm of social life is accelerated, since it is no longer forced to keep time with the life of nature" (Dawson, *Progress and Religion*, 212).

37 Roberto Marchiò, "The Vortex in the Machine: Futurism in England," *International Futurism in Arts and Literature*, ed. Günter Berghaus (Berlin: De Gruyter, 2012), 107. Contrast Charles III, "For

thought "machinery is the greatest Earth-medium,"[38] it was stridently nativist, claiming Nordic ownership over the origin of the machine and casting itself directly against the dominant art of the day, Morris's Arts & Crafts movement.[39] You can imagine how both claims must have sat with Tolkien.

Tolkien clearly set his face against Futurism,[40] an aesthetics and philosophy of history that shaped the first half of the twentieth century, and resonates still.[41] The manifestoes and art of the movement proposed, says the Italian historian of fascism[42] Emilio Gentile, "an acceleration of the rhythms of time, the invention and multiplication of technical means for the domination and exploitation of nature, an expansion of energies both human and material, an intensification of individual and collective life through struggle, a new sense of the world."[43] The movement heralded fascism. Mussolini: "I formally declare that without Futurism there would never have been a fascist revolution."[44] Benedetto Croce: "To anyone with

---

Modernism, by its unrelenting emphasis on the quantitative view of reality, limits and distorts the true nature of the Real and our perception of it" (Charles III, Introductory Comments, Sacred Web Conference, 2006: http://www.sacredweb.com/conference06/conference_introduction.html).

38 Giovanni Cianci, "Futurism and the English Avant-Garde: the Early Pound between Imagism and Vorticism," *Arbeiten Aus Anglistik Und Amerikanistik* 6, no. 1 (1981): 16.

39 Cianci, "Futurism and the English Avant-Garde: the Early Pound between Imagism and Vorticism," 12.

40 C. S. Lewis published an anthology in reply to Vorticism (Philip Zaleski & Carol Zaleski, *The Fellowship: The Literary Lives of the Inklings* [New York: Farrar, Straus and Giroux, 2015], 93).

41 King Charles III includes a picture of the Boccioni in his 2010 *Harmony*, where he argues that this WW1 art movement inaugurated our modernism, and that its ideal of the human as "a machine-like being" remains basic to our ethos (*Harmony: A New Way of Looking at Our World* [London: HarperCollins, 2010], 168–71). His discussion forms part of his argument that modernity is an age of fracture, breaking with the wisdom of previous civilizations, which believed that we are set in a cosmic, divine order (*Harmony*, 148–50). He argues that Aquinas was one of the last thinkers to see our cosmic place clearly.

42 Italian fascism celebrated the Great War for accelerating history: Jorge Dagnino, "The Myth of the New Man in Italian Fascist Ideology," *Fascism* (Leiden: Brill, 2016).

43 Emilio Gentile, "The Conquest of Modernity: From Modernist Nationalism to Fascism," *Modernism/modernity* 1, no. 3 (1994): 60.

44 As quoted by Gentile, and Gentile adds: "the principal exponents of Futurism were among the founding fathers of the fascist movement and firmly adhered to the totalitarian regime" (Gentile, "The Conquest of Modernity: From Modernist Nationalism to Fascism," 55).

a sense of historical connections, the ideal origins of fascism are to be found in Futurism."[45]

One offspring of the movement is Noise Music: innovations at the time included instruments made of mechanical saws, *aeromusica* (predicated on aircraft),[46] music liberated from harmony, and compositions like *Symphony of Mechanical Forces*, which integrated sirens and industrial engines with the orchestra.[47] One music manifesto of the movement runs:[48]

> We enjoy creating mental orchestrations of the crashing down of metal shop blinds, slamming doors, the hubbub and shuffling of crowds, the variety of din, from stations, railways, iron foundries, spinning wheels, printing works, electric power stations and underground railways. Nor should the newest noises of modern war be forgotten.[49]

Thrilling to the sounds of modern war, with frenzied writing, the manifesto invokes a fresh orchestration:

> Every 5 seconds siege cannons gutting space with a chord ZANG-TUMB-TUUMB mutiny of 500 echoes smashing scattering it to infinity. In the center of this hateful ZANG-TUMB-TUUMB area 50 square kilometers leaping bursts lacerations fists rapid fire batteries. Violence ferocity regularity this deep bass scanning the strange shrill frantic crowds of the battle Fury breathless ears eyes nostrils open! load! fire! what a joy to hear to smell completely *taratatata* of the machine guns screaming a breathless under the stings

---

45 As quoted by Gentile, "The Conquest of Modernity: From Modernist Nationalism to Fascism," 56.

46 Tolkien disliked airplanes, calling them "Mordor-gadgets." Despite Christopher serving in the RAF in WW2, Tolkien believed an air force an *intrinsic* evil (*Letters*, 105 #92). Tolkien was proud of his infantry service but held "war-aircraft in special horror." He drew trench maps in WW1 using aerial reconnaissance (chapter 2).

47 Giovanni Lista, "Futurist Music," in *Italian Futurism 1909–1944*, 116–19.

48 Contrasting markedly with Tolkien's account of music, Wyndham Lewis thought: "A man could make just as fine an art in discords, and with nothing but 'ugly' trivial and terrible materials, as any classicist did with only 'beautiful' and pleasant means." (Wyndham Lewis, "The Exploitation of Vulgarity," *Blast* 1 [June 20, 1914]: 145).

49 Luigi Russolo, "The Art of Noises," https://web.archive.org/web/20100305212012/http://120years.net/machines/futurist/art_of_noise.html.

slaps *traak-traak* whips *pic-pac-pum-tumb* weirdness
leaps 200 meters range Far far in back of the orchestra pools
muddying huffing goaded oxen wagons *pluff-plaff* horse
action *flic flac zing zing shaaack* laughing whinnies
the *tiiinkling jiiingling* tramping 3 Bulgarian battalions
marching *croooc-craaac.*

Compare only the slowness of the Ents—Treebeard's eyes "filled
up with ages of memory and long, slow, steady thinking" (*LotR* II,
452)—with the influential Futurist manifestoes of Fillipo Marinetti, described by Wyndham Lewis as the "intellectual Cromwell
of our time."[50] In 1916, Marinetti published a manifesto *The New
Religion—Morality of Speed*, where the dynamism of the motor
car "extends the crater of Etna." He fantasizes about committing a
homicide with "a blinding automobile headlight."[51]

A new machine-based vitalism—Marinetti's "electric hearts"—
based on velocity, Marinetti claims, "its essence being an intuitive
synthesis of all forces in movement, is naturally *pure*. Slowness, its
essence being the rational analysis of forms of exhaustion in repose,
is naturally *unclean*. After destroying traditional good and evil, we
are creating a new good, speed, and a new evil, slowness."[52] Via speed,
Marinetti imagines an attack upon moral order itself. In his aesthetic
metaphysics, the structure of disgust is inverted.[53] Kolnai argues that
disgust is a primary moral orientation: reason places things in order,
the disgusting is marked by its appearing to us as something out
of place (chapter 4). Marinetti thought speed uproots us from the

---

[50] Roberto Marchiò, "The Vortex in the Machine: Futurism in England,"
106. No English Catholic has a good word for Cromwell, so one can imagine Tolkien's reaction.

[51] Filippo Marinetti, "Let's Murder the Moonlight," in *Futurism: An Anthology*, ed. Lawrence
Rainey, Christine Poggi, and Laura Wittman (New Haven, CT: Yale University Press, 2009), 57.

[52] Filippo Marinetti, *The New Religion—Morality of Speed*, in *Futurism: An Anthology*, 225.

[53] Inversion was a theme for Marinetti. He even published a cookbook which "was less of a nutri-
tional treatise and more an act of cultural electrification, razing the rudiments of classical cuisine
in favor of new, bizarre ones—an allegory of the aggression, radicalism, and obsession with novelty
at the heart of Futurism" (https://artmejo.com/how-italian-futurism-influenced-the-rise-of-fas-
cism/#).

cosmos. Tolkien worries that anti-cosmological ideas[54] are, curiously, basic to science fiction writing:[55]

These prophets often foretell (and many seem to yearn for) a world like one big glass-roofed railway station. But from them it is as a rule very hard to gather what men in such a world-town will do. They may abandon the "full Victorian panoply" for loose garments (with zip-fasteners), but will use this freedom mainly, it would appear, in order to play with mechanical toys in the soon cloying game of moving at high speed.[56]

Marinetti: "The artist exposes himself as the priest who conjures up the catastrophe in technics." He imagines an apocalypse wrought by tramcars, which "rumbled by outside, ablaze with colored lights, like villages on holiday suddenly struck and uprooted by the flooding Po."[57] In 1909, he wrote "Let's Murder the Moonlight." Compare his scenario with Melkor's slaying of the Two Trees. Marinetti:

A cry went up in the airy solitude of the upper plateau: "Let's murder the moonlight!" Some of us ran to nearby waterfalls; gigantic wheels were hoisted, and turbines transformed the velocity of the waters into electromagnetic spasms that climbed up wires suspended on high poles, until they reached luminous humming globes. So it was that three hundred electric moons, with rays of blinding chalky whiteness, cancelled the old green queen of love affairs.[58]

In Melkor's second assault on Arda, he knocks down the two lamps that first lit Middle-earth (S, 36). Light is restored by Yavanna, her

---

54 Leader of English Futurism Wyndham Lewis's play, *The Enemy of the Stars*, published in *Blast* magazine, cast the cosmos as a machine ("Throats iron eternities, drinking heavy radiance, limbs towers of blatant light, the stars poised, immensely distant, with their metal sides, pantheistic machines," *Blast* 1, 64) hostile to humans ("The stars shone madly in the archaic blank wilderness of the universe, machines of prey. . . . He rose before this cliff of cadaverous beaming force, imprisoned in a messed socket of existence," *Blast* 1, 64).

55 Tolkien was well-versed in this literature (*Letters*, 377 #294).

56 https://coolcalvary.files.wordpress.com/2018/10/on-fairy-stories1.pdf, 31.

57 https://www.societyforasianart.org/sites/default/files/manifesto_futurista.pdf. Cf. Manfred Hinz, "The Future and Catastrophe: The Concept of History in Italian Futurism," in *The Promise of History: Essays in Political Philosophy*, ed. Athanosios Moulakis (Berlin: De Gruyter, 1986), 182–83.

58 Marinetti, "Let's Murder the Moonlight," in *Futurism: An Anthology*, 59.

singing birthing the Two Trees (S, 38). Perpetually blossoming, Elves date the beginning of history to the "Opening Hour": the first hour of the elder tree—Telperion—coming to maturity. Morgoth plots a third assault. Looking down on "the Guarded Realm," Melkor sees the Valar at "a high feast for the praising of Eru." The gods singing and dancing, Morgoth, with his untrusty ally, the spider, Ungoliant, makes a rush for the trees. Spearing each tree, he wounds them, "their sap poured forth as it were their blood, and was spilled upon the ground. But Ungoliant sucked it up, and going then from Tree to Tree she set her black beak to their wounds, till they were drained" (S, 76).

Now, compare both Marinetti and Melkor with Tolkien's example of streetlights from *On Fairy Stories*:

> These lamps may be excluded from the tale simply because they are bad lamps; and it is possible that one of the lessons to be learnt from the story is the realization of this fact. But out comes the big stick: "Electric lamps have come to stay," they say. Long ago Chesterton truly remarked that, as soon as he heard that anything "had come to stay," he knew that it would be very soon replaced—indeed regarded as pitiably obsolete and shabby. "The march of Science, its tempo quickened by the needs of war, goes inexorably on . . . making some things obsolete, and foreshadowing new developments in the utilization of electricity": an advertisement. This says the same thing only more menacingly. The electric street-lamp may indeed be ignored, simply because it is so insignificant and transient.[59]

And consider the lovely image of Lúthien. Surprised by Beren, she "slipped suddenly down among the white hemlocks and hid herself beneath a very tall flower with many spreading leaves; and here she looked in her white raiment like a splatter of moonlight shimmering through the leaves upon the floor."[60] As Clausewitz observed, in war, attack must up the tempo.[61] Marinetti: "A racing automobile with its

---

59 https://coolcalvary.files.wordpress.com/2018/10/on-fairy-stories1.pdf, 30.

60 J. R. R. Tolkien, *Beren and Lúthien*, 42.

61 Clausewitz, *On War*, 84–85.

bonnet adorned with great tubes like serpents with explosive breath ... a roaring motor car which seems to run on machine-gun fire."[62] To Marinetti's Smaug, contrast Tolkien, on the nexus of power and speed:

> The Enemy in successive forms is always "naturally" concerned with sheer Domination, and so the Lord of magic and machines; but the problem: that this frightful evil can and does arise from an apparently good root, the desire to benefit the world and others—speedily and according to the benefactor's own plans—is a recurrent motive. (S, xiii-iv)

Hence, the creation of the world by the Holy Ones—the Valar—happened slowly. About God: "And he spoke to them, propounding to them themes of music." This cerebral laying out was then turned to song by the gods, but only slowly do the Valar harmonize: "for each comprehended only that part of the mind of Ilúvatar from which he came, and in the understanding of their brethren they grew but slowly. Yet ever as they listened they came to deeper understanding, and increased in unison and harmony" (S, 15). God then makes a revelation and shows them the interweaving, their cosmic polyphony: "that through you great beauty has been wakened into song." Incomplete knowledge, patience, and beauty all linked. Melkor looks on with hatred, stung, that for the Valar, "Earth was become as a garden for them."[63]

Like Melkor, Futurists chafe under the cosmos:

> Our hearts were filled with an immense pride at feeling ourselves standing quite alone, like lighthouses or like the sentinels in an outpost, facing the army of enemy stars encamped in their celestial bivouacs. Alone with the engineers in the infernal stokeholes of great ships, alone with the black spirits which rage in the belly of rogue locomotives, alone with the drunkards beating their wings against the walls.[64]

62 https://www.societyforasianart.org/sites/default/files/manifesto_futurista.pdf.

63 J. R. R. Tolkien, *Morgoth's Ring: The Later Silmarillion*, ed. Christopher Tolkien (Boston: Houghton Mifflin, 1993), 27.

64 https://www.societyforasianart.org/sites/default/files/manifesto_futurista.pdf.

Futurism is an "immanentist apocalypse," a violent attack on our cosmic standing.[65] Contrast Marinetti's hopes and fantasies—at one point he imagines himself as an artillery shell—with Gandalf, a Bliss-friend. Tolkien defines a Bliss-friend as "one loyal to the Valar, content with the bliss and prosperity within the limits prescribed" (*Letters*, 347 #257). Tolkien explains that *The Silmarillion* is about a rebellion against a prohibition. Fans of the films, but new to *The Silmarillion*, are often stunned to learn that Galadriel begins as a rebel against the gods (*Letters*, 386 #297), one of the Elves who brings ruin on her people (*Letters*, 148 #131). Refusing obedience, Tolkien thinks, is a core theme of myth.[66] Tolkien used Gandalf's battle with the Balrog at Moria to dramatize obedience. In the last section of the chapter, I turn to an opposite case, the Númenórean invasion of Valinor. I assess the fall of Númenor as an "immanentist apocalypse" and extend Bradley Birzer's good observation that Sauron is a Gnostic sage.[67] Protesting their cosmic standing, they were already primed to wage revolutionary war on the gods: "And they said among themselves: 'Why do the Lords of the West sit there in peace unending, while we must die and go we know not whither, leaving our home and all that we have made?'" (*S*, 264).

Analogia Entis and Gandalf

Futurism was a Gnostic rebellion against the *analogia entis* (analogy of being). Tolkien says that of all the Wizards only Gandalf

---

65 Leveque, "Futurism's First War: Apocalyptic Space in F. T. Marinetti's Writings from Tripoli," *Romance Notes* 55, no. 3 (2015): 426–27, 431.

66 Prohibition is one of the deep teachings of myth: "Even where a prohibition in a fairy-story is guessed to be derived from some taboo once practiced long ago, it has probably been preserved in the later stages of the tale's history because of the great mythical significance of prohibition. A sense of that significance may indeed have lain behind some of the taboos themselves. Thou shalt not—or else thou shall depart beggared into endless regret. The gentlest "nursery-tales" know it. Even Peter Rabbit was forbidden a garden, lost his blue coat, and took sick. The Locked Door stands as an eternal Temptation" (https://coolcalvary.files.wordpress.com/2018/10/on-fairy-stories1.pdf., 16).

67 Bradley Birzer, *J. R. R. Tolkien's Sanctifying Myth* (Wilmington, DE: Intercollegiate Studies Institute, 2009), 98.

thoroughly passes the tests posed to him (*Letters*, 200 #156). I now tie the *analogia entis* to Gandalf's sacrifice in his combat with the Balrog.

In 1932, the Polish-German Jesuit Erich Przywara innovatively restated Thomas Aquinas's metaphysics of analogy. He both put Aquinas in a modern register and, as a matter of historical interpretation, argued that Aquinas's metaphysics operationalized the Fourth Lateran Council of 1215. Edicts following that ecumenical council included a condemnation of Joachim de Fiori. Przywara is a reaction to malformations Fiori introduced into theology, the political implications of which Voegelin takes up.[68]

The Council argued that Joachim undersold the transcendence of God, tending to see God's nature as merely a collective of persons rather than "a certain supreme reality, incomprehensible and ineffable."[69] The Council stated that an earthly, natural realization of "supreme reality" is impossible, for "one cannot note any similarity between creator and creature, however great, without being compelled to observe an ever greater dissimilarity between them" (*AE*, 73). The upshot, says Przywara, is that the Church teaches "discretion": that the right attitude to our cosmic situatedness is deference to our condition, not a lusting after transfigurations. Twistedness is bound to result because we are sure to get things wrong. Tolkien:

> If we go up the scale of being to "other living things," such as, say, some small plant, it presents shape and organization: a "pattern" recognizable (with variation) in its kin and offspring; and that is deeply interesting, because these things are "other" and we did not make them, and they seem to proceed from a fountain of invention incalculably richer than our own. (*Letters*, 399 #310)

Sounding a Pascalian note,[70] Tolkien argues that deference to the world's value architecture—"As for 'other things' their value resides in

---

68 Eric Voegelin, *The Collected Works of Eric Voegelin*, vol. 30, *Selected Correspondence 1950–1984* (Columbia: University of Missouri Press, 2007), 46.

69 https://www.papalencyclicals.net/councils/ecum12-2.htm#2.

70 Pascal, *Pensées*, 46–50 #149.

themselves: they ARE, they would exist even if we did not" (*Letters*, 399 #310)—is required because even a small plant's organization exceeds our imaginative powers. Tolkien recommends Bombadil, because his is a humble mind, a true scientific mind:

> ... he is then an "allegory," or an exemplar, a particular embodying of pure (real) natural science: the spirit that desires knowledge of other things, their history and nature, *because they are "other"* and wholly independent of the enquiring mind, a spirit coeval with the rational mind, and entirely unconcerned with "doing" anything with the knowledge. (*Letters*, 192 #153; emphasis original)

Tolkien appreciates change; he is, by his own characterization, historically-minded. However, misadventure waits upon the promethean. Refinements in the mechanical and liberal arts must be developed with discretion, alert to our finitude. This is what Tolkien means by saying "a man is both a seed and in some degree also a gardener" (*Letters*, 240 #183). Tom and Goldberry are gardeners, and Tolkien can only compare Lúthien's movement in dance to the "the rose gardens of Valinor where Nessa dances on the lawns of never-ending green."[71] "Fairy-stories may invent monsters that fly the air or dwell in the deep, but at least they do not try to escape from heaven or the sea."[72] Here, we see Tolkien's Catholicism. The core lesson of the Council, Przywara: "The language proper to the mind of the church is one of an aristocratic and sober distance from the 'enthusiasms' of Charismatics, Pneumatics ..." (*AE*, 374).[73] Gandalf is no Pneumatic.

The leading Protestant theologian of the twentieth century, Karl Barth, appreciated Przywara's brilliance, and enjoyed his company, but the *analogia entis* horrified him. He cast the *analogia entis* as an "invention of the Antichrist," thinking it posited too great a grasp of God by metaphysical reasoning. The dismay was reciprocated. In

---

71 J. R. R. Tolkien, *Beren and Lúthien*, 41.

72 https://coolcalvary.files.wordpress.com/2018/10/on-fairy-stories1.pdf, 31.

73 For my elaboration, please see *Erich Przywara and Postmodern Natural Law* (Notre Dame, IN: University of Notre Dame Press, 2019).

Carpenter's telling, the Inklings had a strong dislike of Barth, whom all the Christian youth at Oxford seemed to be reading.[74] Despite Barth's reaction, the impact of Przywara on Catholic thought was significant, in part through his greatest student, Hans Urs von Balthasar. In 1937, Balthasar published *Prometheus*, a book Voegelin credits with the core insight of his own work:[75] the role of Gnosticism in modern ideological movements.

In a 1953 letter to the Austrian phenomenologist Alfred Schütz, Voegelin relays that he had been chatting with Karl Barth. He mentioned the chat because Schütz had taken him to task over the prioritizing of Christian thought, claiming that philosophy grew well enough in the orientation of Plato and Aristotle. Voegelin counters that he has no personal stake in Christianity, but Schütz is not right. There are degrees of differentiation and Christianity is the most complete. Christianity offers a "maximally differentiated experience," a symbol or style of thinking in which the refinement of personal psyche can be most completely articulated. To illustrate, Voegelin observes a "philosophical-technical consequence": today, no one would think to recount a mystical experience in terms of Plato's myth; that myth has been surpassed by a language derived from the idea of a grace from outside transforming consciousness. This is prominent in the film version of *LotR* when Arwen, to save Frodo from his wounding by a Morgul blade, asks the gods that whatever grace has been given her might pass to him.

Replying to Schütz, Voegelin goes on to say that "maximally differentiated experience" is secured by the *analogia entis*. A potent illustration is the loss of Gollum. In his 1964 BBC television interview, Tolkien says the tragedy of the story is the loss of Gollum, his near-repentance on the path to Cirith Ungol cut short by the actual hero of the story, Sam. It is an achingly sad scene.[76] What is critical

---

74 Humphrey Carpenter, *The Inklings* (Boston: Houghton Mifflin, 1979), 134.

75 See Jürgen Gebhardt's editor's introduction in *The Collected Works of Eric Voegelin*, vol. 25, *History of Political Ideas*, vol. 7: *The New Order and Last Orientation* (Columbia: University of Missouri Press, 1999), 6.

76 Lee, "Tolkien in Oxford," 157–58.

about Gollum's act—issuing from a mind so scrambled by malice—
is why he reaches out to Frodo so tenderly. It is because Frodo's quest
is a submission to the *analogia entis*. His kindness to the repellant
Gollum stems from his patience, his persevering against a Gnostic
power, the Ring, a resistance by which he suffers horribly and that
is destroying him. In Frodo, Gollum sees someone trying to hold
open differentiation. Gollum is alert to this phenomenon. Though
slavering and smelly, and earning the nickname "Stinker" from Sam,
Gollum is always very particular about washing his hands, "my nice
hands" (TT, 608-610). About Frodo, Tolkien:

> It seems clear to me that Frodo's duty was "humane" not politi-
> cal. He naturally thought first of the Shire, since his roots were
> there, but the quest had as its object not preserving of this or
> that polity, such as the half republic half aristocracy of the Shire,
> but the liberation from an evil tyranny of all the "humane"—
> including those, such as "easterlings" and Haradrim, that were
> still servants of the tyranny. (*Letters*, 240–41 #183)

Frodo's is a "posture of distance" (Przywara), to which, in a brief
moment, Gollum aspires. This posture—the *analogia entis*—is,
thinks Voegelin, an example of symbolization, "the refusal to reduce
the experience of transcendence to axioms as demanded by Enlightenment philosophes."[77] Marx is an example: "Marx never made
the *sacrificium intellectus;* instead he proposed speculative intellectual theses that can be proposed only when the abyss separating the
divine from the human has not been experienced." In a moment, we
shall see that Gandalf makes the *sacrificium intellectus.*

Voegelin distinguishes "eschatological Christianity" (Protestant)
and "essential Christianity" (Catholicism). Like Przywara, he explains
the difference in terms of establishment and restraint. "Eschatological consciousness is the core of manifest Christian religiousness"
and politically explosive. Unlike the Ancients, the Middle Ages saw

---

77 "Dogmatics is a symbolic web which explicates and differentiates the extraordinarily complicated religious experiences." For the Schütz letter, see: https://voegelinview.com/christianity-s-de-
cisive-difference-pt-1/.

varied revolutionary movements, all "subeschatologies" of "the official eschatology." The Middle Ages witnessed "a widely diversified field of tensions between institutionalized Christianity and the eschatological movements raising rival claims to public status."[78] Voegelin's twist on Pryzwara is the claim that the Church not only had its own quarrelsome progeny but was a stimulant to a rival, Gnosticism. Original to the ancient Mediterranean, Gnosticism was contemporary with the emergence of Christianity—a rival, contends Voegelin, not a Christian heresy.[79] However, the *prevalence* of Gnostic political movements is a consequence of Christianity, derivative of its differentiation.[80]

Gnosticism was given legs by the New Testament: "Considering the history of Gnosticism, with the great bulk of its manifestations belonging to, or deriving from, the Christian orbit, I am inclined to recognize in the epiphany of Christ the great catalyst that made eschatological consciousness an historical force both in forming and deforming humanity."[81] Modern politics is a mutation of St. Paul's great symbol, a *kingdom that is truly the end*.[82] As to what is truly the end, on offer are: "the modern apocalyptic visions of the perfect realm of reason, the perfect realm of positivist science in the Comtian sense, or the perfect realm of Marxist Communism."[83]

---

78 Voegelin, *History of Political Ideas*, vol. 7: *The New Order and Last Orientation*, 229–30. Cf. Voegelin, *Selected Correspondence 1950–1984*, 70–71.

79 Voegelin, "Industrial Society in Search of Reason," 171. Cf. "Ersatz Religion," 63.

80 Voegelin, "What Is History?" *Collected Works*, vol. 28, 30–31. More is said in the following section about differentiation, Voegelin's core concept. Fused with Greek science and philosophy, Christianity is the consummate differentiation because it articulates human psychology beyond natural order, isolates elements, and compounds relations, within our psyche, as well as takes hierarchy—or, differently put, alienation—to a fresh level: e.g., modeling the psyche on the mind-bending idea of the Trinity. It is Christianity—"an increasingly self-conscious vision of the divine Beyond" (Eric Voegelin, "The Beginning and the Beyond," in *Collected Works of Eric Voegelin*, vol. 12, *Published Essays: 1966–1985* [Baton Rouge: Louisiana State University Press, 1990], 228)—that decisively breaks the social compactness of cosmological myth. Nonetheless, it is part of the strangeness of Christianity that a wholly other transcendence is not unconnected to the cosmos. Christianity is a cosmological doctrine combining nature, natural law, and the operation of supernaturally given grace. Recall Aquinas's famous formulation: grace perfects nature.

81 Voegelin, *The Ecumenic Age*, 20.

82 Voegelin, *The Ecumenic Age*, 134.

83 Voegelin, "Configurations of History," in *Published Essays: 1966–1985*, 107.

These unlimited, perfectionist, militant movements mimic:[84] *And there shall be no more curse: but the throne of God and of the Lamb shall be in it; and his servants shall serve him. And they shall see his face; and his name shall be in their foreheads* (Rev. 22:3–4).

Yet, one might wonder: Why is apocalyptic politics bad? Voegelin proposes: 1) lack of pragmatism—the correction of the world sought by the apocalyptic drive is so divergent from the pragmatic needs of people that political order is subverted; 2) cancellation of our living in a cosmos, which twists our sense of embodiment and environment; and thus 3) a perverse accounting of our human standing in reality with inevitable malformations of our mental health and moral solidarity. Think of the self-harming cauldron that is Morgoth:

> But in Angband Morgoth forged for himself a great crown of iron. And he called himself King of the World. In token of this he set the Silmarils in his crown. His hands were burned black by the touch of those hallowed jewels, and black they remained ever after; nor was he ever free from the pain of burning, and the anger of the pain. That crown he never took from his head, though its weight became a deadly weariness. (*S*, 81)

Political sobriety demands appreciating that, metaphysically, the heart of created reality is a *potentia obedientialis*, an inclination to reside patiently suspended between cosmos and transcendence. Melkor utterly refuses to give obedience. Aquinas points out that disobedience is a classic marker of vanity.[85]

Contrast Gandalf in his battle against the Balrog. Tolkien's description of its significance deserves to be quoted in full:

> Gandalf alone fully passes the tests, on a moral plane anyway (he makes mistakes of judgement). For in his condition it was for him a *sacrifice* to perish on the Bridge in defence of his companions, less perhaps than for a mortal Man or Hobbit, since he had a far greater inner power than they; but also more,

---

84 "Among the modern apocalypses there should especially be reckoned certain "philosophies" of history that achieve a transfiguration of society, not by divine intervention, but by revolutionary action of man." (Voegelin, "Anxiety and Reason," 66)

85 Aquinas, *On Evil*, 349.

since it was a humbling and abnegation of himself in conformity to "the Rules": for all he could know at that moment he
was the *only* person who could direct the resistance to Sauron
successfully, and all *his* mission was vain. He was handing over
to the Authority that ordained the Rules, and giving up personal hope of success. (*Letters*, 200 #156)

This is a rich passage, but most critical is not only Gandalf's obedience but the apparent inconsistency of his obedience with what he
knows of his own situation. To use Voegelin's phrase, he makes the
sacrificium intellectus: he obeys against his own better judgement or,
more positively put, he offers himself up in trust: "from trust in Eru
the Lord everlasting, that he is good, and that his works shall all end
in good."[86] Indeed, as Tolkien later explains, even the gods did not
know the purpose of this sacrifice. "He was sent by a mere prudent
plan of the angelic Valar or governors; but Authority had taken up
this plan and enlarged it, at the moment of its failure" (*Letters*, 200
#156). Both Gandalf's being and action embody the *analogia entis*.
He is a high being yet limited in knowledge. On mission for the gods,
his obedience realizes a still greater mission about which he and they
know nothing. Gandalf illustrates the ever greater of the *analogia
entis* in his "the posture of distance."

The battle at the Bridge depicts Tolkien's philosophy of history—
incomplete knowledge, sobriety, and patience. In fact, a dramatization of his obediential metaphysical aesthetics. Gandalf's sacrifice is
a foretaste of the Second Music of the Ainur. Firmly planted in the
cosmos, Gandalf submits to a revelation that he awaits. And which
does come: "Naked I was sent back—for a brief time, until my task
is done" (*Letters*, 203 #156). He parallels Ulmo. Melkor is described
by Eru as "immoderate" and "without restraint" (*S*, 19). Contending
with Melkor's creation, Eru transforms it. This recuperative creation
transcends Ulmo's incomplete knowledge: "Truly, Water is become
now fairer than my ear imagined, neither had my secret thought

---

86 J. R. R. Tolkien, *Morgoth's Ring*, 245.

conceived the snowflake, nor in all my music was contained the falling of the rain" (*S*, 19).

Ulmo and Gandalf contrast with Futurism's metaphysical aesthetics of vanity; its machine perfectionism literally has in its sights the cosmos. Voegelin:

> One should, on the contrary, speak of the illusion of disappearance, for under the dominance of modern Gnosticism and scientism the cosmos has been relegated to a position so subordinate that its presence has become almost unbelievable. An ardent Communist, for instance, would be greatly surprised if he learned that by his activities he participates in a cosmological rite of renewal in order to assuage his anxiety of existence."[87]

Gnosticism apes Revelation and so, unsurprisingly, apocalyptic war follows in its wake. The difference is that the consequences of the apocalypticism are crushing rather than redeeming, crushing because the cosmos is recalcitrant and resists false dominion. This is why Marinetti has to imagine himself an artillery shell. Let us follow Voegelin's reasoning on this and see how it tracks with Númenor's war on the gods.

Gnosticism and Númenóreans

The West, Voegelin contends, is inescapably the experience of a Christian civilization prone to falling back on the less differentiated. This is what happened during the Enlightenment when the *analogia entis* was abandoned. Thus, Voegelin: "One of the great tasks ahead of us is a renewal of the analogical meaning of symbols, a new philosophy of myth and revelation."[88] "The apocalyptic movements have become socially dominant to such a degree that today we are

---

87 Voegelin, "Anxiety and Reason," 66. All politics, according to Voegelin, addresses a metaphysical vertigo (Voegelin, *The Ecumenic Age*, 74). In this sense, human nature is unchanging. Unchanging because we cannot escape either the anxiety that we are suspended over a metaphysical abyss (think of the whirlpool example at the start of Descartes's *Meditations*), or the anxiety resulting from our encounter with the transcendent, an order not of human making: the stars, the verities of reason, or the grace of God (Voegelin, *Israel and Revelation*, 129).

88 Voegelin, *Selected Correspondence 1950–1984*, 371.

living in an age of apocalyptic politics. . . . Today it would be significant if, not a poet but anybody at all, would write *not* an apocalypse for a change."[89] Happily, a non-apocalyptic politics is Tolkien's very project.

Nietzsche contends that the age of the Last Man—the age of the bourgeois Whig humanitarian (us!)—will not be peaceable; worse, it will consist of a political order of happiness without dignity that concludes in callousness. In an article on Nietzsche's prophecy of future catastrophic war, Voegelin says of those wars that "while they have motives they have no orientation towards purposes."[90] The reason is dislocation. Nietzsche has the Last Man ask: "What is a star?" The question stems from the Last Man's complete indifference to all that is not his product.[91] We saw this theme in Futurism. The anti-cosmic is anti-civilizational, for it collapses differentiation. Not a great leap into the future, but a modern reprimitivism, in fact.

Voegelin's philosophy of history is subtle. It is neither a Whig progressivism nor a Spenglerian tale of decline. The latter figures in Tolkien scholarship, where Tolkien is viewed as a declinist:[92] Middle-earth's Golden Age slowly but surely erodes, commentators appear to agree. The immediate problem with this reading is that there never was a Golden Age: war, from the very start, mars Middle-earth, and Melkor's hate gains him some striking early successes. Voegelin helps us see that Tolkien's philosophy of history is more nuanced than the declinist's. In Voegelin's telling, Westernized countries can never fall back into polytheism.[93] This is not because Christianity eradicated all memory of the old gods, but because there is a buffer separating us moderns from a polycentric politics

---

89 Voegelin, *Selected Correspondence 1950–1984*, 481.

90 Eric Voegelin, "Nietzsche, the Crisis and the War," *The Journal of Politics* 6, no. 2 (1944): 180.

91 Voegelin, "Nietzsche, the Crisis and the War," 179.

92 The conventional take is that Tolkien's is a Plotinian philosophy of history: reality as a falling away from a perfect Model, what Robley Evans in *Mythlore* terms *degenerative recurrence*. For Evans, see "Tolkien's World-Creation: Degenerative Recurrence," *Mythlore* 14, no. 1 (1987): 5. Cf. Potts, "'Evening-Lands': Spenglerian Tropes in *Lord of the Rings*," *Tolkien Studies* 13 (2016): 158, 164.

93 Eric Voegelin, *The New Science of Politics* (Chicago: The University of Chicago Press, 1966), 123.

built around the ancient divinities of peoples.[94] There is carnage, but not because of decline. Gnosticism is a buffer: it is a marring agent but also full of energy and enterprise. In *Progress and Religion*, Dawson observes: "And the same spirit reappears in the revolutionary political and socialist reformers of the nineteenth century, all of whom had an almost apocalyptic belief in the possibility of a complete transformation of human society—an abrupt passage from corruption to perfection, from darkness to light."[95] Voegelin: "The stage is set for the divine messengers who abandon created reality altogether and concentrate on the Gnosis of the redemptive exodus from the cosmos."[96] Decline is not quite the right image, then, for modern primitivism is entrepreneurial. It is an amped-up exodus from the cosmos wrought by perfectionist technologies: "evil spirits have grown lustily in these vessels."[97] As the Futurists made clear, it is the acceleration that is alluringly homicidal. Gnosticism fuels a modern primitivism[98] because of a fateful exaggeration of one of the elements of Christ:[99] Christ in the stillness before and after creation. Gnosticism is apocalyptic because it *exclusively* invokes Christ *nunc stans*. The meaning of Christ crucified, the history of the life of Jesus, including His *enduring* suffering,[100] does not give the Gnostic pause.

Decline is also not quite the right image because if Gnosticism is always latent in the West, so is Christian renewal. Meaning: a fresh possibility wherein cosmos and Revelation are held in tension. Such a renewal is found in Tolkien. Númenor falls, but a remnant, the

---

94 This would be the basis of a Voegelin critique of Dugin's Eurasianism.

95 Dawson, *Progress and Religion*, 5.

96 Voegelin, *The Ecumenic Age*, 26.

97 Voegelin, "Nietzsche, the Crisis and the War," 188.

98 Futurism artist Henri Gaudier "created stylized 'primitive' line drawings, calligraphic sketches of animal forms, and a series of drawings progressively reducing realistic forms to geometrical shapes and interrelated planes and masses. He also made pastel drawings of stylized machines or machine-like shapes. These, along with his other highly stylized and abstract drawings and his geometricized carvings, placed his work directly within the main tendencies of the Vorticist painters" (Wees, *Vorticism and the English Avant-Garde*, 135–36).

99 Voegelin, *The Ecumenic Age*, 20.

100 Aquinas stresses that in heaven Christ's wounds are scarred over, not that they vanish. Please see my *Ecstatic Morality and Sexual Politics* (New York: Fordham University Press, 2005), 88–89.

Faithful, having fled Gnostic Númenor before the amphibious invasion of Valinor, survive. They are the Faithful because they are obedient to the gods. They suffer persecution and martyrdom because they refuse to trammel the *analogia entis*. Put more abstractly, they suffer because they want to hold open differentiation. Of course, in true Biblical fashion, they lose their way yet again, but this is what Voegelin's Gnostic latency theory would predict. Denethor is a good example of this latency bubbling up once more in Gondor.

Differentiation is a critical Voegelian term of art and requires some explaining. First, a detailing of Voegelin's theory, then a lengthy application to Númenor. [101]

Voegelin maintains that the tension between compactness and differentiation is native to consciousness as such. "The maximum of differentiation" is Greek philosophy twinned with Christianity,[102] where it culminates in ideals of personal liberty, being an evolution in the history of civilizations.

A research collaborator with Voegelin, Maria König, argued that the transition from compactness to differentiation was discernible in Paleolithic artifacts. An example of compactness, ancient objects show an initial ritual use of spheroids. A symbol of the human—and our Neanderthal counterparts—enclosed in wholeness. Spheroids gave way to the ritual use of cups and skulls. With their openings, the half-spheres of cups and skulls mimicked life under a vault, with heaven and earth distinguished. König also thought that the discovery of so many skulls around springs spoke to a notion of a netherworld, too; another differentiation, therefore.[103] König's research into the tripartite consciousness of the Paleolithic confirms a Voegelin thesis: "The history of symbolization is a progression from compact to differentiated experiences and symbols."[104]

---

101 Voegelin, *Collected Works of Eric Voegelin*, vol. 28, "What is History?" 30–31.

102 Voegelin, *The New Science of Politics*, 79, 164.

103 For an excellent discussion, see Barry Cooper, *Paleolithic Politics* (Notre Dame, IN: University of Notre Dame Press, 2019).

104 Eric Voegelin, *Order and History*, vol. 1, *Israel and Revelation* (Baton Rouge: Louisiana State University Press, 2001), 5.

I agree with Meredith Veldman's comment on Tolkien's overall metaphysical stance: "Truth reveals itself not only in 'the facts' but also in the mythological wisdom that transcends those facts tallied by ear and eye."[105] However, a use of myth that affirms persons is a delicate thing, and this is where Voegelin is so helpful to Tolkien studies. In his history of civilizations, Voegelin argues that early civilizations were gripped by an overwhelming sense of cosmos. He argued that the first political form was cosmological empire: polities keyed to the experience of celestial and seasonal change, their rulers standing at the center of geographical space.[106] For example, the Babylonian king was the axis through which ran the points of the compass. Of himself, Cyrus said, "I am Cyrus . . . King of the four quarters of the world."[107] This compactness gave way to a partial differentiation under pressure from ecumenic empires. With the extension of empire more and more strangeness was encountered and this eroded the surety of geographical consistency, sparking historical consciousness, a way to explain differences in mores. Alexander is an example of geography partly dislodged by history. Alexander the Great declared: "When you address yourself to me, address me as the King of Asia."[108] Alexander did not think himself one with the cosmos, like Cyrus, but a portion only (Augustine's *civitas terrena*).[109] Alexander expresses an awareness of otherness: his was an ecumenic empire, reflecting a change in consciousness wherein historical understanding is prominent.

The compactness of cosmological empire means that freedom and individual flair were hamstrung.[110] Even more differentiation than is on offer in ecumenic empire is required if personal identity is

---

105 Veldman, *Fantasy, the Bomb, and the Greening of Britain*, 81.

106 Voegelin, "Anxiety and Reason," 59.

107 Voegelin, *The Ecumenic Age*, 149.

108 Voegelin, *The Ecumenic Age*, 154.

109 Voegelin, "What Is History?" 32.

110 For Voegelin, human nature, in part, is fixed: no political symbol can "remove the soul and its transcendence from the structure of reality" (Voegelin, *The New Science of Politics*, 165).

to come to the fore.[111] More intense symbols of differentiation arose in Greece and Israel. Greek letters describe the soul in dynamic relationship with transcendent values:[112] an experience consummated in Christianity,[113] with Jesus preaching that not a sparrow falls from the sky without God's grace-filled permission: *Are not two sparrows sold for a farthing? and one of them shall not fall on the ground without your Father* (Matt. 10:29). In Judeo-Christianity, the lock of the cosmos on the human spirit is sprung: the prime value of persons becomes apparent to consciousness: "'He is a good mathematician,' you will say. But I am not concerned with mathematics: he would take me for a proposition.' He is a good soldier.' He would take me for a place under siege" (*Pensées*, 204 #605).

But now, we return to the problem at the start: insufficient beauty. The Númenóreans are blessed yet dissatisfied. Why is the cosmos adorned with stars not enough for us? Why does the refinement of the arts and sciences that elevate us so much not satisfy? We have vast libraries, the internet, fashion and glamour galore, and yet Pascal's paradox remains: "The more enlightened we are the more greatness and vileness we discover in man" (*Pensées*, 206 #613). Voegelin argues that the high moral adventure required by Christian belief is insupportable, and that the resulting anxiety is a key Gnostic driver. The Christian call to faith is to live in belief, and not certainty, to potentially experience the aridity of the Dark Night of the Soul (*NSP*, 122). It is a humbling call. Our reason is offended by this call to incompleteness,[114] by the call to an obedience completed by a grace whose source is wholly without us (*Pensées*, 237 #781).

---

111 "In its order every society reflects the type of men of whom it is composed. One would have to say, for instance, that cosmological empires consist of a type of men who experience the truth of their existence as a harmony with the cosmos" (Voegelin, *The New Science of Politics*, 62).

112 "In the symbolic form of the myth, thus, Plato recognizes the philosopher's role in history as that of the man who is open to reality and willing to let the gift of the gods illuminate his existence" (Voegelin, *The Ecumenic Age*, 184).

113 Eric Voegelin, *Order and History*, vol. 1, *Israel and Revelation*, 87. Plato could not deliver full differentiation because, for the Greeks, an abiding symbol is "intracosmic gods" (Voegelin, *Collected Works of Eric Voegelin*, vol. 12, "The Gospel and Culture," 194).

114 "All Gnostic movements are involved in the project of abolishing the constitution of being, with its origin in divine, transcendent being, and replacing it with a world-immanent order of being, the perfection of which lies in the realm of human action. This is a matter of so altering the structure

In explaining secularization in the West, Voegelin argues that many had not "the spiritual stamina for the heroic adventure of the soul that is Christianity." Exhausted, the modern Westerner falls "back on a less differentiated culture of spiritual experience," one that removes doubt (*NSP*, 123–24).[115] This is immanentization. Furthermore, on account of Judeo-Christianity, the problem is amped up: we now worry the cosmos is suspended over nothing (*creatio ex nihilo*). This generates a hallmark of Christian civilization, intense anxiety (see Pascal, Kierkegaard, and the most anxious of all, Hume). It is anxiety that opens the door to Gnosticism. And, compounding the problem yet further, Scripture supplies a model of compactness for an escape:[116] *And I John saw the holy city, new Jerusalem, coming down from God out of heaven, prepared as a bride adorned for her husband* (Rev. 21:2). Biblical apocalypse proposes a city—not the Shire!—as an end to imperfection forever.[117] In modernity, this idea migrates to the philosophies of history proposed during the Enlightenment: "Among the modern apocalypses there should especially be reckoned certain 'philosophies' of history that achieve a transfiguration of society, not by divine intervention, but by revolutionary action of man."[118] It is because the symbols of modern mass movements trade on the Christian idea of perfection that Voegelin dubs such movements "ersatz religion."

It is striking that Tolkien's 1951 letter to Milton Waldman outlines in some detail the religious problem posed by Sauron and the Númenóreans: Númenor is utterly destroyed in an apocalypse, a judgment on a civilization that was great despite its cultic practice of human sacrifice (*S*, 273). Theirs is an apocalyptic politics or ersatz religion. Ersatz religion has six core features:

---

of the world, which is perceived as inadequate, that a new, satisfying world arises. The variants of immanentization, therefore, are the controlling symbols. . . ." (Voegelin, "Ersatz Religion," 75).

115 Cf. Voegelin, "Industrial Society in Search of Reason," 44.

116 Voegelin, "Ersatz Religion," 66.

117 In Comte, the positivist Church is a unity of cities (Richard Vernon, "Auguste Comte and the Withering-Away of the State," *Journal of the History of Ideas* 45, no. 4 (1984): 553.

118 Voegelin, "Anxiety and Reason," 66.

1. Dissatisfaction with the world.
2. The problem is the world, not us.
3. The belief that salvation from the world is possible.
4. The order of being will have to be changed in history to correct its fault lines.
5. The salvific change in history must come through human agency.
6. Knowledge—gnosis—of how to effect the transformation is "the central concern of the Gnostic," who is seeking "the construction of a formula for self- and world salvation." Gnosticism thus has a prophetic cast.[119]

We can use these six core elements as a rubric to assess Tolkien's Catholic political vision. The Númenórean situation is the following. The angelic guardians of Middle-earth, the Valar, live in the Undying Lands and have placed a prohibition on visits. They have laid down the Ban of the Valar which, in the case of the Númenóreans, denies travel by sea so far westward that sight of the island of Númenor is lost (*Letters*, 204–5 #156; *LotR*, Appendix A, 1013). A bewilderment falls upon anyone daring to break the Ban (S, 246 & 248). Should any remain oriented enough and get past the enchantment, the punishment is death (S, 249). When the Númenóreans rebel against the Ban, God not only destroys their armada but unleashes an apocalypse: [120] God rends the land, and their kingdom—"the Land of Gift"—falls into the sea, and the people, cities, and civilization of Númenor are lost (S, 279). What goaded the Númenóreans to wage war and break the Ban?

1. **Dissatisfaction with the world.**
   "The Númenóreans began to hunger for the undying city that they saw from afar, and the desire of everlasting life, to escape from death and the ending of delight, grew strong upon them; and ever as their power and glory grew greater their unquiet

---

119 Voegelin, "Ersatz Religion," 64–65.
120 J. R. R. Tolkien, *Unfinished Tales* (Boston: Houghton Mifflin, 1980), 165.

increased" (*S*, 263). The Númenóreans complain of being mortal: "Why should we not go even to Aman, and taste there, were it but for a day, the bliss of the Powers? Have we not become mighty among the people of Arda?" (*S*, 264). The Elves explain to the Númenóreans that even they do not know why death is "the Doom of Men": "We who bear the ever-mounting burden of the years do not clearly understand this; but if that grief has returned to trouble you, as you say, then we fear that the Shadow arises once more and grows again in your hearts" (*S*, 265). Even the Valar do not understand. The Elves tell the Númenóreans: "Nonetheless, many ages of Men unborn may pass ere that purpose is made known; and to you it will be revealed and not to the Valar" (*S*, 265).

2. **The problem is the world, not us.**

On the one hand, there is the Enemy: "But there were some that turned from evil and left the lands of their kindred, and wandered ever westward; for they had heard a rumour that in the West there was a light which the Shadow could not dim. The servants of Morgoth pursued them with hatred . . ." (*S*, 259). In this line of the story, the problem is "us," so to say, it's a case of "man-made" evil, as it were, and not a protest at the condition of the cosmos itself. Evil befalls Middle-earth because Melkor hates beauty: "and the beauty of the Earth in its Spring filled him the more with hate" (*S*, 36). There is an agent marring the cosmos. On the other hand, Morgoth's machinations through Sauron only have purchase because the Númenóreans chafe at the limited knowledge that is their lot. In the absence of knowledge, they complain that they must trust:[121] "For of us is required a blind trust, and a hope without assurance, knowing not what

---

121 "Even when a prohibition in a fairy-story is guessed to be derived from some taboo once practised long ago, it has probably been preserved in the later stages of the tale's history because of the great mythical significance of prohibition. A sense of significance may indeed have lain behind some of the taboos themselves. Thou shalt not—or else thou shalt depart beggared into endless regret. The gentlest 'nursery-tales' know it. Even Peter Rabbit was forbidden a garden, lost his blue coat, and took sick. The Locked Door stands as an eternal Temptation" (https://coolcalvary.files.wordpress.com/2018/10/on-fairy-stories1.pdf, 33).

lies before us in a little while" (*The Silmarillion*, Akallabêth, 265). They complain about the mystery of their Doom, but are warned: "Beware! The will of Eru may not be gainsaid; and the Valar bid you earnestly not to withhold the trust to which you are called" (*S*, 265). Gnostics are intolerant of limited knowledge, and in consequence, "the truth of the open soul; a whole area of differentiated reality that had been gained by philosophy and Christianity was ruined" (*NSP*, 163). Sauron completes their ruin, but the Númenóreans had primed the pump. Before the Númenóreans are corrupted utterly through the practice of human sacrifice introduced by Sauron, they lost their moral bearings when their adventurism morphs into predation, plundering and leveeing taxes on the weaker population of ordinary men (*S*, xxii–iii). Despite "the bliss of Westernesse," to the Númenóreans "their own land seemed to them shrunken, and they had no rest or content therein, and they desired now wealth and dominion . . ." (*S*, 266).

3. **The belief that salvation from the world is possible.**
There is no technology fine enough to obscure the problem of time built into the constitution of men and Elves. According to Tolkien, what ennobles human life is living with growing things, *temporal* things. This requires enduring time, the very thing that provokes the Númenóreans. Time is wrapped up with what Gandalf identifies as the source of health. He says Gollum suffers, for "he ceased to look up at the hill-tops, or the leaves on trees, or the flowers opening in the air," and when Gandalf tries to reach through the chaos of Smeagol's mind, he talks to him of green things: "It was actually pleasant, I think, to hear a kindly voice again, bringing up memories of wind, and trees, and sun on the grass, and such forgotten things" (*FR*, 53). Éowyn is described as "a healer, and loved all things that grow and are not barren" (*RK*, 943). In his own way, Sam is a healer, and, returning from war, he plants saplings to replace the "specially beautiful and beloved trees" destroyed by Saruman and "all through the winter

he remained as patient as he could, and tried to restrain himself from going round constantly to see if anything was happening" (*RK*, 1000). The Númenóreans, however, lose the orientation set by growing things, they forsake the time-signature of growing things because they are impatient: "But Atanamir was ill pleased with the counsel of the Messengers and gave little heed to it, and the greater part of his people followed him; for they wished still to escape death in their own day, not waiting upon hope" (*S*, 265–66). They are seduced by Sauron's talk of other worlds: "And still, if they should at the last come to the end of those lands and seas, beyond all lay the Ancient Darkness.'And out of it the world was made. For Darkness alone is worshipful, and the Lord thereof may yet make other worlds to be gifts to those that serve him, so that the increase of their power shall find no end'" (*S*, 271). In consequence, the Númenóreans begin to believe that if there is to be salvation, it must be salvation *from* the Middle-earth. According to Voegelin, it is part of Gnostic lore that there be a Sage who appears to transcend the normal limits of the cosmos and out of whose assured mind comes salvation. The Sage is an overman phenomenon.[122] Sauron fits the image of the overman. When the Eagles of the West "bore lightning beneath their wings" as a warning to Númenor, and a portent of what would befall their rebellion, "Sauron stood there upon the pinnacle and defied the lightning and was unharmed; and in that hour men called him a god" (*S*, 277).

4. **The order of being will have to be changed in history to correct its flaws.**

An "immanentist apocalypse" aims at a radical and thorough going change of order, a *renovatio mundi*. This is what the Númenóreans seek in wanting to live on Valinor. Sauron eggs them on: "And he said: 'The Valar have possessed themselves of the land where there is no death; and they lie to you concerning

---

122 Voegelin, *New Science of Politics*, 80. Cf. Fukuyama on Hegel's account of Napoleon as a Gnostic sage, *The End of History*, 199.

it, hiding it as best they may, because of their avarice, and their fear lest the Kings of Men should wrest from them the deathless realm and rule the world in their stead'" (S, 274).[123] This appetite runs counter to the logic of fairy stories. Such stories offer relief not *renovatio*. Fairy tales, thinks Tolkien, have their own peculiar structure, different from other literature. They offer an *eucatastrophic* moment, when there is a brief joyous turn, "a sudden and miraculous grace: never to be counted on to recur." It is an *evangelium*, "giving a fleeting glimpse of Joy."[124] A temporary relief from a condition that must be endured patiently, therefore, whilst the Númenóreans seek a novel and permanent change of condition.

5. **The salvific change in history must come through human agency.**

    "Thus the fleets of the Númenóreans moved against the menace of the West; and there was little wind, but they had many oars and many slaves to row beneath the lash. The sun went down, and there came a great silence" (S, 278). So vast an armada that "the light of the setting sun was cut off by the cloud of the Númenóreans" (S, 278). Ar-Pharazôn plots: "he brooded darkly, thinking of war" (S, 270). Melkor schemes: "for even then he had secret friends and spies among the Maiar" (S, 36). Their activism contrasts with the orthodox actors in the plot, those who are Elf-friends. Amongst them, there is a strong sense of other-worldly agency. There are many examples of angels visiting inhabitants of Middle-earth (S, 238–39, 299–300). In *The Silmarillion*, Túor is visited by Ulmo, "one of the greatest of the *Valar*, the lord of seas and waters" (*Letters*, 386 #297). Elrond's stewardship of Middle-earth is, after a manner, always other-worldly, as one of his foremothers is Melian, a Maia (S, 261). And, of course, there is Gandalf. And with the Númenórean invasion even the Valar

---

123 As Bradley Birzer points out, Sauron gives a Gnostic reading of Númenórean theology with Ilúvatar cast as the "God of Darkness" (Birzer, *J. R. R. Tolkien's Sanctifying Myth*, 98).

124 J. R. R. Tolkien, *Tolkien on Fairy Stories*, 75.

trust to a divine visitation: "Then Manwë upon the Mountain called upon Ilúvatar, and for that time the Valar laid down their government of Arda" (S, 278). There are also portents of other-worldly intervention. As the Númenóreans gather themselves for war, they grow afraid. "'Behold the Eagles of the Lords of the West!' They cried. 'The Eagles of Manwë are come upon Númenor!' And they fell upon their faces" (S, 277).

6. **Knowledge (gnosis) of how to effect the transformation is "the central concern of the Gnostic;" seeking "the construction of a formula for self- and world salvation."**

"For with the aid and counsel of Sauron they multiplied their possessions, and they devised engines, and they built ever greater ships" (S, 274) and "they broke the Ban of the Valar, and sailed into forbidden seas, going up with war against the Deathless, to wrest from them everlasting life within the Circles of the World" (S, 278). As the kings of men grow in ambition, they even take names of the Valar for themselves (S, 267–68). A sign that they turn away from the measure of the cosmos and turn to their own devices is that the Númenóreans stop tending the White Tree (S, 268), birthed by the aratar, Yavanna (S, 59). Though the Elves explain to the Númenóreans "the fate and fashion of the world," and that death is not a punishment (S, 264–65), "the fear of death grew ever darker upon them, and they delayed it by all means that they could; and they began to build great houses for their dead, while their wise men laboured unceasingly to discover, if they might, the secret of recalling life, or at least of the prolonging of Men's days" (S, 266).

The wisest of the Númenóreans know that Gnosticism is apocalyptic. Amandil warns his household: "But hold you ever in readiness, for the end of the world that we have known is now at hand" (S, 276). As the kings of men brood on war against the Valar, the throne changes hands, and briefly the royal line of Númenor recalls the legacy of their founder Elros, brother of Elrond. Tar-Palantir reorients the throne: "The White Tree he tended again with honour; and he prophesied, saying that when the tree perished, then also would the line of the Kings come to its end. But his repentance was too late to appease the anger of the Valar with the insolence of his father" (*S*, 269). Tar-Palantir tries to reconnect rule with the green growth of Yavanna. Like Gandalf, Éowyn, and Sam he conveys Tolkien's conviction that sympathy with flora is a training in steadfast obedience to the rule of harmony with the cosmos.

Fussell argues that "war is the ultimate anti-pastoral," but Tolkien confounds this. Fussell thinks war writers sometimes turn to myth, enchantment, and pastoralism to flip their experience of war. In this light, Tolkien is not particularly original and perhaps not even a worthy guide to the problem of war—an example of a "bizarre inverse quest" (Fussell)—being an escapist, not really contending with the true cost of war.[125] Grafting this reading onto Tolkien misses something. Gardening plays a role in his Tory account of war because it ruminates on the high worth of the world without embracing militarism (fascism) or dismissing bourgeois suavity (communism) or subverting historically settled patterns of life (progressive humanitarianism). Gardening is emblematic of the civilizing "aristocratic distance" (Przywara) that depends on the rank of value tones. The civilizational work of gardening is twofold, in fact. It looks upwards at the value tones, the transcendental architecture of aesthetics, and it quite literally makes us look down, at the condition of the soil, and the geography of a place.

One of Tolkien's signature beliefs, I propose, is that gardens are not an escape from war, they are part of it. In this, he belongs to a soldiering tradition. Clausewitz observes that "military movements are practically impossible in heavily wooded country," and that intense cultivation, "where the land is cut up by numerous ditches, fences, hedges, and walls,"[126] creates friction in military operations. In the absence of intense cultivation, there is a security problem. Tolkien confirms the point made by the great theorist of war:

---

125 Croft, *War and the Works of J. R. R. Tolkien*, 28–29.
126 Clausewitz, *On War*, 349.

> In later days Gondor built a bridge over the upper Limlight, and often occupied the narrow land between the upper Limlight and Anduin as part of its eastern defences, since the great loops of the Anduin . . . had many shallows and wide shoals over which a determined and well-equipped enemy could force a crossing by rafts or pontoons, especially in the two westward bends, known as the North and South Undeeps.[127]

Keen attention to flora and the cultivation of land is not simply tactical—think of the use of forests lines in the Ukraine War to cope with drones—but strategic. It was the British Tory Mackinder who made this evident when founding the science of geopolitics on the eve of WW1. Placing Tolkien alongside Mackinder, the next chapter explores the geopolitics of Arda. Specifically, the claim is that Tory thinking about land and strategy is a critical plank in Tolkien's "cosmogonical drama" to restrain Gnosticism. Gnostics can have no sincere geopolitics.

---

127 J. R. R. Tolkien, *Unfinished Tales* (New York: Ballantine, 1991), 273.

2

Geography
and Mirkwood

"A map is a weapon."
Lt. Col. Ewan Maclean Jack, cartographer
with the British Expeditionary Forces, WW1

"A man is both a seed and
in some degree also a gardener."
J. R. R. Tolkien, *Letters*, 240 #183

In 1904, Sir Halford Mackinder, geographer and Director of the London School of Economics, delivered a lecture, "The Geographical Pivot of History."[1] The lecture has earned him the moniker "father of geopolitics." He argued not only that geography is the principal driver of history but, startlingly, he affirmed the primacy of land power over sea power. Disturbing to English ears—since the potency of sea power is "part of [Britain's] folklore"[2]—Mackinder's argument nonetheless tracked British strategy in the runup to the First World War. His thinking helps us frame some useful questions about Tolkien.

---

1 Halford Mackinder, "The Geographical Pivot of History," *The Geographical Journal* 170, no. 4 (December 2004): 298–321; hereafter GPH.

2 Brian Holden Reid, "The British Way in Warfare: Liddel Hart's Idea and Its Legacy," *RUSI Journal* 156, no. 6 (2012): 70.

Did Tolkien favor the geographical school of history?[3] Ralph Wood thinks so, since for Tolkien, "geography is hugely determinative for the way people think and act."[4] Playing on the word *theophany*, Patrick Curry insightfully speaks of Tolkien as proposing a geophany[5], and Gerard Hynes talks of Tolkien's geomythology.[6] About the Elves, Sam comments: "Now these folk aren't wanderers or homeless, and seem a bit nearer to the likes of us: they seem to belong here, more than Hobbits do in the Shire. Whether they've made the land, or the land's made them, it's hard to say, if you take my meaning" (*FR*, 351).

Which way did Tolkien lean on the great strategic question: land or sea?[7] More concretely, how did twentieth-century British strategic thinking shape the battlescape of a seminal piece of English literature, "a tale about a war" (*Letters*, 197 #154; *FR*, 14)? We know he thought about these things:

> The wide lands south of Mirkwood, from the Brown Lands to the Sea of Rhûn, which offered no obstacle to invaders from the East until they came to the Anduin, were a chief source of concern and unease to the rulers of Gondor. But during the Watchful Peace the forts along the Anduin, especially on the west shore of the Undeeps, had been unmanned and neglected. After that time Gondor was assailed....[8]

Indeed, sometimes the geographical experience of an infantryman pops off the page: "The Company were footsore and tired; but they trudged along the rough and winding track for many miles" (*FR*, 293).

A half century ago in the pages of *Mythlore*, Paul Lloyd argued that the *post*-WW1 theory of indirect war shapes *LotR*. He relies on

---

3 For an introduction, see Morris, *Geography is Destiny*.

4 Wood, "Tolkien and Postmodernism," *Tolkien among the Moderns*, 257–58.

5 Curry, *Defending Middle-earth*, 157.

6 Gerard Hynes, "'Beneath the Earth's Dark Keel,' Tolkien and Geology," *Tolkien Studies* 9 (2012): 28–29.

7 For Tolkien's use of contemporary earth sciences, see Kristine Larsen, "Medieval Organicism or Modern Feminist Science? Bombadil, Elves, and Mother Nature," in *Tolkien and Alterity*, ed. Christopher Vaccaro and Yvette Kisor (London: Palgrave, 2017), 95.

8 J. R. R. Tolkien, *Unfinished Tales* (New York: Ballantine, 1980), 308.

the work of Sir Basil Henry Liddell Hart, a contemporary of Tolkien's who was gassed at the Somme. A critic of the General Staff's performance in WW1, Liddell Hart argued that on the runup to WW1, British thinkers fell under the spell of Continental planners and catastrophically began to think in terms of land power. The traditional strategy of British arms, contends Liddell Hart, was indirect, relying on the surprise and mobility of nimble expeditionary forces backstopped by sea power.[9] Had Britain persisted in what he dubbed "the British way in warfare," the slaughter of massed conscript armies bogged down in Flanders would have been avoided. Lloyd: "From the very beginning Gandalf consistently follows the rule of strategy expressed by Liddell Hart in his classic work on strategy." By contrast, Sauron and Saruman throw mass ranks of infantry onto fortified positions.[10] Lloyd's tack is to contrast the lack of imagination shown by Sauron with Gandalf's agile thinking in always pulling off a surprise. He does not add, but he could have done, that Aragorn storms onto the Pelennor Fields from boats, and that Frodo and Sam operate behind the lines like special forces. These elements of the story seem to comport with indirectness, and so Lloyd's thesis has legs. Nonetheless, fifty years on, I think it is time to revisit Lloyd's claim.[11] *Pace* Lloyd, it is British WW1 strategic thinking that shapes the battlescape of *LotR*, not the post-WW1 critical reaction.

In general, the place of WW1 in Tolkien's life cannot be gainsaid. In the BBC interview towards the close of his life, Tolkien recalls still walking about Oxford in his uniform, even after having been released from service. Specifically, he recalls being back in

9 B. H. Liddell Hart, *The British Way in Warfare* (London: Penguin, 1942), v.

10 Paul Lloyd, "The Role of Warfare and Strategy in *Lord of the Rings*," *Mythlore* 3, no. 3 (1976): 5–6.

11 One reason to revisit Lloyd's argument is that Liddell Hart is no longer viewed as a reliable witness to the war in which he fought. John Mearsheimer observes that his view of the General Staff as nincompoops only became popular as the threat of WW2 intensified (John Mearsheimer, *Liddell Hart and the Weight of History* [New York: Cornell University Press, 1988], 11). Ian Morris points out that sending field armies to the Low Countries, to defend Britain's counterscarp—the nation's first line of defense—has been fixed policy since Elizabeth I (Morris, *Geography Is Destiny*, 51–52); cf. Michael Howard, *The British Way in Warfare: A Reappraisal*, Neale Lecture in English History, vol. 5 (London: Jonathan Cape, 1974), 15.

Oxford when Bulgaria fell out of the war, September 1918. This is an interesting detail, because Tolkien links an event in his life to an historical moment on the Eastern Front, a war Churchill dubbed *The Unknown War*. It shows both that Tolkien followed the late events of the war, even events little known to regular folk, and that these events remained vivid fifty years later. It would be completely unsurprising, then, for Tolkien to take note of the debate that arose after the war respecting its strategic character.

Nonetheless, to be clear, my point is not that Tolkien was fixated on WW1—though he'd be well within his rights to be so—and even less is it my point to make Tolkien play umpire between feuding British strategists as to who got WW1 right or wrong.[12] The point of this chapter is to show that Mackinder's geopolitics is of apiece with Toryism—during the Great War, Mackinder was the conservative Member of Parliament for Glasgow—and gave Tolkien a strategic way to think about his great love, flora. In addition, Mackinder's geography made vivid for his contemporaries the great divide in mythology between land and sea. This is the lesson Schmitt took from Mackinder, and one that Tolkien addresses in the tale of *The Mariner's Wife*.

As to specifics, the argument of this chapter has five parts: 1) proposes that, like Mackinder, Tolkien thought geography and history intimates; 2) explores the myth of the rivalry between land and sea in Tolkien's *The Mariner's Wife*; 3) summarizes briefly Mackinder on land power and British strategy running up to WW1; 4) examines the role of gardening in Tolkien and how it tracks one of

---

12 This caution noted, if the chapter helps Tolkien studies clean up its comments in and around WW1, then that's all to the good. Tolkienists can do better than: "And indeed, rather than solving anything, World War 1, a war ignited by little more than happenstance and rash judgement, laid the foundations for the even more global Second World War" (Witt & Richards, *The Hobbit Party*, 122). There was nothing rash about it, Mearsheimer documenting that in the original calculations the British planned to jump in mid-way through the conflict in big enough numbers to command the peace after the French and Germans had destroyed themselves (Mearsheimer, *The Tragedy of Great Power Politics*, 159–60). In a debate that kicks off a recent collection of essays on Tolkien and the Great War, Glenn Peterson repeats the blundering General Staff account of WW1—with Tom Shippey and John Bourne, rightly relying on recent historical studies, pushing back forcefully. See the dueling essays opening *"Something Has Gone Crack": New Perspectives on J. R. R. Tolkien in the Great War*, ed. Janet Brennan Croft and Annika Röttinger (Zollikofen, Bern: Walking Trees Publishers, 2019).

Mackinder's strategic insights about geography; and, lastly, 5) compares Tolkien to his contemporary, Carl Schmitt, the great German strategist whose work on war also emerged from the First World War. Having linked land power, gardening, and war, the close of the chapter points to Tolkien's belief that the common Tory appreciation of land also needs a value theory. This is a point of dispute between Schmitt and Tolkien, which I take up in chapter 3 on war aims.

Tolkien and Geography

It is not sheer coincidence that *LotR* is, as Tolkien himself explains on the first line of his foreword to the second edition of *LotR*, "a history of the Great War of the Ring." Serving in the signal corps at the Battle of the Somme—described by Tolkien biographer John Garth as "the biggest battle the world had yet seen"[13] and by Mackinder himself as "the longest battle in the world's history"[14]—Tolkien would have used tactics that he learnt during officer training, as well as from combat experience. It is very much worth noting that David Jones describes signalers as "a group of men apart, of singular independence and resource." He writes: "Accustomed as they were to lonely nocturnal searchings for broken telephone wires, they usually knew the geography of the trenches better than most of us."[15] To communicate at a distance, the Elves use a *glathralvas* or flashing glass. Carl Hostetter usefully compares this crystal with the signaling instrument Tolkien used during the war, the heliograph. A mirrored signaling device, its training manual observes that, in arid lands and from elevation, the Morse code generated by manipulating the heliograph could be seen some seventy miles away. The manual continues, however, that in Europe, with its fog, mist, and haze, alternative means of communication also might be required.[16] This last links to an important point made by Robert Collins that,

---

13 Garth, *Tolkien and the Great War*, 147.

14 Halford Mackinder, *The World War and After* (London: George Philip & Son, 1924), 117.

15 Jones, *In Parenthesis*, n. 32, 197.

16 J. R. R Tolkien, *The Nature of Middle-earth*, 354.

for Tolkien, water is not a simple good. He points out that mist and snowflakes, some of which are tinged with malice, only result once Eru has neutralized the discord in the musico-metaphysics of the world introduced by Melkor.[17]

Given a rough wartime schooling in geography,[18] did Tolkien learn strategy from Mackinder?

Of Tolkien, Darryl Jones says, he "was one of the great writers about Englishness."[19] In Tolkien's mind, the Hobbits are English! To his son, Christopher, fighting in WW2, Tolkien recommends "keep up your hobbitry in heart" (*Letters*, 78 #66). From the most prominent English author of the twentieth century, what should we expect: Is land or sea primary in his epic? In his 2006 Caird Lecture inaugurating The Research Centre at the British Maritime Museum, Greenwich, Harvard historian David Armitage took as his theme the elephant and the whale: the great Biblical opposition between God's terrifying pets, the Behemoth and the Leviathan. In myth, they represent the land and sea powers.[20] Armitage cites the French priest and Enlightenment historian, the Abbé Reynal, who argued in 1777: "It is since this revolution, which hath, as it were, submitted the earth to the sea, that the most important events have been determined on the ocean." Let's call Reynal the anti-Mackinder.

Born an Englishman in 1892, at the summit of British sea power, did Tolkien agree with Reynal and depict the earth submitted to the sea? He certainly dreamt that way, but terrifyingly. In a 1965 letter, Tolkien relays that for years he had a recurring dream: a "stupendous and ineluctable wave advancing from the Sea or over the land, sometimes dark, sometimes green and sunlit" (*Letters*, 361 #276).

17 Robert Collins, "'Ainulindalë': Tolkien's Commitment to an Aesthetic Ontology," *Journal of the Fantastic in the Arts* 11, no. 3 (2000): 259.

18 In a 1940 letter to his son Michael, who had recently posted to his regiment, Tolkien comments: "War is a grim hard ugly business. But it is as good a master as Oxford, or better" (J. R. R. Tolkien, *The Letters of J. R. R. Tolkien: Revised and Expanded Edition*, 61 #38a).

19 "Foreword," in *Tolkien: The Forest and the City*, 6. Tolkien's interest even extended to the most English communities in the USA (Shippey, *The Road to Middle-earth*, 223).

20 David Armitage, "The Elephant and the Whale: Empires of Land and Sea," *Journal for Maritime Research* 9, no. 1 (2007): 23–36.

Yet *LotR*'s first words, "When Mr. Bilbo Baggins of Bag End," and Tolkien's use of maps point the other direction, towards Mackinder.

In a 1954 letter, Tolkien apologizes to a proofreader: "I am sorry about the Geography. It must have been dreadfully difficult without a map or maps." He then goes on to explain: "I wisely started with a map, and made the story fit. . . ." (*Letters*, 177 #144). Yves Lacoste, founder of the French school of geopolitics, would not be surprised: "Within any governing body and its administrative structure, geographical observation and historical narrative are indispensable for considering a strategic situation and preparing either a political or a military operation. Over the centuries, this has been one of the major functions of geography."[21] Tolkien's major works— *The Hobbit, The Lord of the Rings*, and *The Silmarillion*—all have maps. The greatest novel, Leo Tolstoy's *War and Peace*, contains no maps, despite the setting being Russia's mobilization to fend off Napoleon's 1812 invasion. Why do Tolkien's works include maps?

From 1915 to 1919, Tolkien was a lieutenant in the Lancashire Fusiliers. He was a gifted pen and ink artist, and learnt about maps as part of an officer's fieldcraft.[22] A trench map drawn by Tolkien in 1916 is extant.[23] Tolkien made around 30 maps. As evident from letters, he fussed over them his entire life. He thought his son, Christopher, a much better cartographer, and it is his son's reworking of a Tolkien map[24] that appears in the first edition of *LotR*.[25] As Paul Lloyd points out, this map shows very clearly the Gap of Rohan, the easiest route for Sauron to come from the East into the West. He comments: "Once his armies are past the gap, no further natural barriers exist

21 Yves Lacoste, "Geography, Geopolitics, and Geographical Reasoning," *Hérodote* 146, no. 3 (2012): 6.

22 Matthew Edney, "British military education, mapmaking, and military 'map-mindedness' in the later Enlightenment," *The Cartographic Journal* 31 (1994): 14.

23 *The Tolkien Family Album* (Boston: Houghton Mifflin, 108), 40.

24 The use of red on Tolkien's original map may echo the use of red on WW1 trench maps: https://www.nypl.org/blog/2015/05/15/WW1-map-division.

25 https://www.tor.com/2020/01/22/celebrating-christopher-tolkiens-cartographic-legacy/#comments.

to block him."[26] However, the map of Wilderland, appearing in the first edition of *The Hobbit*, shows that Tolkien's strategic geography is more fine-grained than Lloyd suggests. The Wilderland map depicts three natural barriers—the Misty Mountains, the Great River of Wilderland, and Mirkwood—and a curious line, Edge of the Wild. In Tolkien's tales, pathways, hedges, bogs, fens, forests, rivers, marshes, mountains, shires, and cities, aid (*RK*, 814–15) and hinder (*FR*, 86) adventurers, and even their songs (*TT*, 464).

Those only familiar with the *LotR* films are sometimes surprised when they start the books that they move at a walking pace—it takes an absolute age for Frodo and his friends to get out of the Shire. "There were no paths in the undergrowth, and they did not get on very fast" (*FR*, 87). Here Tolkien observes a soldier's experience of land and war: terrain matters, or, as Clausewitz puts it, "the very smallest feature of the ground."[27] The land of the Shire is described in detail—comparable to the long descriptions of desert landscapes in Colonel T. E. Lawrence's WW1 classic, *The Seven Pillars of Wisdom*. Tolkien's close friend Robert Gilson—killed on the first day of the Somme—described No Man's Land as "the most absolute barrier that can be constructed between men."[28] Having witnessed the Somme's No Man's Land himself, Tolkien was keenly aware of the tight relationship between land and shared political life. Hobbits "possessed from the first the art of disappearing swiftly and silently, when large folk whom they do not wish to meet come blundering by . . . ," and have this skill not by magic but on account of "a close friendship with the earth" (*FR*, 1). For Tolkien, the history of war and peace has a geography: "But there were some that turned from evil and left the lands of their kindred, and wandered ever westward; for they had heard a rumour that in the West there was a light which the Shadow could not dim. The servants of Morgoth pursued them with hatred. . . ." (*S*, 259).

26 Lloyd, "The Role of Warfare and Strategy in *Lord of the Rings*," 4.
27 Clausewitz, *On War*, 109.
28 Garth, *Tolkien and the Great War*, 155.

Tolkien and the Sea's False Promise

During the Great War there was a split in the thinking of the British Cabinet about war aims. The options were total victory in Europe—the position of the British Prime Minister, Lloyd George—and a rival, majority position, the safety of the Empire, a goal that could tolerate concessions to Germany in Europe. Implicit in the minority, but prevailing, position was the primacy of good order on land, and, in the second, the primacy of sea.[29] This tension is unsurprising, since the rivalry between land and sea is a principal part of myth. Tolkien addressed the rivalry in *The Mariner's Wife*, a tale that, on balance, shows he thought the sea a false friend.

In Tolkien's mythology, desire for immortality and perfection drives history, but, critically, this driver is mapped. The immortality pole of his lore is across the sea, the Undying Lands—the seat of the gods—including the island of Tol Eressëa. The sea is a lure, therefore, but ambiguous,[30] disquieting,[31] dislocating (*TT*, 492), saddening,[32] and ravenous:[33] "Melendur looked coldly on the enterprises of his son [Aldarion], and cared not to hear the tale of his journeys, believing that he sowed the seed of restlessness and desire of other lands to hold."[34] Melendur thinks sea power expansionary, a position

---

29 George Cook, "Sir Robert Borden, Lloyd George and British Military Policy, 1917–1918," *The Historical Journal* 14, no. 2 (1971): 372.

30 Hamish Williams, "Tolkien's Thalassocracy and Ancient Greek Seafaring," *Tolkien Studies*, 17 (2020): 144–45.

31 Matthew Dickerson has pointed out the characterization of the sea in *The Silmarillion* as "a great unquiet" (Matthew Dickerson, "Water, Ecology, and Spirituality in Tolkien's Middle-earth," in *Light Beyond All Shadow: Religious Experience in Tolkien's Work*, ed. Paul E. Kerry and Sandra Miesel [Madison, NJ: Fairleigh Dickinson University Press, 2011], 17).

32 "It was at that time that she [Galadriel] received Nenya, the White Ring, from Celebrimbor, and by its power the realm of Lórinand was strengthened and made beautiful; but its power upon her was great also and unforeseen, for it increased her latent desire for the Sea and for return into the West, so that her joy in Middle-earth was diminished" (J. R. R. Tolkien, *Unfinished Tales* [Ballantine], 249).

33 Tolkien's early spider fiend was Gloomweaver, about whom the Valar speculate she was "bred of mists and darkness on the confines of the Shadowy Seas" (Garth, *Tolkien and the Great War*, 258).

34 J. R. R. Tolkien, *Unfinished Tales* (Ballantine), 184.

developed at length by Schmitt in his 1942 fable of war, *Land and Sea*. Gandalf seems to share Melendur's anxiety, speaking of the "seas of war" (*TT*, 586).[35] Mythology, Schmitt documents, depicts land power contending with sea power through the image of a behemoth trying to take bites out of the leviathan whilst the whale uses its great flippers to try to seal shut the jaws of the bull. The struggle is literally elemental,[36] and biblical, too: *Fear ye not me? saith the LORD: will ye not tremble at my presence, which have placed the sand for the bound of the sea by a perpetual decree, that it cannot pass it: and though the waves thereof toss themselves, yet can they not prevail; though they roar, yet can they not pass over it?* (Jer. 5:22).[37] Perhaps this biblical image stands behind Aragorn's talk of the Sundering Seas (*FR*, 189).

Rival loyalties to land and sea bedevil the Númenórean royal household. The idea of an elemental sundering affecting kingship is found in a heated exchange between Melendur and Aldarion. Aldarion has been away at sea for years and his father questions how being away from home for so long can prepare him for rule. Aldarion replies: "'Do I not study men all my days?' said Aldarion. 'I can lead and govern them as I will.'" Melendur retorts: "'Say rather, some men, of like mind with yourself.'"[38] Myth, contends Schmitt, depicts conflict between fish-humans and land-humans.[39] Tolkien

---

35 Another line of interpretation sees land power as the problem. Glen Goodknight believes Tolkien follows Celtic tradition, which situates the immortality pole to the West, whilst in C. S. Lewis's metaphysical geography, a Biblical orientation figures, with the immortality pole in the East. Goodknight reasons that the Celtic tradition did this not only because of the appeal of the sea in myth, but also because the experience of the East was as an origin of strange and barbarous visitors. In this interpretation of Tolkien, land power is the threat and the sea a sanctuary (Glen Good-Knight, "A Comparison of Cosmological Geography in the works of J. R. R. Tolkien, C. S. Lewis, and Charles Williams," *Mythlore* 1, no. 3 [1969]: 21).

36 Schmitt, *Land and Sea*, 11–13.

37 Mark Deckard has pointed out to me that in "the Old Testament/Ancient Near East imagery the sea is normally seen as representative of Chaos, something to be feared and never to be tamed. Hence, the crossing of the Red Sea and the Jordan river both picturing God as in control of the seas, and specifically of Leviathan, the creature in Job. Similarly, Christ calms the storm/walks on water again demonstrating no Chaos" (private communication 5/9/2022). Adam Smith notes the ancient Egyptians had antipathy to the sea and finds the same in India, too (Smith, *The Wealth of Nations*, vol. 1, 367).

38 J. R. R. Tolkien, *Unfinished Tales* (Ballantine), 186.

39 Schmitt, *Land and Sea*, 5–9.

plays with the idea, Melendur suggesting that, at best, Aldarion could rule fish-humans. Identifying with the sea, Aldarion justifies his preference: "'The mariner who is single of purpose and not tied to the shore goes further, and learns better how to deal with the sea.'" Melendur corrects him: "'And you do not 'deal with the sea,' Aldarion, my son. Do you forget that the Edain dwell here under the grace of the Lords of the West, that Uinen is kind to us, and Ossë is restrained? Our ships are guarded, and other hands guide them than ours. So be not overproud. . . .'"[40] Melendur accuses Aldarion of vanity, mistaking his place, for he is a land-human and not a fish-human, for only by the grace of the gods does he travel the seas.

The Ban of the Valar stands behind Melendur's anxiety about the future direction of Númenor under the rule of his son.[41] Prophetically, he fears Númenor as a sea power, that an expansionary policy will ultimately break the Ban and be disastrous for Númenor. That Ban is something like the American Monroe Doctrine, which outlaws foreign power military buildup in the Western hemisphere. The difference is that the American Ban is the threat of retaliation—it triggered the 1917 deployment of American troops to the Western Front[42]—whereas in Tolkien a bewilderment falls about anyone daring to break the Ban (S, 246 & 248). Should any remain oriented enough and get past the enchantment, the punishment is death (S, 249). It is the wisdom of the gods that the kings of men focus on soil more than venture upon the seas.[43]

The kindly Melendur thinks good rule has a geography. He chides Aldarion: "Rather would I have had you beside me, than any news or gifts from the Dark Lands. This is the part of merchants and explorers, not of the King's Heir. What need have we of more silver and gold, unless to use in pride where other things would serve

---

40 J. R. R. Tolkien, *Unfinished Tales* (Ballantine), 186.

41 J. R. R. Tolkien, *Unfinished Tales* (Ballantine), 200.

42 Ian Morris argues that Germany encouraging Mexico to invade Texas was the trigger for American involvement (Morris, *Geography is Destiny*, 383).

43 Cf. Elizabeth Hoiem, "World Creation as Colonization: British Imperialism in 'Aldarion and Erendis,'" *Tolkien Studies* 2 (2005): 79.

as well? The need of the King's house is for a man who knows and loves this land and people, which he will rule."[44] The gods—and God—agree. We saw in chapter 1 that when the Númenóreans finally do rebel against the Ban, God does not merely destroy their armada but, pretty astonishingly, unleashes an apocalypse. God near eradicates a civilization on account of its vanity: "for the light of the setting sun was cut off by the cloud of the Númenóreans" (S, 278). Little survives the apocalypse,[45] though, significantly, the tale *The Mariner's Wife* comes down to later peoples of Middle-earth. In the legendarium, the tale survives, Tolkien says, because its love story tells how Númenor became involved in the politics of Middle-earth (*Letters*, 360 #276).

The tale has three principal characters. Melendur, an astronomer king, who ponders his kingdom's place in the cosmic order. Aldarion, a figure of sea power, and Erendis, the land. Aldarion and Erendis are in an ill-fated marriage, a story about land contending with the sea. During their long courtship, Aldarion declares "the desire of the Sea still holds me."[46] Though he tries to spend time ashore to please Erendis, "suddenly the sea-longing took him as though a great hand had been laid on his throat, and his heart hammered, and his breath was stopped." He delays his marriage again and again, complaining to his father, "the hard ground of stone wounds my feet."[47] For her part, Erendis listens to his tales of adventure, but: "'I rejoice that the world yet holds such things as you tell of; but I shall never see them. For I do not desire it: to the woods of Númenor my heart is given. And, alas! if for love of you I took ship, I should not return. It is beyond my strength to endure; and out of sight of land I should die. The Sea hates me. . . .'"[48] Erendis loves the woods, but Aldarion

---

44 J. R. R. Tolkien, *Unfinished Tales* (Ballantine), 186.

45 As Patrick Curry points out, by the time of the action conveyed in *LotR*, Tolkien refers to the Undying Lands and Númenor as having existed in a "mythological time" of Middle-earth, so altered is the geography (Patrick Curry, *Deep Roots in a Time of Frost* [Walking Tree Publishers, 2014], 33).

46 J. R. R. Tolkien, *Unfinished Tales* (Ballantine), 186.

47 J. R. R. Tolkien, *Unfinished Tales* (Ballantine), 194–95.

48 J. R. R. Tolkien, *Unfinished Tales* (Ballantine), 196.

looks at trees as timber. He is careful to replant with trees the forests he levels for his ships, yet the destruction of the woods[49] poisons the mind of Erendis: trees begin to irk her, their use in ships representing the tightening grip of the sea on the land. "Fearing the Sea, and begrudging to all ships the felling of trees which she loved, she determined that she must utterly defeat the Sea and the ships, or else be herself defeated utterly." Ultimately, she shies away from the fight and takes sanctuary. Erendis seeks the hinterland, pastures free even of trees, so as to be as far from the sea as possible. The marriage is torn apart by their rival loyalties, and Erendis departs their marital home in Armenelos and takes their daughter with her. Erendis is not without fault, nor is she altogether a good mother, but the greater fault seems to lie with her husband. For his part, Aldarion spends ever longer at sea, and it stokes his vanity: "Life on land was irksome to him, for aboard his ship he was subject to no other will, and the Venturers who accompanied him knew only love and admiration for the Great Captain."[50]

Things are admittedly complicated. Against those who think water has a unitary, positive value for Tolkien—a symbol of hope, longing, or mourning—Norbert Schürer convincingly shows that there is little stability in how Tolkien treats water. He notes that the sea is sometimes presented as sinister and that the predominant forms of water in Tolkien are mist, fog, and cloud—concerns of an infantryman in signals—not the sea.[51] *Frodo's Dreme*, a poem also named "The Sea-Shell," hints at the sea as false promise:[52] the pilgrim venturing to new land in great expectation the sea becomes murky, and the poem's basic tone is disappointment.[53] Nonetheless, as a reward for his war service, Frodo gets to take the sea passage in the

49 Gareth Hynes "Empire, Deforestation and the Fall of Númenor" in *Tolkien: The Forest and the City*, 128.

50 J. R. R. Tolkien, *Unfinished Tales* (Ballantine), 188.

51 Norbet Schürer, "The Shape of Water in J. R. R. Tolkien's *The Lord of the Rings*," *Mythlore* 40, no. 1 (2021): 21–41.

52 Cf. Shippey, *The Road to Middle-earth*, 282.

53 Perhaps a reflection of Revelation 21.1, where the remaking of the world in the Apocalypse does not include the sea.

company of immortal Elves. Born of mortal stock, Frodo will not live forever, even in the Undying Lands. Yet, Frodo's sanctuary on the blessed land closes the loop (*Letters*, 104 #91); on his journey to war, Frodo had a dream of the Undying Lands (*FR*, 132). Some, like "Bright Eärendil" transcend the rivalry. A great mariner, "Eärendil came never back to the lands that he had loved" (*S*, 259).[54] John Garth has wondered about the role of biography: stricken by recurring trench fever, Tolkien convalesced by the North Sea in 1917 which, says Garth, "haunted so much of what Tolkien wrote."[55] Importantly, as the tale concludes, Melendur relinquishes the throne in favor of Aldarion, bowing to his great knowledge of Middle-earth gained from his seafaring. Sauron is stirring, and Melendur fears he does not have the strategic comprehension to rightly guide Númenor. Aldarion's development of Númenor's naval prowess lays the foundation for the amphibious landings that turn the tide of war in Middle-earth, Númenor coming to the relief of Lord Elrond.[56] It is delicate, therefore, but, on balance, Aldarion, a figure of the sea and vanity, seems to reveal Tolkien's preference: land over sea. The catastrophe seafaring brings to Númenor and the role of pasturage and flora, at least in the hands of Hobbits, if not Erendis, points

---

54 Even here, there is a complication. In *The Silmarillion*, Túor is visited by Ulmo, "one of the greatest of the *Valar*, the lord of seas and waters" (*Letters*, 386 #297). Túor, a man, marries Idril, an Elf, and Lord Elrond is their grandson. The visit of Ulmo gives Túor "an insatiable sea-longing," which he transmits to Eärendil, his son. One of Tolkien's very earliest inventions, Eärendil was already percolating in 1914. A great mariner, Eärendil becomes piacular. A status in Roman law: a person or a thing held to be "piacular" is judged culpable, though not guilty. Adam Smith explains the ancient law (*The Theory of Moral Sentiments*, 107). Tolkien: "But Eärendil, being in part descended from Men, was not allowed to set foot on Earth again, and became a Star shining with the light of the Silmaril" (*Letters*, 386 #297). The story of Eärendil might seem to put emphasis on the primacy of the sea but, in fact, it confirms Tolkien's skepticism: Eärendil is ambiguous. A "herald star," as Tolkien explains, but also piacular for having trod upon forbidden land dedicated to the gods. He is an exile, forbidden the land, yet also a figure of hope. What he is *not* is a good illustration of Robley Evans's assessment of Tolkien's philosophy of history. "Structurally and morally, the reduction of free will in history, which Túrin's madness symbolizes, becomes not only sentimental but also pathetic, so that action itself becomes suspect, insanely idealistic and possessive. Choice is so reduced that the last protagonist, Eärendil, can only escape to the stars. . . ." ("Tolkien's World-Creation: Degenerative Recurrence," 8). The last phrase is strange, since Eärendil is punished, but the bigger point is that the history of Eärendil reflects the struggle between land and sea power.

55 Garth, *Tolkien and the Great War*, 235.

56 J. R. R. Tolkien, *Unfinished Tales* (Ballantine), 250–51.

decisively, I think, towards land as most strategically significant in Tolkien's thinking.

This tracks with Mackinder's turn to land power. With more detail about the thinking of the Tory Mackinder, we can better gauge Tolkien's own strategic thought.

Mackinder and WW1 Strategy

About WW1, Mackinder says, "it tested all the results of history."[57] In his 2014 book *First World War—Still No End in Sight*, Frank Furedi describes WW1 as the "great dividing line" in modern European civilization.[58] The war still shapes our imagination, he contends. Furedi sees a crisis in self-belief at the origin of the war. Europe was turning to mass politics, with all its attending media, putting pressure on the principle of dynastic descent, which anchored the legitimacy of monarchical rule throughout Europe. Legitimacy was fraying because the idea of self-rule was afoot.[59] An alternate view, Mackinder's, is that not crisis, but strategic dynamics were at play.[60]

Mackinder calls accounts like Furedi's—where ideas drive change—"the literary conception of history" (GPH, 423). By contrast, he argues that European civilization is a consequence of the Russian steppe: a response to "a blow," Mackinder says, "from the great Asiatic hammer striking freely through the vacant space" (GPH, 427).[61] He argues that for a thousand years, Europe's formation was stimulated by horsemen raiding from the east, their mobility, and thus possible domination, halted by "the surrounding forest and mountains" (GPH, 427). Of interest to Tolkien, Mackinder goes on: "A rival mobility of power was that of the Vikings in their boats" (GPH,

---

57 Mackinder, *The World War and After*, 192.

58 Frank Furedi, *First World War—Still No End in Sight* (London: Bloomsbury, 2014), 12.

59 Furedi, *First World War—Still No End in Sight*, 41–44, 240.

60 Mearsheimer, *The Tragedy of Great Power Politics*, 188.

61 Cf. Smith, *The Wealth of Nations*, vol. 2, 692.

427). Away from their boats, however, Viking mobility waned and both England and France consolidated power under the stimulus of the Norse."Mobility upon the ocean is the natural rival of horse and camel mobility in the heart of the continent" (GPH, 432). Europeans took the Viking lesson to heart, and with the discovery of the "Cape road" to the Indies, the West gained fresh strategic power, able to add pressure on the steppe from the rear (GPH, 432).[62]

Sea power had been delivering strategic advantage since the eighteenth century, but thought Mackinder, by 1904 railways had shifted the balance back in favor of the steppe. Due to lack of timber and stone, roads could not unlock the potential of the steppe—as roads had done for the Romans in Italy—but railways restored the "Asiatic hammer"[63]: the steppe laced with railways promises wheat, cotton, minerals, fuel, and population, a totally fresh kinetic power.[64] For this reason, Mackinder calls Russia the "pivot area" of world history.

The strategic consequence? France in particular, Mackinder argues, must ally with the sea powers, so the country can be used as a bridgehead for allied deployments (GPH, 436). Critically, for England, this alliance is the only way to protect her sea power: the threat stemming from the bridgehead compels land power to concentrate its forces on land and not divert resources to dabble in the sea. This was the deep logic of Lord Wellington's role in Portugal[65] and the best way to defend India (GPH, 436).

---

62 There is a subtlety sometimes skipped over. Mackinder was no mere materialist or geography determinist. He noted that of equal significance to land was the failure of Rome to make Roman the peoples wedded to Greek. The Russians (the Graeco-Slav, as he calls them) owe their identity to Byzantium and the great sea powers to the Pontiff. He writes: "Thus the modern land-power differs from the sea-power no less in its source of ideals than in the material conditions of its mobility" (GPH, 433). In a footnote, Mackinder relays that at the lecture this sentence proved controversial, but, despite the debate, he stands by the claim.

63 Mearsheimer points out that the French invested heavily in railways in Russia to balance against Germany by strengthening the threat from the East (Mearsheimer, *The Tragedy of Great Power Politics*, 70).

64 Echoing Mackinder, Lord Curzon, in a 1907 lecture at the Sheldonian, argued that the Mahdi had not been defeated so much by British arms at the Battle of Omdurman (where Churchill fought), but by the light railway stretching across Egypt (*Frontiers: The Romanes Lecture* [Oxford, 1908], 17).

65 It might seem that Wellington's campaign in Portugal serves Liddell Hart's thesis well, but as Steven Ross points out, by 1808 the British were sure—and not for the first time in their long history—that their earlier hit-and-run tactics were insufficient and the commitment to a Continen-

The calculus of Mackinder is grim. Liddell Hart argued that the attritional strategy of the Western Front was a ghastly mistake.[66] Not so, says Mackinder: it was necessary to leech power away from Germany to safeguard the wider Empire. In 1912, Britain's Foreign Secretary, Sir Edward Grey stated that protection of the British Isles depended on keying British sea power to a British land war in Europe.[67] He was giving voice to a decision already made.[68] Lord Hankey was Secretary of the War Council during WW1. In his 1961 *The Supreme Command 1914–1918*—compiled from his wartime notes—the octogenarian Hankey recalled a 1911 Committee of Imperial Defence meeting: "From that time onwards there was never any doubt what would be the Grand Strategy in the event of our being drawn into a continental war in support of France. Unquestionably the Expeditionary Force, or the greatest part of it, would have been sent to France as it actually was in 1914."[69]

How does the British turn to land power register in our great English author? With the turn to the land, "the very smallest feature of the ground" (Clausewitz) becomes important. I agree with Jessica Seymour: in Tolkien studies, it is too simple to oppose green things as peaceful and barren spaces as presaging violence. Seymour points out that forests are frequently places of foreboding in Tolkien, and my argument—that green things have strategic value—means gardening, husbandry, and forestry concern boundaries, and thus peace in light of the possibility of war.[70]

---

tal land war was necessary (Steven Ross, "Blue Water Strategy Revisited," *Naval War College Review* 30, no. 4 [1978]: 58–66, and especially 62).

66 Liddell Hart, *The British Way in Warfare*, 29. Cf. B. H. Liddell Hart, *Strategy: The Indirect Approach*, 168–69.

67 Paul Kennedy, *Strategy and Diplomacy 1870–1945* (London: George Allen & Unwin, 1983), 57.

68 Samuel Williamson, *The Politics of Grand Strategy: Britain and France Prepare for War, 1904–1914* (Cambridge, MA: Harvard University Press, 1969), 111–14.

69 Kennedy, *Strategy and Diplomacy 1870–1945*, 58.

70 Jessica Seymour, "Nature and Beauty in the Hearts of Dwarves," in *Representations of Nature in Middle-Earth*, ed. Martin Simonson (Zollikofen, Bern: Walking Tree Publishers, 2015), 32.

Strategy and Gardening,

He threatens the Men of Rohan and draws off their help from Minas Tirith, *even as the main blow is approaching from the East.*

—Gandalf on Sauron's maneuvers (*TT*, 486)

Steeped in the Bible,[71] Tolkien never lived in a disenchanted world.[72] He seems always to have firmly believed in the now-out-of-fashion Catholic idea of the Guardian Angel, about which he spoke many times. Neither of the World Wars[73] dented his faith;[74] rather, they conformed to its near-pessimism. In a wartime letter to Christopher, Tolkien elaborates a fascinating ontology of Guardian Angels (*Letters*, 66 #54). Much of this ontology he reports as given to him in a vision (*Letters*, 99 #89). Angels making visits to inhabitants of Middle-earth are part of the myth (*S*, 238–39).[75] In the Bible, nations themselves have Guardian Angels (Dan. 10:13). There is a different Biblical theme even more resonant for Tolkien: Mary Magdalene *turned herself back, and saw Jesus standing, and knew not that it was Jesus. Jesus saith unto her, Woman, why weepest thou? whom seekest thou? She, supposing him to be the gardener, saith unto him, Sir, if thou have borne him hence, tell me where thou hast laid him, and I will take him away* (Jn. 20:14–15).

---

71 Shippey observes, "unlike many men of his age, he had not been alienated even by the Great War from the traditions in which he had been brought up" (Shippey, *The Road to Middle-earth*, 217).

72 He seems to have had an interest in ghosts: John Garth, "Revenants and Angels: Tolkien, Machen, and Mons," in *"Something Has Gone Crack": New Perspectives on J. R. R. Tolkien in the Great War*, 180.

73 Tolkien was always proud of his regiment, the Lancashire Fusiliers (Tom Shippey, "Tolkien as a Post-War Writer," *Mythlore* 21, no. 2 [1996]: 85, n. 5).

74 For this reason, I worry about the surety of those who think Tolkien experienced WW1 as trauma. This claim of Molly Hall seems hard to support: "It is through this moment, the transpiring of both a bodily dismemberment (Frodo's finger) and a fall (Gollum's body), which I insist one must read the whole of *The Lord of the Rings'* response to the trauma of WW1" (Molly Hall, "Narrating the Missed Encounter with the Loss of a World," in *"Something Has Gone Crack": New Perspectives on J. R. R. Tolkien in the Great War*, 244). It seems at least plausible that the many examples of dismemberment for crime—e.g., Beren's theft of the Silmaril and Frodo continuing the Baggins theft from Gollum—are Tolkien channeling ancient ideals of punishment.

75 J. R. R. Tolkien, *Unfinished Tales* (Ballantine), 410–11.

Though remaining on Middle-earth, the High Elves, Tolkien relays in a letter, still desire "the unchanging beauty of the Land of the Valar. Hence the making of the Rings; for the Three Rings were precisely endowed with the power of preservation, not of birth" (*Letters*, 177 #144). This aping of Valinor is itself a problem. The rings were made "to preserve all things unstained" and Elrond expresses the wish they had never been made (*FR*, 262). Elrond's regret illumines the depth of the strategic problem facing the allies. The surface problem is real enough: Sauron's forces are far more numerous (*FR*, 242), the allies are divided,[76] and though they have Sauron's master weapon (*S*, 287), it must not be used. Its power is perverse, only capable of generating darkness (*FR*, 253 & 261). Should the West use the Ring, victory would be pyrrhic (*RK*, 861).

The deeper strategic issue had long been in the offing: a false stress on preservation, instead of growth. Gandalf clarifies the war aim of the West: to get rid of Sauron, "uprooting the evil in the fields that we know, so that those who live after may have clean earth to till" (*RK*, 861). It is for this reason that the Hobbits are so important. They have not been immune from diminishment with passing years (*FR*, 1), but they are gardeners, and creative with it, too: "But all accounts agree that Torbold Hornblower of Longbottom in the Southfarthing first grew the true pipe-weed in his gardens" (*FR*, 8).

Tolkien had a very definite value order, and into the story line of the Númenóreans he weaves the criticism that preservation can fold into embalming. It must not. He explains:

> [Elves] wanted to have their cake and eat it: to live in the mortal historical Middle-earth because they had become fond of it (and perhaps because they there had the advantages of a superior caste), and so tried to stop its change and history, stop its growth, keep it as a pleasaunce, even largely a desert, where they could be "artists"—and they were overburdened with sadness and nostalgic regret. In their way the Men of Gondor were similar: a withering people whose only "hallows" were their tombs. (*Letters*, 197 #154)

---

76 A point well made by Lloyd ("The Role of Warfare and Strategy in *Lord of the Rings*," 4).

Despite Tolkien being, without question, an old-fashioned, conservative English patriot—maybe, even better said, a Worcestershire man (*Letters*, 54 #44)—he held life, not remembrance, as his core value. History cannot, and must not, be arrested (*Letters*, 116 #101), and key to life well lived is a right relation to land. A paragraph from a 1955 letter takes us to the center of Tolkien's value preferences:

> There are of certain things and themes that move me specially. The inter-relations between the "noble" and the "simple" (or common, vulgar) for instance. The ennoblement of the ignoble I find specially moving. I am (obviously) much in love with plants and above all trees, and always have been; and I find human maltreatment of them as hard to bear as some find ill-treatment of animals. (*Letters*, 220 #165)

Gardening figured prominently in Tolkien's life, and does so, also, in *LotR*. He was a keen plantsman:[77] "I am in fact a Hobbit (in all but size). I like gardens, trees, and unmechanized farmlands; I smoke a pipe, and like good plain food (unrefrigerated), but detest French cooking; I like, and even dare to wear in these dull days, ornamental waistcoats" (*Letters*, 288–89 #213).

Illustrative of the importance of flora is *The Silmarillion*. Evil befalls the Elves on account of their lust of jewels containing light from The Two Trees. The jewels possess, therefore, what all desire, "the unsullied light of Paradise" (*Letters*, 387 #297). They bring corruption, however, for they are light arrested, held in suspension by jewels that are inorganic.[78] The problem repeats for Bilbo, whose lust for the Ring "uprooted" him (*FR*, 61). Gollum suffers similarly: "he ceased to look up at the hill-tops, or the leaves on trees, or the flowers opening in the air," and when Gandalf tries to reach through the chaos of his mind, he talks to Gollum of green things: "It was actually

---

77 Walter Judd and Graham Judd, *Flora of Middle-earth: Plants of J. R. R. Tolkien's Legendarium* (Oxford: Oxford University Press, 2017), 3.

78 Verlyn Flieger points out that the Silmarils are something of an oddity. On the one hand, light is one of the great civilizational principles and a staple of medieval philosophies of light, yet Fëanor's jewels cause catastrophe. I would resolve the oddity by stressing not the light but their being jewels. For Flieger's point, "Jewels, Stone, Ring and the Making of Meaning" in *Tolkien in the New Century*, ed. John Houghton et al. (Jefferson, NC: McFarland & Co., 2014), 66–67.

pleasant, I think, to hear a kindly voice again, bringing up memories of wind, and tress, and sun on the grass, and such forgotten things" (*FR*, 52–53).

Tolkien explains that Samwise Gamgee, Frodo's gardener (*FR*, 81), is the story's "chief hero." Sam, he further explains, was modelled on the British "Tommy" he came to esteem in the trenches: "My Sam Gamgee is indeed a reflexion of the English soldier, of the privates and batmen I knew in the 1914 war, and recognized as so far superior to myself."[79] What is the difference between jewels and gardens? Unlike the Silmarils, gardens must be tended. Gardens and gardening make you tenderer. The gardener, armed with hoe and shears, is a tough-minded protector: controlling, but ultimately obeying the logic of plants, humbly attuning craft to the seeds of life. Sam is a true knight, for he combines toughness with tenderness.[80] And the strategic value of being a plantsman?

In his survey of the strategic situation of *LotR*, Paul Lloyd rightly notes the larger geological and geographical framework, but he skips the more concrete: "There was not as yet any sign of a path, and the trees seemed constantly to bar their way" (*FR*, 109). Furthermore, he contends that the story line of Sam and Frodo conforms to Liddell Hart's indirect war: "From the very beginning Gandalf consistently follows the rule of strategy expressed by Liddell Hart."[81] Liddell Hart's basic complaint was that Britain had adopted the "Continental" way of war, with massed ranks, whereas English arms succeeded historically by oblique sallies, on the back of British superiority at sea. As Tom Shippey points out, historical studies now show that the idea of lines of men going "over the top" just to be mowed down is a false image of WW1: generals used all manner of infantry tactics to eke out an advantage.[82] Furthermore, it is a somber

---

79 https://johngarth.wordpress.com/2014/02/13/sam-gamgee-and-tolkiens-batmen/

80 For a philosophical account of knight-errantry, see Adam Ferguson, *An Essay on the History of Civil Society*, 191–93.

81 Lloyd, "The Role of Warfare and Strategy in *Lord of the Rings*," 4.

82 Tom Shippey & John Bourne, "A Steep Learning Curve: Tolkien and the British Army on the Somme," in *"Something Has Gone Crack": New Perspectives on J. R. R. Tolkien in the Great War*, 14–15.

fact that British losses at the Somme were proportionally the same as losses at Malplaquet and Waterloo.[83] WW1 was not the aberrant military venture that Liddell Hart proposes.

There are massed ranks actions in *LotR*. The massed calvary charge of the Rohirrim—"the hoofs of wrath"—at the Pelennor Fields has Théoden encouraging the troops: "Arise, arise, Riders of Théoden! Fell deeds awake: fire and slaughter!" (*RK*, 820). Aragorn also leads the remnant of the allies directly against the Gates of Mordor, which brings us to an important point. You might think the operation of Sam and Frodo an example of indirection, but you could also treat Aragorn's reasoning as a carbon-copy of Mackinder's idea of the Western Front: direct confrontation as a way to pre-occupy German resources so as to keep their eye off Britain's core strategic vulnerability. In WW1 a peer competitor developing a rival sea power able to target India, and in *LotR* possession of the Ring. Gandalf, at the "very brink," wants to keep the Enemy's Eye off the true strategic vulnerability (the Ring) of the Allies:

> He is watching. He sees much and hears much. . . . He studies the signs. . . . His Eye is now straining towards us, blind almost to all else that is moving. So we must keep it. . . . But we must at all costs keep his Eye from his true peril. . . . We must push Sauron to his last throw. We must call out his hidden strength, so that he shall empty his land. We must march out to meet him at once. . . . We must walk open-eyed into that trap, with courage, but small hope for ourselves (*LotR* V.9.861–62).

Likely some such words were spoken at the 1911 Committee of Imperial Defence meeting when the fate of the British army in the Great War was, in fact, sealed.

It would not cross Sam's mind to embalm the light of the trees of Valinor: not from lack of imagination, but because his value preference forbids it. By contrast, Sauron and Saruman have no gardens, and, as Tolkien explains, they introduce a false theology—"worship of the Dark" (*Letters*, 156 #131), a "Satanist religion" (*Letters*, 205

---

83 Morris, *Geography is Destiny*, 381.

#156)—replacing fertility with sterility (Sauron's "scorched earth policy" [*Letters*, 179 #144]). Mordor is a rank scape, a twisted nursling of Sauron's resentment (*RK*, 900). Not even Bombadil, a potency of botany, could survive the apocalyptic sterility of a Sauron victory (*Letters*, 179 # 144). Saruman's power base, Isengard, begins its war effort with the destruction of the forests (*TT*, 463). This is not accidental. Critically, plants, but most especially the planting of trees, delivers strategic value. Mackinder argued that it was forests that curbed the mobility of armies from the East. Forests are barriers and historically have offered the West sanctuary from the steppe.[84]

Mackinder's idea is in Tolkien. It is a point you see in Tolkien's Wilderland map, where Mirkwood is so prominent. Merry expresses the idea, saying of the Old Forest, "everything in it is very much more alive" (*FR*, 108). Treebeard: "Those were the broad days! Time was when I could walk and sing all day and hear no more than the echo of my own voice in the hollow hills. The woods were like the woods of Lothlórien, only thicker, stronger, younger" (*TT*, 458). When Merry and Pippin are in Fangorn, Pippin finds the place inhospitable to Hobbits: "And I don't like the thought of trying to get through it either. Nothing to eat for a hundred miles, I should guess" (*TT*, 451). Early in their journey, the Hobbit adventurers are warned: "'But you won't have any luck in the Old Forest,' objected Fredegar. 'No one ever has luck in there'" (*FR*, 105). After Gandalf's charge at Helm's Deep, the orcs scattered: "The Orcs reeled and screamed and cast aside both sword and spear. Like a black smoke driven by a mounting wind they fled. Wailing they passed under the waiting shadow of the trees; and from that shadow none ever came again" (*TT*, 529). Treebeard, a strategic potency overlooked by Saruman ("I told him many things that he would never have found out by himself; but he never repaid me in like kind" [*TT*, 462]), sees the Enemy clearly: "For if Sauron of old destroyed the gardens, the Enemy today seems likely to wither all the woods" (*TT*, 465). Ultimately, Sauron is an

---

84 Ukraine forces suffered badly in 2023 during the Russo-Ukraine War when the battles moved from pine forests, which facilitated the smaller Ukraine army's partisan-like attacks, to the steppe, where the Russian advantage in fires proved decisive.

assault on the metaphysical principle: "A man is both a seed and in some degree also a gardener" (*Letters*, 240 #183). His strategic target is greenery, things that grow. Pippin observes their strategic value: "he thought he saw groves of trees. But they were moving! Could it be that the trees of Fangorn were awake, and the forest was rising, marching over the hills to war?" (*TT*, 475).

With Mackinder, Tolkien affirms the central significance of gravid land. *Pace* his co-religionist, the Abbé Reynal, for Tolkien, the earth has not, and must not, submit to the sea. Peace depends upon it.[85]

The Shire

This state of mind in which the soldier derives his conception of the strategic scene is brought primarily by the matter of geography.
— J. C. Wylie, *Military Strategy*, 1967

As we close this chapter, where does Tolkien sit alongside other strategic thinkers? Mackinder argues that the first dynamic of strategy is the pressure land power puts on sea power. Not all strategists think in terms of geography—far from it. Nowhere does Francis Fukuyama mention geography in his justly famous *The End of History*, yet the book dominated American strategy for nearly three decades after the fall of the Berlin Wall. Fukuyama's great opponent, John Mearsheimer, thinks fear, not geography, basic. Carl Schmitt opens his seminal *The Nomos of the Earth*, thusly, "I am much indebted to geographers, most of all to Mackinder" (*NE*, 37–38). Schmitt and Tolkien are worth comparing.

Schmitt commentator Eileen Kennedy thinks WW1 the formative event of Schmitt's political thinking.[86] His most important work,

---

85 I cannot agree with Pamina Camacho, who says Tolkien had no problem with the "sea-power paradigm," even casting Britain as a Phoenician trading civilization: "Cyclic Cataclysms, Semitic Stereotypes and Religious Reforms: A Classicist's Númenor," in *The Return of the Ring: Proceedings of the Tolkien Society Conference 2012*, vol. 1, ed. Lynn Forest-Hill (Edinburgh: Luna Press, 2016), 205.

86 Elizabeth Kennedy, *Constitutional Failure: Carl Schmitt in Weimar* (Durham, NC: Duke University Press, 2004), 111.

The Concept of the Political, opens with a dedication to August Schaetz of Munich, killed on the Rumanian front in 1917. In 1917, Schmitt was a military civil servant in Munich with responsibility for surveillance of leftist peace groups.[87] Schmitt's later thought is derived, in part, from Mackinder. Land, argues Schmitt, "contains law within herself, as a reward of labor; she manifests law upon herself, as fixed boundaries; and she sustains law about herself, as a public sign of order" (*NE*, 42). The earth's seasons reward labor, for her fertility generates rule of law: initially, the boundaries of the crops and partitions of the fields. Language itself develops around these partitions.[88] This is why law, observes Schmitt, is originally a fence-word, meaning a place to dwell (*NE*, 74–75).

We see this theme of good order when Tolkien writes of Hobbits: "for they love peace and quiet and good tilled earth: a well-ordered and well-farmed countryside was their favourite haunt" (*FR*, 1). And, again, in Gildor's warning: "But it is not your own Shire. Others dwelt here before hobbits were; and others will dwell here again when hobbits are no more. The wide world is all about you: you can fence yourselves in, but you cannot for ever fence it out" (*FR*, 82).[89] Land orients, an insight Erendis (rightly) fears Aldarion will not appreciate:

> "I have journeyed with you by ship, lord. Before I give you my answer, will you not journey with me ashore, to the places that I love? You know too little of this land, for one who shall be its King." Therefore they departed together, and came to Emerië, where were rolling downs of grass, and it was the chief place of sheep pasturage in Númenor; and they saw the white houses

---

87 Reinhard Mehring, *Carl Schmitt: A Biography* (Cambridge: Polity, 2014), 76–77. Schmitt was a lawyer and assigned to draft a legal justification for a state of siege: a document relied upon in 1919 amidst anti-revolutionary combat with the Bavarian Soviet Republic—ending in the trial and execution of a thousand-plus anarchists and communists (R. Mehring, *Carl Schmitt: A Biography*, 98).

88 Schmitt, *Writings on War*, 123–24.

89 There is, then, a quite literal relationship between law and Arda in Tolkien. Though Douglas Kane has an article, "Law and Arda" (*Tolkien Studies* 9 [2012]), he does not address how legal ideas are literally rooted.

of the farmers and shepherds, and heard the bleating of the flocks.[90]

Tolkien argues that the fecundity of land stabilizes the strategic situation. A feature of the reign of Aragorn at the close of *LotR* is: "Mirkwood had fallen under the domination of a Power that hated all living things but was restored to beauty and became Greenwood the Great before the end of the story" (*Letters*, 420 #339).

Tolkien tweaks Mackinder in one subtle and critical way. In a 1975 *Mythlore* article, Willis Glover observes: "In contrast to the classical effort to understand history in the context of nature, the Bible understands nature in the context of history."[91] Mackinder (mostly) derives history from nature, land being near-deterministic. Tolkien's geography operates alongside history (*Letters*, 80 #69). The efforts of land to orient us well is swamped, its compass muddled by the history of wickedness. And yet, despite this history, plants and trees make their appeal, and some, like the Hobbits, harken. Trees and flowers are not only strategic; obedience to their appeal points to hope (*Letters*, 100–101 #89). I say more about this at the end of the book when discussing the *simbelmynë* on the barrows of the kings of Rohan.

This chapter has shown that there is a Gothic twist to Tolkien's pastoralism. Verlyn Fleiger speaks insightfully of the flinty undertow in Tolkien. An example is Tolkien's belief that flora are a part of war. I have shown that his thinking about gardening and land power is of a piece with the geopolitics of the Tory Mackinder. The next chapter continues with links between Tolkien and British Toryism but, in addition, in pondering why the Shire is worth defending, I posit parallels between Tolkien and German Toryism. Specifically, I look at the Shire in light of Carl Schmitt's geopolitics, but with an important caveat. Schmitt and Tolkien share a common ideal of the land, but Schmitt was a value minimalist and the monarchical Tolkien a value maximalist. In this regard, I find significant continuity between

---

90 J. R. R. Tolkien, *Unfinished Tales* (Ballantine), 191.

91 W. B. Glover, "The Christian Character of Tolkien's Invented World," *Mythlore* 3, no. 2 (1975): 6.

Tolkien and the German arch-Tory, the value theorist Max Scheler. When Scheler came to prominence around the time of WW1, he was a Catholic philosopher and his influence on Catholic thought in the twentieth century can hardly be overstated.

3

War Aims
and the Shire

"And hobbits as miserable slaves would please
him far more than hobbits happypy and free.
There is such a thing as malice."
Gandalf, about Sauron (*FR*, 48)

In *The Lord of the Rings* the conflict is
not basically about "freedom," though that is
naturally involved. It is about God, and His
sole right to divine honour.
(*Letters*, 243 #183)

This chapter is about war aims. Wanting to be sole Creatrix, Melkor's war aim is to remove liberty. His is a challenge to the sovereignty of God, and thus freedom, for Eru makes free creations (*S*, 43–44). Sent to Middle-earth to safeguard God's sovereignty, Gandalf's war aim is to preserve Hobbits "happy and free." In Tolkien's telling, "happy and free" requires preserving the Shire, specifically the sacred boundaries that orient a free civilization. Gandalf's defense of the Shire is a symbolization of a larger work, the "liberation from an evil tyranny of all the 'humane'—including those, such as 'easterlings' and Haradrim, that were still servants of the tyranny" (*Letters*, 241 #183). In a proposition: Melkor's war aim is to increase tyranny by diminishing God's rule, whilst Gandalf's war aim is to preserve liberty by amplifying God's rule. This chapter explores Tolkien's reflection on the relationship between rule and liberty. Put differently, why bother defending the Shire?

Chapter 1 discussed Gandalf's submission to God at the battle with the Balrog at the bridge of Khazad-dûm. Tolkien explains that Gandalf, without complete knowledge of why his sacrifice was required, "was handing over to the Authority that ordained the Rules, and giving up personal hope of success." This obedience "was a humbling and abnegation of himself in conformity to 'the Rules.'" What are "the Rules" that make us "happy and free"?

Tolkien fought for England and saw droves of men die for England. In his *Letters*, Tolkien is explicit: he would not die for the British Empire and certainly not for what he despised, "Americo-cosmopolitanism" (*Letters*, 65 #53). Tolkien was willing to die for a place, "my little hayfield" (*Letters*, 348 #257), but not for other places (British Empire) or no place (cosmopolitanism). Wars, he believes, should not be fought for imperial ambition or capitalist humanitarianism. We are back to our Tory dispute with the Whigs. Adam Smith argues that the division of labor erodes the integrity of family and weakens the connection of families to specific places.[1] Under the effects of the division of labor, therefore, we would expect that wars will be increasingly fought for "Americo-cosmopolitanism."[2] And, sure enough, as John Mearsheimer points out, in the last thirty years the "benevolent" US has been at war for two thirds of the time.

In the last chapter, we explored Tolkien's reflection on the strategic value of flora and gardening. In this chapter, we draw out the significance of Tolkien's claim that his idea for the Ents came from the leaf-mold. By this, I propose he meant that land and civilizational

---

1 Smith, *The Theory of Moral Sentiments*. Cf. Schmitt, *Writings on War*, 91.

2 For a summary of what this is as a matter of US security policy, see Mearsheimer, *The Tragedy of Great Power Politics*, 9 and 46–47.

orientation go together. The Shire is a *cosmion* (Voegelin). What propositions attach to this symbol? The boundaries of a place are basic to rule of law. This idea was basic to medieval English village life, and Carl Schmitt takes up the idea in his talk of the *nomos* of the earth. The English Distributists had the same idea. This chapter contends that Tolkien's *cosmion* closely approximates Max Scheler's argument for the estate as an antidote to the "hostile modern spirit." Specifically, Tolkien's Catholic Toryism takes seriously Schmitt's idea of the *manring* as a feature of war, but critically supplements it with an axiology that links place to "the Rules" of God. This delivers a war aim: for Tolkien, it is worth fighting for the sacred boundaries of a place where eccentricity prevails. Eccentricity is, I think, a core value for Tolkien, one justifying going to war.

Hobbits Happy and Free

Tolkien: "There's nothing in *The Lord of the Rings* except that it's a foundation of one's feeling for trees, flowers and England generally."[3] Tolkien planned to dedicate his lore "to England; to my country" (*Letters*, 144 #131; cf. 250 #190),[4] yet the books and films are an astonishing global phenomenon. Why? Maybe the world over there is an appetite for Elves, Hobbits, Wargs, Nazgûl, and nasty little fellows like Gollum. Maybe its success speaks to the voyeur in us: the appeal of wandering inside one man's densely constructed fantasy; or maybe it is because we sense that the fantasy world that is Middle-earth is jammed full of moral, political, philosophical, and religious ideas with which we wrestle and perhaps have some sympathy. Maybe we agree with Tolkien that the Hobbits are happy and free? More, perhaps we sense that they are happier and freer than us?

---

3 S. Lee, "Tolkien in Oxford," 163.

4 Tolkien is quite unusual in this. After the Great War, writing national histories fell out of favor. The historical interest in world history, and even the efforts of philosophers of history to find the transcendental operators, arose from a real distaste for nation, seen as the culprit for the losses of WW1. Dawson falls into this camp, too, and that might explain the absence of the theme in *Progress and Religion*. For this background to the writing of history in the period, see Joseph Stuart, *Christopher Dawson: A Cultural Mind in the Age of the Great War* (Washington, DC: The Catholic University of America Press, 2022), 142–48.

The appeal of the Hobbits registers in the oddest of places. Palantir Technologies is a spy technology company in Silicon Valley. Its founder is Alexander Karp, a philosophy PhD. The CIA is one of Palantir's clients, as are other US security agencies. Amongst many spy coups, Palantir worked out that al-Qaeda suicide bombers are transported throughout the Middle East using the established human trafficking networks of organized crime. Palantir Technologies gets its name from the *palantír*, the seeing ball of *LotR* that allows face-to-face communication at a distance, a sort of Zoom *avant la lettre*. Company reps report that they are expected to return to the head office in Silicon Valley on a regular basis, as Alexander Karp is nervous, as they put it, lest they "lose touch with the vibe of the Shire."[5]

Some might be nervous that America's security agencies are tended by a man who lives to some significant degree in Tolkien's fantasy world. Howsoever that may be, Palantir Technologies is another indicator of the way in which Tolkien's masterpiece of English literature is woven into contemporary sensibility. That it is so, ought to puzzle us. After finishing his law degree at Stanford, Karp moved to Frankfurt and there earned his doctorate in political philosophy. The Frankfurt School of political philosophy is a famed iteration of the New Left, a progressive politics born out of the student unrest of 1968. What is the relationship between Tolkien and the New Left? Nothing, except perhaps the anxiety that not all is well with us.

What's Wrong with Us?

Tolkien: "I do find this Americo-cosmopolitanism very terrifying. . . . For I love England" (*Letters*, 65 #53). What is this Americo-cosmopolitanism? Here are two contrasting images of the city. The first is from David Hume; the second, Tolkien. Hume argues that civilization relies on the intimate relationship between

5 Siobhan Gorman, "How Team of Geeks Cracked Spy Trade," *WSJ*, September 4, 2009.

commerce and refinement in the arts and sciences. These combine in the city. Hume writes:

> The more these refined arts advance, the more sociable men become.... They flock into cities; love to receive and communicate knowledge; to show their wit or their breeding; their taste in conversation or living, in clothes or furniture. Curiosity allures the wise; vanity the foolish; and pleasure both. Particular clubs and societies are everywhere formed: Both sexes meet in an easy and sociable manner; and the tempers of men, as well as their behavior, refine apace. So that, beside the improvements which they receive from knowledge and the liberal arts, it is impossible but they must feel an increase of humanity, from the very habit of conversing together, and contributing to each other's pleasure and entertainment.[6]

The city is an allure of fashion, opulence, and vanity. It incites what is best about us, argues Hume, our "relish for action," quickness of mind, and our very humanity. The city, for the Scot, is a beachhead in the Whig transformation of civilization. This transformation is ongoing: urbanization is a global phenomenon and accounts for massive contemporary migrations. Hume would certainly militarily defend a fashionable city, but would he the Shire?

Middle-earth has its share of magnificent cities but, interestingly, in *LotR* they are mostly marked by decay. Gondolin was long ago overrun by Orcs, Osgiliath is in ruins, Dwarrowdelf a tomb, Rivendell is emptying, and the White City sparsely populated. Pippin, coming to the White City for the first time, is struck by its grandeur and power:

> Yet it was in truth falling year by year into decay and already it lacked half the men that could have dwelt at ease there. In every street they passed some great house or court over whose doors and arched gates were carved many fair letters of strange and ancient shapes: Pippin guessed of great men and kindreds that had once dwelt there; and yet now they were silent, and no footstep rang on their wide pavements, nor voice was heard

---

6 Hume, "Of Refinement in the Arts," *Essays Moral, Political and Literary*, 271.

in their walls, nor any face looked out from door or empty window. (*RK*, 736)

And at the heart of the White City: "A sweet fountain played there in the morning sun, and a sward of bright green lay about it; but in the midst, drooping over the pool, stood a dead tree, and the falling drops dripped sadly from its barren and broken branches back into the clear water" (*RK*, 736). Tolkien does not celebrate cities, as does David Hume.[7] Rather is he sympathetic to Vincent McNabb, the Anglo-Irish Dominican and spiritual director of the anarcho-syndicalist workshop of Ditchling. McNabb: the "unceasing Nazareth cry is: 'Come back, not to Ur, Memphis or Jerusalem, but to Nazareth, lest you prepare another Golgotha.'"[8] Why are cities sacrificial? It is on account of the division of labor.

In *The Silmarillion*, the great Númenórean city of Armenelos is consigned to the sea by the wrath of Eru as punishment for the human sacrifice practiced there (*S*, 271–74). In *The Hobbit*, Erebor is a wreck occupied by the worm, Smaug, and the Elves, at least, think the Dwarves rather invited Smaug with their greed. Greed sacrificing persons is intrinsic to the division of labor.[9] Ferguson:

> Manufactures, accordingly, prosper most, where the mind is least consulted, and where the workshop may, without any great effort of imagination, be considered as an engine, the parts of which are men. . . . But if many parts in the practice of every art, and in the detail of every department, require no abilities, or actually tend to contract and to limit the views of the mind, there are others which lead to general reflections, and to enlargement of thought.[10]

The late-Victorian, German social theorist Ferdinand Tönnies elaborates. About the ancient city of Rome:

---

7 Charles Huttar, "Hell and The City: Tolkien and the Traditions of Western Literature," in *A Tolkien Compass*, ed. Jared Lobdell (Chicago: Open Court, 2003), 128–30.

8 Vincent McNabb, OP, *Nazareth or Social Chaos* (Norfolk, VA: IHS, 2010), 5.

9 An unrestrained celebration of the division of labor finds its way into some Tolkien scholarship (Witt and Richards, *The Hobbit Party*, 149).

10 Ferguson, *An Essay on the History of Civil Society*, 174–75.

The rule of Rome over the *orbis terrarum*, which has its material foundation in commerce, brings all cities closer to the one city, and gathers together all the shrewd, bargaining, prosperous individuals, the entire ruling elite of this boundless empire, all haggling together in the Forum. It erases their differences and inequalities, gives them all the same outward appearance, the same language and form of expression, the same currency, the same culture, the same covetousness and the same curiosity. The abstract human being, the most artificial, "routinized" and sophisticated of all machines, has been conjured up and constructed, and can be observed—like an apparition—in the bright unglamorous light of day.[11]

The commercial city erases peoples' "differences and inequalities" and literally makes the human anew on the model of a routinized machine. Many today intuit that there is an unacceptable twisting of values inside much of our commercial civilization. Whether in film and television or local shops and bars, a common complaint heard about our world of work is the way in which persons are disregarded, as mechanistic management practices prioritize short-term profits. That which is highest, persons, and that which is finest, the life of the mind, arts, hobbies, and craft, play second fiddle to what is least inspiring, routinization. Ferguson's Tory anxiety about the division of labor is Tolkien's.

Though Boromir speaks lovingly about the White City (*FR** 45), and Aragorn and Arwen renew it (*RK*, 950–51), nonetheless the Shire, a constellation of villages, is most to Tolkien's taste.[12] This preference includes an important philosophical point.

Famously, *LotR* opens with Tolkien telling us that Hobbits are in "close friendship with the earth," and "do not and did not understand or like machines more complicated than a forge-bellows, a water-mill, or a hand-loom" (*FR*, 1). Their craft is slow, and so their

---

11 Ferdinand Tönnies, *Community and Civil Society* (Cambridge: Cambridge University Press, 2001), 217.

12 Which does not mean he thought it a utopia. As Philip Irving Mitchell points out, there are significant and abiding divisions and suspicions in the Shire ("Conceptions of the Pastoral in The Fellowship of the Ring," *Approaches to Teaching Tolkien's The Lord of the Rings and Other Writings*, 109).

consumption of the earth is slow. In chapter 1, we saw Tolkien oppose the cult of speed in Futurism. In his BBC interview, Tolkien complains that "multiplication makes everything faster now."[13] The first page of *The Silmarillion* begins with war: the first page of *LotR* begins with what is worth defending.

The Leaf-Mold

Hobbits do not constitute a commercial civilization trading far and wide and dedicated to perpetual innovations in the arts and sciences because they are not in thrall to the division of labor. Most people are charmed by Bilbo, and the Shire,[14] but not all. Some are irked. Hugo Brogan relies on Fussell to criticize Tolkien for "gross dichotomizing": Tolkien's use of gardens is dismissed as a merely typical English literary conceit—one intended to evade a fuller assessment of the Great War.[15] As already shown, this point misses the strategic significance of flora. Gardening is not an alternative to war, for Tolkien; it is a component part. David Jones provides a dark example: "faery-bright a filigree with gooseberries and picket-irons—grace this mauled earth." Gooseberries were barbed-wire spheres made "at leisure, by day" and tossed out at night to thicken the entanglements in front of trenches.[16] Brogan misses something even deeper, though. The division of labor can only be humanized if some part of a civilization escapes its logic. The Shire is a symbolization of this Tory insight.

Here is a very Hobbity thing from *our* Middle Ages. Gangdays, or Rogation Days, persisted in the villages of the British Isles from before the Norman Conquest and for a thousand years after:

---

13 Lee, "Tolkien in Oxford," 163.

14 Anna Vaninskaya comments that Tolkien's anti-industrialism has been discussed *ad nauseum* (Anna Vaninskaya, "Tolkien: A Man of His Time?" in *Tolkien and Modernity*, ed. Frank Weinreich & Thomas Honegger [Zollikofen, Bern: Walking Tree Publishers, 2006], 7).

15 Brogan, "Tolkien's Great War," 353–54, 361.

16 Jones, *In Parenthesis*, 35 & n. 13, 194.

Led by the priest and carrying the Cross, banners, bells, and lights, the men of the village went in perambulation about the boundaries of the village. They beat its bounds. The small boys who went with the procession were thrown into the brooks and the ponds or had their buttocks bumped against the trees and rocks which marked the bounds, so that they should remember them the better. . . . The bounds of his village were the most important bounds he knew.[17]

Whiggery and the division of labor is a threat to these boundaries. Tolkien's symbol is not a wholesale rejection of the division of labor; rather, it calls for the marginalization of the division of labor in orienting political order. The point can be illustrated by two elements of Tolkien's biography.

I contend that Tolkien is a symbolist, and the Shire a symbol, a *cosmion* of a free life. As already noted, symbols are complex, housings sub-theses that need explication. Because symbols are not simplistic, it is possible to both like some aspects of brutalist architecture and nonetheless prefer trees before almost all things, and such appears to have been the case with Tolkien. Tolkien lived in two houses in Oxford. In the BBC interview, he notes that the house on Manor Road had been knocked down for a new, brutalist library. He says: "There's an enormous combined English and Law library built there, which isn't bad, I think, at all. At any rate, there's a lot of it inside that is very good, anyway."[18] In the same interview, he says:

I haven't the slightest recollection whatsoever—I normally preserve a very bright visual recollection of where I was, where I am and things that are associated with what I'm looking at. I shall always remember, for instance, this chap dangling the green lights. . . .—but I haven't the slightest recollection of anything, the position, where the window was, myself, or the thoughts, anything that came out of the whole of the Ent chapter. That came straight out of the leaf-mold. There was

17 George Homans, *English Villagers of the Thirteenth Century* (London: Russell & Russell, 1960), 368.
18 Lee, "Tolkien in Oxford," 163.

no difficulty and no sense of trouble of composition, but it must have been sort of burgeoning there. I don't know if that's a good example.[19]

Tolkien offers a cautious approval of brutalist buildings and a full-throated one of trees. The idea of basic orientations coming out of the leaf-mold—fallen leaves decaying and reentering the soil as fertilizer—answers a critical need after the Whig Settlement, and its issuance, *AirSpace*.[20] Understanding this need is critical to good politics, and thus, per Clausewitz, any account of war.

The Hostile Modern Spirit

In eighteenth-century Britain, the Tories lost to the Whigs on what would henceforth hold sway over the culture. The Tories defended the inheritance of the Middle Ages, where most people lived on the land, either as parts of estates owned by the Church and aristocracy, or as small farmers or yeomanry.[21] Town and city life was marginal in orienting culture.[22] The Whigs sought to reverse this emphasis and transform the country from being largely agricultural to primarily commercial, with culture basically oriented by city living.[23] Adam Smith was clear about one of the implications: under the Whig Settlement there would be a gradual dissolving of familial and territorial loyalties.[24] Over a century after the Whigs vanquished the Tories, Tolkien, along with other Tories, expressed dismay at what the Whigs had wrought.[25] The disgruntlement has never abated.[26]

---

19 Lee, "Tolkien in Oxford," 159.

20 *AirSpace* picks out a non-place where geography and local political realities do not matter: https://www.theverge.com/2016/8/3/12325104/airbnb-aesthetic-global-minimalism-start-up-gentrification.

21 W. G. Hoskins, *The Midland Peasant* (New York: St. Martin's Press, 1957), 59, 244.

22 Hoskins, *The Midland Peasant*, 79.

23 Benjamin Disraeli, *Whigs and Whiggism* (London: John Murray, 1913).

24 Smith, *The Theory of Moral Sentiments*, 222–23.

25 Dawson, *Progress and Religion*, 8–9.

26 Good examples are Waugh's *Brideshead Revisited*, the television version being a huge cultural hit in the 1980s; and the modern Western TV series, *Yellowstone*, as well as its various spinoffs in the US.

A countercultural movement helped put Tolkien on the map. Amongst hippies in the seventies, regard for Frodo led the way.[27] To this day, many self-consciously liberal people—the New Left— enthuse about *LotR*. Many, on hearing about Tolkien's Catholic conservatism, are puzzled: "I don't like religion, and I certainly don't like conservatism," they declare, and then they wonder: "So why do I like *The Lord of the Rings* so much?" Meredith Veldman thinks that Tolkien and the New Left are linked by a shared romanticism.[28] The truth of this thesis hinges on how you think of romanticism. In *Political Romanticism,* Schmitt argues that it owes much to Whiggery, and in the hothouse of Marxist loyalty the New Left was quickly identified as Whiggery.[29] I am arguing that Tolkien is postliberal, but the New Left is not postliberal. Its iconic thinker, Jürgen Habermas, still invokes "the acceleration of history" and the spirit of revolutionary abstract rationality radiating outwards from the West towards the East.[30] In other words, a philosophy of history that Tolkien loathed as "Americo-cosmopolitanism;" a philosophy of history that became globally prominent with Fukuyama's famous formulation. Nonetheless, Tolkien—a self-identified establishment conservative—shares the same dissatisfactions with the modern world held by the average shopper at a Whole Foods or Waitrose supermarket. It is only the anxiety that is common, not the political solution.

What is his worry? Around 1917, Max Scheler wrote an essay, "Christian Love and the Twentieth Century: An Address." It is a profound meditation on WW1. During the Great War, Scheler launched bitter attacks on vanity and was then at the height of his reputation as the leading Catholic theorist of his generation. Reflecting after WW1 about his childhood, Sir Winston Churchill wrote: "The character of society, the foundations of politics, the methods

---

27 Jane Ciabattari, "Hobbits and Hippies: Tolkien and the Counterculture," *BBC News*, November 19, 2014.

28 Veldman, *Fantasy, the Bomb, and the Greening of Britain*, 304–7.

29 Isaac Deutscher, "Marxism and the New Left," 1967: https://www.marxists.org/archive/deutscher/1967/marxism-newleft.htm.

30 Jürgen Habermas, "What Does Socialism Mean Today? The Rectifying Revolution and the Need for New Thinking on the Left," *New Left Review* (September–October 1990): 8, 15.

of war, the outlook of youth, the scale of values, are all changed, and changed to an extent I should not have believed possible in so short a space without any violent domestic revolution."[31] The conservative Churchill viewed WW1 as a catastrophe; it buried entire the *ancien régime* and inaugurated a new age. Scheler, no less a conservative than Churchill, saw matters differently: WW1 was a market war, the fullest flowering of a commercial revolution wrought in the British Isles in the 1700s; occurring in 1914 because at that moment the last vestiges of Christian culture amassed in the Middle Ages were finally exhausted. WW1 was no watershed; it inaugurated nothing that had not been gestating for centuries. Such a war could only happen because the idea of European solidarity, an inheritance of Christendom, was finally supplanted by a moral psychology in which sympathy was twisted out of all recognition into the phenomenon of the spiritual vampire (this interesting idea about our moral psychology is discussed in chapter 6).

When the war started, Scheler was a rabid supporter of the German cause. By 1917, however, Scheler thought WW1 a commercial war, stemming from a twisted spiritual attitude. He breaks down this attitude into the seven attributes of what he calls the "hostile modern spirit." First, Scheler's list of attributes, then the role each plays in Tolkien.

Think of Scheler's list as a Tory manifesto. Headlining the modern spiritual force hostile to the care of the person is humanitarianism. Six other attributes follow: doctrinaire individualism or socialism; the absolute state; exclusive cultural nationalism; competition and rivalry; communities built exclusively by contract, where property holding functions to group people in class identities; and finally, "the bourgeois-capitalist economic ethos of unrestricted production and accumulation of capital" (*EM*, 366). These attributes, Scheler argues, each displaced Tory values, older ways of human relating. For example, humanitarianism displaced the Christian commandment to personal love, sacrifice, and service. Not for the

---

31 Winston Churchill, *A Roving Commission* (New York: Charles Scribner's Sons, 1930), vii.

liberal humanitarian is the Psalmist's *offer up the sacrifice of justice* (Ps. 4:6). Sure that the law is just a reflection of her will, the global humanitarian is nonplussed by the idea of obedience to law. The six other displaced values Scheler identifies are: "the Christian idea of the moral solidarity of autonomous persons," feudalism, national cultures linked as members of a world-culture, intellectual and spiritual work spanning nations and multiple generations, discrete peoples living in solidarity, and moral principles directing economic activity to supply "the needs of the community" (*EM*, 366). Each value figures in Tolkien, and the list provides the *value framework* or axiology for Tolkien's account of war and civilization.

Axiology

The idea of reality saturated with values was made famous by Scheler.[32] He is part of an elite club: philosophers credited with developing far-ranging ethical systems. They are few. His account has had a profound impact on European thought, and especially in Catholic circles, and not least in the thinking of Saint John Paul II and Benedict XVI. Scheler argues that persons in their judgments and acts defer to "the mysterious laws of the interresonance of love and hate" (*die geheimen Gesetze des Echos von Liebe und Hass*). Ordering our primary orientation to the world through love and hate is the ready access we have to discrete, extra-mental value-tones.[33] A civilization's moral history is the relationship between the acts of

---

32 "Indeed, it is as if the *axiological nuance* of an object . . . were the *first* factor that came upon us. . . . A value precedes its object; it is the first 'messenger' of its particular nature" (M. Scheler, *Formalism in Ethics and Non-Formal Ethics of Values*, 18).

33 Jonathan McIntosh's book on Aquinas and Tolkien overstates the anti-modernism of Tolkien. In my opinion, McIntosh is too wedded to a university movement in Catholic theology of the early 2000s, Radical Orthodoxy. His sympathy with this stridently anti-modern movement leads him to the position: "Tolkien's realism is thoroughly anti- and pre-modern, even Thomistic." In evidence, he cites Tolkien (*Letter* 399 #310) writing of things that "their value resides in themselves: they ARE, they would exist even if we did not." Since Thomas does not use the language of value, McIntosh is forced to admit: "What precisely Tolkien means by 'value' is not immediately evident." If we think Tolkien alert to value theory, which delivers a robust moral and aesthetic realism in a modern register, it is clear what he meant. And, indeed, Tolkien does talk like this in another letter (chapter 6). What's important about this phrasing is that no one ever regularly speaks like this: only those reading philosophical works about morals. For the McIntosh, see *The Flame Imperishable: Tolkien, St. Thomas, and the Metaphysics of Faerie* (Brooklyn, NY: Angelico Press, 2017), 90.

persons and this "invisible Order" (*EM*, 35; *FE*, 324–25). Scheler thought commercialism a distortion of the core resonances of reality (chapter 6). As we have already seen, Melkor's creations—the perverted Elves—are a distortion of the governing music of Eru. Whiggery is also distorting because it unmoors us from the shape of the land that delivers political order and frames war.[34]

I think one of the most curious features of Tolkien's remarkable popularity is that his conservatism[35]—he describes himself as a "reactionary back number" (*Letters*, 65 #53)—contrasts markedly with the dominant ethics of the West today, namely, our global humanitarianism.[36] Like Scheler, what registers with Tolkien is an older ethic, the Christian call to personal service: "Greater love has no one than this, that one lay down his life for his friends (John 15:13)."[37] Chapter 1 discussed in detail the full significance of Gandalf's sacrifice at Khazad-dûm. Each of the heroes in *LotR* is prepared to lay down his or her life for a friend: think of Aragorn's reaction to the death of Boromir (*FR** 45) or Éowyn's assault on the Captain of the Nazgûl (*RK*, 823–24). Think here also of Gandalf's reaction when Frodo agrees to be the Ring-bearer: Sir Ian McKellen does a lovely acting job when he betrays a sudden but subtle sadness at the thought of Frodo's sacrifice (*FR** 27).

If we continue with Scheler's list, we see that each hero stands in a fixed community, for example, Gimli *the Dwarf*. And yet eccentricities prevail, e.g., Bilbo, very much a Hobbit, is odd in being bookish,[38] fashion-forward, so to say—and a Hobbit, moreover, who has had

---

34 Dawson—in a passage we know resonated with Tolkien—formulated this point, thusly: Of the Victorian fashion for top-hat and frockcoat, though it spread across the globe like no other costume, it was "out of touch with the life of nature and of human nature as well" (J. R. R. Tolkien, *Tolkien On Fairy-Stories*, 72).

35 Cf. Kilby, *Tolkien & The Silmarillion*, 53.

36 For example, Verlyn Fleiger invokes humanitarianism, *There Would Always Be a Fairy Tale: Essays on Tolkien's Middle-earth* (Kent, OH: The Kent State University Press, 2017), 91.

37 Adam Ferguson remarks that personal service is not so much Christian as that Christianity makes explicit one of the inclinations of natural law (*An Essay on the History of Civil Society*, 16–24).

38 This is one reason Tolkien amusingly says: "They're not a very common type in universities. Though I do know, I won't mention his name in public, I know a most perfect example of a University Hobbit, both in size, appearance, and general sentiments" (Lee, "Tolkien in Oxford," 163).

an "adventure," unlike the other homebody Hobbits (see the nice comic opening at *H1** 4). Tolkien's heroes have group solidarity yet are characters, autonomous persons, with foibles and personal trajectories of their own.

Middle-earth is feudalistic.[39] Independent kingdoms and personages are linked by ascending and descending lines of authority and allegiance: Hobbits know they live under the King's law (*FR*, 9); Rohan owes loyalty to Gondor by ancient custom;[40] Denethor is steward only; all grasp that Lord Elrond's age and office commands deference; and Bombadil has authority over the Barrow-wights even (*FR*, 139). I discuss this more in chapter 6.

Scheler lamented the competition and rivalry implicit in the oftentimes garish, strident, and harsh tones of nationalistic music and art, indifferent to the style forms of high common cultures, those of Hinduism, Islam, China, Japan, and the Christian West. The great cities of Gondor are centers of civilization—built by survivors of Númenor (chapter 1)—"works marvelous and strong" (*S*, 291); these points of civilization, contrasted sometimes with the rude culture of Rohan (*TT*, 567; *RK*, 737), are clearly tone-setting.[41] Tone-setting, too, is the craftsmanship of the Dwarves, but whatever universal appeal it has pales under the appeal and authority of the language, lore, craft, and music of the Elves, who are tasked with the healing and adornment of the earth (*S*, xix). Particular craft cultures abound in Middle-earth, but there is a universal appreciation of things Elvish—though Dwarves, master craftsmen themselves, only grudgingly acknowledge the fact. Even Melkor defers to Elvish craft by placing the Silmarils in his crown.

---

39 Cf. Jane Chance, "The Lord of the Rings," *Understanding The Lord of the Rings*, 221–26.

40 J. R. R. Tolkien, *Unfinished Tales* (Ballantine), 323–24.

41 Tolkien's dust jacket design for *The Hobbit* is regarded as a modern classic of design. It owes something to his appreciation of Japanese art, which dates to his college days, and reflects a keen focus on the Arts and Crafts movement. See Michael Organ, "Tolkien's Japonisme: Prints, Dragons, and a Great Wave," *Tolkien Studies* 10 (2013): 105–122. One of Tolkien's favorite composers, Carl Maria von Weber, was the first Western composer to use Chinese music in his compositions. The tunes came to the West through the Jesuit missions (https://theamericanscholar.org/air-from-the-east/).

Rivalry is perhaps inadequate to describe the bitterness that exists between Elves and Dwarves (*H1** 2; *S*, 235; *FR*, 332 & 334). Betrayals have caused the bitterness, but there is also a mutual incomprehension about the sorts of things loved by the Dwarves and Elves. This incomprehension is the backdrop to the unlikely blossoming of friendship between Gimli and Legolas. At the Council of Elrond, Gimli stoutly repeats the ancient Dwarf adage, "Never trust an Elf!" Adversity and courage quickly draw Gimli and Legolas together, however. When the Fellowship, already tested and damaged, arrives at the borders of Lothlórien, the Elf watch says Dwarves may not enter the home of Galadriel. Legolas protests with his kinsmen (*FR*, 334). What cements their understanding, however, is poetry.

Journeying with the Fellowship, Legolas marvels at the trees he passes, but Gimli is afraid of them (*TT*, 533). By the same token, Legolas is astonished that Gimli can find rocks so interesting. There is a beautiful episode after the Battle of Helm's Deep—I say a little more about it in chapter 6—when Gimli speaks lovingly of the beauty of the caves there. He tells Legolas:

> Strange are the ways of Men, Legolas! Here they have one of the marvels of the Northern World, and what do they say of it? Caves, they say! Caves! Holes to fly to in time of war, to store fodder in! My good Legolas, do you know that the caverns of Helm's Deep are vast and beautiful? . . . Immeasurable halls, filled with an everlasting music that tinkles into pools . . . and the light glows through folded marbles, shell-like, translucent as the living hands of Queen Galadriel. . . . And plink! A silver drop falls, and the round wrinkles in the glass make all the towers bend and waver like weeds and corals in a grotto of the sea. (*TT*, 534)

Coming to a new understanding, not just of Gimli but the things Dwarves love, Legolas responds: "'You move me, Gimli,' said Legolas. 'I have never heard you speak like this before. Almost you make me regret that I have not seen these caves'" (*TT*, 535). Later, I discuss Gimli's adoration of the Elf queen, Galadriel: it is a good example of moral consensus, the appeal of certain values that breaks down rigorously held nativist, communal ideals. Here, what matters is that the refinement of Gimli, his mastery of the art of poetry, is a bridge to a "world-culture," as Scheler puts it.[42]

Scheler not only worried about the need to curb the spirit of rivalry by moderating modernity's nationalism, but he was also anxious lest this spirit damage a community's internal solidarity, too. Hume and Smith both dwell upon novelty as a leading attribute of commercial civilization, and novelty breaks with previous generations. Scheler thinks a rich conception of solidarity includes continuing the work of previous generations, an ancestral tradition.[43] This idea is clearly represented in Balin's mountain city of Khazad-dûm. The Fellowship seeks to cross the mountains of Moria. A blizzard, spiked with malice, drives them off the mountain, and they have no choice but to enter Balin's Dwarf city under the mountain. It is a poignant scene: Gimli thrilled to be about to visit his cousin Balin's city, but Gandalf well aware the city fell long ago to Orcs. When all is revealed, Gandalf recounts that the city fell because the greed of the Dwarves for *mithril* meant they mined down into the depths of the mountain only to stir creatures of extreme terror and malice, the fire demons, servants of Morgoth. Despite this greed, the halls and craft are magnificent. Paying little heed to the danger, Gandalf lights the main hall with his staff and the party gape in awe at the pillars of the city, which range as far as the eye can see and rise up into the vault of the mountain (*FR** 34). This is the work of generations, a unity of style and talent rooted in the identity of the Dwarves. I take up this theme in chapter 4 and chapter 6.

Khazad-dûm expresses an inheritance lovingly attended and amplified. Each hero, no matter his or her individual quirks, is profoundly marked by an identity that frames the things they love and

---

42 I think John Ellison is right that there is a remarkable similarity between Tolkien's illustrations and those of Russian folklorist Ivan Bilibin (John Ellison, "Tolkien's Art," 28). Look at The Trolls illustration in *The Hobbit*, then at the third illustration here: http://textualities.net/jennie-renton/the-art-of-ivan-bilibin. Bilibin was, like Tolkien, influenced by Japanese art (Sergei Golynets, *Ivan Bilibin* [Leningrad: Aurora Art Publishers, 1981], 10). See plates 103, 107, and 109 in the Golynets, and the Tolkien plates 2, 3, 14, and 27 in J. R. R. Tolkien, *Pictures by J. R. R. Tolkien* (New York: Willian Morrow, 2021).

43 Cf. Gill, *A Holy Tradition of Working* (n.p.: Lindisfarne Press, 1983), 136–37.

gives to each a home. Each hails from a place. Indeed, so marked is the idea of place in *LotR* that new readers of the books, after only knowing the films, are amazed at just how long it takes Frodo and friends to actually get out of the Shire. Hobbits are great gardeners, and as rooted as the plants they love. And, of course, they are as nourished by the Shire as their plants. Leaving a place, Tolkien wants to insist, should be hard, and the Shire never leaves the longing of the Hobbits of the Fellowship. The reason it is hard to leave a place is that geography is strategic, a point discussed in chapter 2. There is another reason: land and civilizational orientation go together. This explains why Gandalf's war aim is to save the Shire.

Catholic Toryism

The "bourgeois-capitalist economic ethos," with its emphasis on the mobility of capital and labor—globalization—could not contrast more with *LotR*. As we saw, weirdly, cutting edge tracking technologies like Palantir model themselves on the Shire, even when they have so little in common. The ideology of industrialism is utterly rejected in the figure of the depredations of Saruman (*FR** 18) and even commerce itself is a vanishingly small part of Middle-earth (contrast the place of trading and banking in *Game of Thrones*). Though Bilbo is a wealthy Hobbit (*Letters*, 292 #214), the lust of the Sackville-Bagginses for Bag End illustrates, thinks Tolkien, a cramped spirit (*FR*, 67).[44] It is also somewhat perverse as, as a rule, Hobbits are "free from ambition or greed of wealth" (*Letters*, 158 #131). Hints here and there of commerce can be found (*FR*, 6)—moreso in *The Hobbit* (*H1** 8; *H2** 17, 18 & 23)—but the impression given is that commerce and trade are limited in Arda because communities are mostly self-sufficient craft cultures. Interestingly, in the contemporary West, hipsters have made a modified version of

---

44 As Shippey points out, the basic structure of *The Hobbit* is that Bilbo's adventure pulls him away from his bourgeois comforts and makes him a better man. Think of Gandalf's piercing question to Bilbo: When did dollies become so important to you? For Shippey's point, see his *J. R. R. Tolkien: Author of the Century*, 10.

this attitude big business. Congregating in specific neighborhoods, hipster brewers, marijuana growers, barbers, and tattoo artists are making bank.

Though there are dissenters, there is a standard line of Tolkien interpretation that he sympathized with the English Christian social movement of Distributism.[45] I think this is right. Owing something to the anarcho-syndicalists, the theory put an emphasis on collaborations in workshops amongst autonomous workers enjoying the widest distribution of private property, as well as an emphasis on family labor and arable land ownership.[46] Authors of the Catholic movement of Distributism include Belloc, Chesterton, Gill, Jones, and McNabb. I will argue that Tolkien is closest to Scheler's German version.

In England, the epicenter of Catholic Distributism was Ditchling. It was the sort of place that sustained the craft attractive to those, who, like Tolkien, loved "ornamental waistcoats" (*Letters*, 289 #213). The spiritual counselor there was Vincent McNabb, and lead artists were sculptor Eric Gill[47] and artist and poet David Jones. Elizabeth Ward thinks the ideas of Ditchling flirted with fascism, or at best, anarcho-syndicalism.[48] You do not find the former in Eric Gill's writings,[49] but you do the latter.[50] Chapter 1 was devoted to Tolkien's opposition to fascism, and I take up the theme again in chapter 5. Even in this chapter, it will already be clear that Distributism runs counter to the corporate statism typical of fascism.

---

45 Jay Atkins, "On Tolkien's Presentation of Distributism through the Shire," *Mallorn* 58 (2017): 23–28.

46 Vincent McNabb, *The Church and the Land* (Norfolk, VA: IHS Press, 2003), 40, 104–5, 107, 155–56.

47 In what follows, value is found in Gill's social writings. Personally, he was a monster.

48 Ward, *David Jones Mythmaker*, 26–27.

49 In the thirties, Gill veered leftwards, away from Toryism (James Lothian, *The Making and Unmaking of the English Catholic Intellectual Community, 1910–1950* [Notre Dame, IN: University of Notre Dame Press, 2009], 107).

50 Gill, *Work & Property*, 108–10. Cf. Adrian Cunningham, "Eric Gill and Workers' Control," *New Blackfriars* 63, no. 745/746 (1982): 304–11.

Rather than dwelling on fascism, some might think it better to criticize the anarcho-syndicalism of Distributism as just silly.[51] In *The Hobbit Party*, Witt and Richards dismiss Distributism as a romanticization of the English Middle Ages, minimizing the high risk of failure that beset most medieval economies, and they contend, surely suffering the embalming Tolkien condemns. I will come to their account of Tolkien in a moment, but the first thing to worry about is their poor history of the Middle Ages. Certainly, old European churches have Marian shrines where Mary is implored to save the locals from war, famine, and plague. Indeed, to their point, the last famine in England dates to 1597, prior to capital markets.[52] Nonetheless, as William Hoskins shows—he was a contemporary of Tolkien's at Oxford and a specialist in medieval village life—English village life was remarkably stable across a thousand years.[53]

Witt and Richards point out that Tolkien surely knew about Distributism given its high profile then,[54] and in Catholicism today, yet nowhere does he mention the social movement: "sometimes the absence of evidence is evidence,"[55] they contend. However, as Ward has observed, Ditchling was an anarcho-syndicalist workshop—at least in McNabb's mind[56]—and Tolkien does frequently speak approvingly of anarchism, and even self-identifies as an anarchist (*Letters*, 63–64 #52). What is absolutely ruled out is that he was an Ancap, i.e., an anarcho-capitalist or libertarian fan of globalization and commercial rootlessness.[57] Witt and Richards tend in this direc-

---

51 Richards and Witt, *The Hobbit Party*, 158–59. "An aspiration or good intention is one thing, a policy is quite another" (161).

52 Morris, *Geography Is Destiny*, 257.

53 Hoskins, *The Midland Peasant*, xiii–xvi.

54 BBC Radio aired some of their public debates at the time (https://modjourn.org/essay/distributism/).

55 Richards and Witt, *Hobbit Party*, 162.

56 Ward contends that there were tensions between McNabb's idea of Ditchling as a model of industry to care for the worker and the more aesthetic concerns of Gill and Jones (Ward, *David Jones Myth Maker*, 27).

57 For the difference between the Ancap and the Ancom (anarcho-syndicalist), and lots of source material, see M. Malice, *Anarchist Handbook* (Amazon, 2021).

tion themselves.[58] For example, they are critical of Belloc for suggesting that to foster family ownership the state needs to redistribute land [59]—a position Pope Francis advocates,[60] and which even the Tory pope Benedict XVI thought appropriate to manage through political economy.[61]

Pace Witt and Richards, Tolkien echoes McNabb's 1933 *Nazareth or Chaos*, in which Old and New Testament leaders are documented as shepherding their people "out of decadent city organization back to the land." The Shire matches McNabb, "the gentle hills and wide valleys where the God of the hills and valleys had summoned us."[62] Though Erendis is not without her faults, she shares McNabb's valuations:

> Therefore ere long she left Armenelos [the capital city of Númenor], and went to Emerië in the midst of the Isle, where ever, far and near, the bleating of sheep was borne upon the wind. "Sweeter it is to my ears than the mewing of gulls," she said, as she stood at the doors of her white house, the gift of the King; and that was upon a downside, facing west, with great lawns all about that merged without wall or hedge into the pastures.[63]

McNabb's return to Nazareth was not solely to pastures and sheep, but to an alternative model of manufacture. It was a return not merely to the land, but to productive property based upon arable land holdings. Like his contemporary McNabb, Belloc—whom Tolkien admired—argued that the average citizen of the industrial West lived a servile life. His basic claim was that a person is servile unless he or she can step away from laboring for others. This freedom

---

58 Richards and Witt, *Hobbit Party*, 160.

59 Richards and Witt, *Hobbit Party*, 161.

60 Francis, *Laudato Si*, para. 65.

61 Benedict XVI, *Caritas in Veritate* [Encyclical Letter on Charity in Truth], The Holy See, June 29, 2009, chapter 3.

62 McNabb, *The Church and the Land*, 136.

63 J. R. R. Tolkien, *Unfinished Tales* (Ballantine), 201.

only exists if one owns productive land, which grants a degree of self-sufficiency.

The Middle Ages bequeathed garden and cottage industry, as well as the commons, a public space for grazing livestock at the center of English village life,[64] but Whig industrialism gradually stripped all this away.[65] Interestingly, the great Dutch historian Johan Huizinga observes that the commons of the English village functioned as playing fields and fostered modern sporting life.[66] Contemporary home ownership is no replacement for land ownership (see the conceit for a story about land that came to Tolkien's mind when at Mass [*Letters*, 81 #69]), because such an asset is invariably mortgaged, oftentimes requiring two adults' wages to sustain the payments. Wage-servitude is another way to think of the typical person's property today.

Belloc's demand for a free-holding yeomanry sounds like the effusions of nostalgia and utopianism, but, as we just saw, he rejected this. Servility is so repugnant to human dignity that people ought seriously to think about how to generate genuine land distribution. Something like the Shire, pointing to widespread land ownership, with houses and their productive gardens, is basic to Distributism; an example of Pope Leo XIII's "ownership of productive property."[67] Owning such property, as opposed to stock or other capital instruments, commits one not only to participation in a surrounding

---

64 Hoskins, *The Midland Peasant*, 93–95, especially 240.

65 Hoskins, *The Midland Peasant*, 228.

66 Johan Huizinga, *Homo Ludens* (Boston: The Beacon Press, 1955), 197. As explained by Guardini, Catholic liturgy is bounded by doctrine, and there is also an unenclosed commons: "The liturgy wishes to teach, but not by means of an artificial system of aim-conscious educational influences; it simply creates an entire spiritual world in which the soul can live according to the requirements of its nature. The difference resembles that which exists between a gymnasium, in which every detail of the apparatus and every exercise aims at a calculated effect, and the open woods and fields. . . . The liturgy creates a universe brimming with fruitful spiritual life, and allows the soul to wander about it at will and to develop itself there" (Romano Guardini, *The Church and the Catholic and The Spirit of the Liturgy* [New York: Sheed & Ward, 1940], 177).

67 Pope Leo XIII made this point in 1893—and Gill makes much of it (Gill, *A Holy Tradition of Working*, 125–26)—and it is still found in the writings of popes today. For Pope Francis's skepticism towards urbanization, see *Evangelii Gaudium*, para. 73. For Pope Benedict XVI's criticism of an international class of managers divorced from the community and his requirement that capital be invested in the place of its origin, see *Caritas in Veritate*, chapter 3.

world but just that, a surrounding, a belonging, a place. This point is well made in the film version of *The Hobbit*. Bilbo, criticized by Thorin for being overly preoccupied with thoughts about Bag End, retorts that he is there to help the Dwarves precisely because they have no home: all should hanker to belong to a place like Bag End (*H1* 29*). And, of course, the Dwarves do long for a home: think of the wonderful scene when Thorin and Balin finally enter Erebor again (*H2* 26*). Terror first comes to the Shire in the guise of the Ringwraiths. The Nazgûl hunt Frodo. Formerly kings of men but corrupted by the Ring now, severed from all community, they roam the earth on their horses or take to the air on missions for Sauron. Detached from the land, they represent a fascination with mobility that is one of the hallmarks of commercial civilization, but also show that goodness collapses without belonging and home. In a position paper he wrote about government policy respecting the design of, and payment for, WW1 gravestones, Eric Gill argued that local stone masons should be employed. British regiments drew heavily upon specific districts and regions, and Gill thought soldiers hailing from Brighton, for example, should have tombstones made by Brighton masons drawing upon their native styles and stones.[68]

Gill's idea of home even in death shares Tolkien's belief that Hume's city of fashion, vanity, and mobility mistakes the very foundations of civilization. It might be thought that Tolkien's Toryism, his emphasis on a person belonging to some place with an inherited communal identity, runs the risk of making persons epiphenomenal to the dynamics of communities. Tolkien turns this on its head, though: it is the Whig commercial city of the "abstract human being" where this is most likely to happen. This explains Tolkien's hostility to what he called *Theyocracy* and his seemingly odd desire that people go by their personal names only (*Letters*, 63 #52). One of the finest features of Tolkien's work, I think, is the stress he places on the eccentricities of his many characters. Think how *LotR* begins with Bilbo, who is "very peculiar" (*FR*, 21). Eccentricity is seldom

---

68 https://drawingmatter.org/eric-gill-on-designing-war-graves-1919/.

celebrated today, puzzlement or mockery typically the reaction, but Tolkien is of a piece with the Catholic literature of his times in welcoming eccentrics. To read Evelyn Waugh's *Brideshead Revisited* with its love of place, the return of the dying Lord Marchmain to his ancestral home, and Bridey's matchbox collection is little different than reading about Bilbo, his books, and his adventure "there and back again."[69] The eccentricities of Bilbo, Éowyn, and Bombadil, to name only a few, are a way for Tolkien to stress how an inherited identity enhances rather than smothers. To fight for one's land is, implies Tolkien, to fight for personhood.

Catholic Toryism, an Illustration

In my opinion, Scheler's Distributism is closest to the Shire. Scheler thought the West a declining civilization under capitalism (*NS*, 103–7). The problem is that vanity has been made the animating principle of production. The problem is certainly not beauty. Scheler was no Spartan, and Tolkien most certainly was not. In his BBC interview, Tolkien relays a funny encounter with some Hobbits when young (Birmingham youth townies) who made japes at his expense: "I'm rather dressed in the fashion of the day, rather like little Lord Fauntleroy, very unsuitable really."[70] In Tolkien's language the problem is multiplication.[71] Scheler thought craft culture a leaven, a way to undermine the glamorization (chapter 6) of an industrial mentality, where quantification is lauded as a vehicle to acquire luxury.[72] Note Tolkien's seemingly curious complaint that the problem with cars is that modern ones just aren't very good:[73] anyone

---

69 Cf. Peter Wilkin, *Tory Anarchism* (Faringdon, Oxfordshire: Libri, 2010), 72–73. For the significant role of English Catholics in supporting Tory anarchism, see 84–85.

70 Lee, "Tolkien in Oxford," 164.

71 Lee, "Tolkien in Oxford," 150.

72 Gill, *A Holy Tradition of Working*, 116–17.

73 In his BBC interview, Tolkien contends that the problem with cars is their cheap quality, a function of their multiplication (Lee, "Tolkien in Oxford," 115–76).

familiar with classic cars will appreciate his point that production numbers of classics were low because even relatively democratically priced ones—like an Austin Cambridge—included some hand finishing. In Tolkien's terms, the trick is to find a social form that escapes the acquisitive lusts of the Dwarves without flipping over into the primitivism and uniformization of the Orcs (chapter 6). Scheler operationalized this counter-vision in the idea of the estate. *LotR* is a literary imagining of the idea.

The first thing one likely thinks of, when hearing the idea of the estate, is a country estate, a manor with surrounding lands cultivated for food or sport. Scheler's idea does not exclude such estates—and a monastery brewing beer or tending a farm is another example—but an estate is any business organized around place, history, and, especially, family, but providing a sufficiency for itself and its workers.

What need does the estate answer? Smith theorized that one of the distinguishing features of commercial civilization is mobility: whether one thinks of the intellectual agility of workers to absorb new innovations in production, a sales staff and managerial cadre always on the move, or the liquidity of money, mobility characterizes commerce. This mobility is meant to be a great equalizer, a trait common to all touched by commercial civilization. But, in fact, the poor are often excluded. Stripped of assets, they have no solid place from which to start. Put positively, amidst mobility, a point of stability is necessary. But instability is compounded when persons unmoored become individuals—and families, community schools, loyalty directing action, and orienting regional ethos all wither. Vulnerability is the consequence and, as a corrective, government tries to pick up the pieces, relying on increasingly coercive techniques as it frantically tries to stop the disintegration.

The estate—a place where knowledge is gained, innovation exercised, and a space that is also a web of sympathies—cements a person's dignity. The estate is a place of work, a property, or holding, that fosters a standing in the community: it provides a role for self-regulating human effort. Linked to a community, it is a concern of families in a locality. The goal of Distributism is, says Scheler:

to transform the working *class* into an *estate*. An estate is something stable, a standing or a status, something wherein a man is self-sufficient, but which he nevertheless does not freely choose like a profession, since he merely finds himself "placed" there. But to know one's estate is to be truly *at home* in the State, at home in the consciousness of firmly defined and assured lawful rights on which no one may trespass. The idea of the estate and a certain order of estates, according to the values and functions with which each one is concerned, is totally inseparable from the Christian idea of community.[74]

At home in an estate, there is no flitting between commercially generated identities. This stability means there is no "boundless craze to have more and be more,"[75]—vanity!—a distortion of desire Scheler thought culminating in a spiritual vampire (chapter 6). Scheler's vision is found in the Shire:

> The Shire at this time had hardly any "government." Families for the most part managed their own affairs. Growing food and eating it occupied most of their time. In other matters they were, as a rule, generous and not greedy, but contented and moderate, so that estates, farms, workshops, and small trades tended to remain unchanged for generations. (*FR*, 9)

Having many varieties, the estate is a center of privilege, each estate working and perfecting peculiar values. Tolkien's characters bear the lineage of an estate. More about that in chapter 6, and elsewhere I have shown that the fashion marque Brunello Cucinelli is a fair approximation of Scheler.[76] Its business plan stretches between husbandry of land and flair. Indeed, the fashion is firmly rooted in history. The neutral tones of Cucinelli scarves, with one dyed strip running along, is a manner of decoration that dates to fabrics found at Neolithic sites.[77] This brand, solidaristic and personalist, committed to the land and style signatures, is contiguous with the Shire.

---

74 Scheler, *Christian Love and the Twentieth Century*, 399–400.

75 Scheler, *Christian Love and the Twentieth Century*, 397.

76 Please see McAleer & Rosenthal, *The Wisdom of Our Ancestors*, chapter 5.

77 Virginia Postrel, *Fabric of Civilization* (New York: Basic Books, 2020), 110.

I am absolutely sure that Bilbo and Tolkien would love Cucinelli knitwear and suiting!

Manring

In the Shire, each village is, in its own way, an eccentricity. The Gaffer thinks Buckland Hobbits "so queer" and "they fool about with boats on that big river—and that isn't natural" (*FR*, 22). The Ring is the Enemy because hostile to the multiplicity and oddities of estates. The unity sought by the Ring cancels a plurality of manners of life and therewith cancels a host of value orders distributed throughout these manners of life. This is why goodness collapses without place. After a fashion, even cities in Middle-earth are akin to villages. The cities of Arda are for Dwarves, Men, and Elves, not "the abstract human being."[78] Each is a bastion of the distinctive characteristics of their builders. This is because homes generate solidarity, shared values that guide. There is a risk. The life of a place requires a preparedness to protect that home. Solidarity requires a solidification of the enclosure, and now I turn to Tolkien's belief that risk and war are problems inevitably wrapped up with solidarity.

A civilization is always exposed. The cultivation of the land, its buildings, and institutions, runs the risk of drawing unwanted attention. In the last twenty years or so, Carl Schmitt has emerged as one of the most important minds of the twentieth century, a man who is also notorious, tainted by his Nazi associations.[79] As a Catholic, his inspiration is not the Middle Ages but a triad of modern Continental Catholic monarchists, de Bonald (d. 1840), de Maistre (d. 1821), and Donoso Cortés (d. 1853). He mentions them in all his

---

78 Though *our* Arda is made for the abstract human being, and the environmental and social cost is high: https://theconversation.com/keep-buildings-cool-as-it-gets-hotter-by-resurrecting-traditional-architectural-techniques-podcast-190384.

79 Dozens have written on the extent and character of Schmitt's relationship to the Nazis, but the place to start remains Joseph Bendersky's *Carl Schmitt, Theorist for the Reich* (Princeton, NJ: Princeton University Press, 1983). See his important recent assessment, which delves into the Schmitt's Nuremberg interviews. Bendersky contends that these show that Schmitt, though undeniably a sponsor of authoritarianism, was likely not a principled Nazi, but an unappealing opportunist: Joseph Bendersky, "Carl Schmitt's Path to Nuremberg: A Sixty-Year Reassessment," *Telos: A Quarterly Journal of Politics, Philosophy, Critical Theory, Culture, and the Arts* 139 (2007): 6–34.

major works—his *Political Romanticism* provides one of his longer treatments of their significance—and I think Tolkien found some (not all) of their basic insights congenial.

Of the three, Schmitt relies most on de Bonald. Famous for the claim that political legitimacy is historical, an inheritance of a people and a land, de Bonald argues that political life take its bearings from a community bounded by time and space, that human acts take their orientation from a place. Schmitt deepens and darkens this claim, and the Shire illustrates Schmitt's analysis. *The Concept of the Political* (1927) is known for its signature thesis that the friend-enemy distinction is inescapable: inescapable on account of the fact that borders are ineliminable. This is also the core thesis of *The Nomos of the Earth* (1950), where Schmitt argues that an elemental gesture of human life is the manring: forming their bodies into a circle, persons foster face-to-face communication in the manring, but also establish a boundary with their backs (*NE*, 74).[80] The idea is found in McNabb: about Nazareth, he says: "it was a family of families gathered together in aid and defence of life. Within its circuit dwelt the little self-sufficing group of land-workers and hand-workers."[81] A similar idea is found earlier in Ferguson:

> . . . slavery and rapine are first threatened from abroad, and war, either offensive or defensive, is the great business of every tribe. The enemy occupy their thoughts; they have no leisure for domestic dissensions. It is the desire of every separate community, however, to secure itself; and in proportion as it gains this object, by strengthening its barrier.[82]

This idea is found again and again in Tolkien. Amongst many instances, in *The Hobbit* the Dwarves form a manring at the onrush of Elf riders in Rivendell (*H1** 15) and Gandalf uses his staff to light a defensive ring around himself to hold at bay the power of Sauron (*H2** 29). Gandalf does the same in *LotR* when covering the

---

80 Schmitt, *Writings on War*, 113.
81 McNabb, *Nazareth or Social Chaos*, 5.
82 Ferguson, *An Essay on the History of Civil Society*, 122.

retreating cavalry of the White City (*RK** 21). The Ents form up in a manring (*TT*, 474). Dwarves maintain a manring by the cunning strategy of keeping their native tongue secret and only revealing their names in the language of the strangers with whom they are interacting (*Letters*, 175 #144). As Gimli, Legolas, and Aragorn track the Uruk-hai raiding party that has snatched Pippin and Merry, they find themselves strangers in Rohan. Crossing paths with a Rohan contingent of cavalry, Jackson has the Riders of Rohan swirl marvelously round the trackers only to quickly tighten formation into a circle enclosing the trackers that they might be questioned (*TT** 11). At the end of the movie, outside the Black Gates, the hordes of Mordor surround Aragorn's forces, who all then position themselves back-to-back as a manring (*RK** 65).

Manrings are enclosures that mark land with values. "The enclosing ring—the fence formed by men's bodies, the manring—is a primeval form of ritual, legal, and political cohabitation" (*NE*, 74). The Rogation Days of the medieval village are an illustration. In consequence, as at Rome, the city walls were sacred. Borders and veneration are birthed together. Gandalf understands the point perfectly. At the Siege of Gondor, the walls of the White City threatened by Sauron's forces, and Gandalf, arrayed in the glory of the White Wizard, mans the walls. Realizing that Denethor, Steward of Gondor, is unhinged by the threat the city faces, Gandalf calls to the men of Gondor to man the walls: riding through the city on Shadowfax, he shouts again and again, "Prepare for battle! To the walls! Return to your posts!" This is nicely done in the film (*RK** 36).

Walls are prominent in Tolkien: there are the walled havens of the Falas (*S*, 97) and part of the judgement of the Valar against the rebellious Elves is that Valinor is fenced against them (*S*, 88). Melian rings Neldoreth with "an unseen wall of shadow and bewilderment" (*S*, 97). Johan Huizinga (no fan of Schmitt) confirms his point:

> Every place from which justice is pronounced is a veritable *temenos*, a sacred spot cut off and hedged in from the "ordinary" world. The old Flemish and Dutch word for it is *vierschaar*, literally a space divided off by four ropes or, according

to another view, by four benches. But whether square or round it is still a magic circle, a play-ground where the customary differences of rank are temporarily abolished. Whoever steps inside it is sacrosanct for the time being.[83]

Tied to the land, the manring is a normative enclosure: Schmitt writes, "*nomos* means dwelling place, district, pasturage; the word *nemus* has the same root and can have ritual significance as forest, grove, woods" (*NE*, 75). The entire community and its laws are given an orientation from one place towards other places (*NE*, 74–75; 42),[84] including, as far back as Neolithic graves, the afterlife.[85] *LotR* abounds in loving descriptions of pasturage and forests, descriptions that express Tolkien's conviction that personal dramas have a geography and history. Think of this vivid geographical statement of the manring by Boromir:

> Believe not that in the land of Gondor the blood of Númenor is spent, nor all its pride and dignity forgotten. By our valour the wild folk of the east are still restrained, and the terror of Morgul kept at bay; and thus alone are peace and freedom maintained in the lands behind us, bulwark of the West. But if the passages of the River should be won, what then? (*FR*, 239)

Like Plato and Aquinas, Tolkien rejects self-creation, insisting that not all that is new is good (*S*, xiii & *FR*, xv). In Schmitt's 1970 *Political Theology II*, he argues that vanity celebrates what is new, the novel, the *novum*, but forgets the *ovum*. *LotR* begins in Hobbiton, literally in a hole in the ground, from whence emerges the Hobbit, Bilbo. It begins at Bag End and, far from Bilbo's adventure being a journey of self-creation, it is a tale of "there and back again." The *ovum* is an historical community (de Bonald) rooted in fertile

---

83 Huizinga, *Homo Ludens*, 77.

84 Schmitt, *Writings on War*, 123. See also Hannah Arendt, *The Human Condition* (Chicago: The University of Chicago Press, 1958), 64, n. 64.

85 The graves of senior members of early human communities were also aligned with the heavens (Morris, *Geography Is Destiny*, 66–69). It is also a seemingly curious feature of early human settlements that the houses of the dead were more substantial than those of the living, with the likely explanation being the veneration due to the ancestors who are the glue of the community (http://www.spoilheap.co.uk/burial.htm).

pasture:"the solid ground of the Earth is delineated by fences, enclosures, boundaries, walls, houses, and other constructs" (*NE*, 42). This working up of the land elaborates the "orders and orientations of human social life" (*NE*, 42). Elrond, appointing the Fellowship, makes the point: "This is the hour of the Shire-folk, when they arise from their quiet fields to shake the towers and counsels of the Great" (*FR*, 264). For this reason, dwellings in Middle-earth are melded into the land. Bag End is under the hill, Dwarrowdelf is built into a mountain (Caradhras), and Minas Tirith about one (Mount Mindolluin) (*S*, 304). Amidst the trees of Lothlórien, the seat of Galadriel and Celeborn is the city Caras Galadhon, the City of Trees (*FR*, 344–45). Civilization itself, then, is always, in Pope Leo XIII's phrase, "that portion of nature's field."

Geography and Law

Schmitt's own lack of moral character and his throwing in his lot with the Nazis for a time—for how long is contested—makes it is easy to think that his talk of the manring is really a surrogate for virulent nationalism, a valorization of wars of aggression, and imperial expansion. Yet it is an implication of the foregoing that a crucial theme for Schmitt is defense, not attack. Schmitt's manring restricts personal agency to bearings derived from the land and a community's past. A solidaristic enclosure deferring to the land is evident in the mines of Moria for the Dwarves, Lothlórien for the Elves, and, behind hedges, the Hobbit houses inside the knolls of the Shire. A lovely example from *The Silmarillion* is the Girdle of Melian.

Married to the Elvenking, Thingol, Queen Melian, being of "divine race," an Ainur, or one of The Holy Ones, casts a defensive ring around Doriath. Melian, by her Girdle, "Doriath defended through long ages from the evils without." With the death of her beloved Thingol at the hands of Dwarves, her spirit breaks and part of the defensive wall, the river of Esgalduin, is weakened: "The enchanted river spoke with a different voice, and Doriath lay open to its enemies" (*S*, 234). This image of the defensive Girdle or ring repeats in the City of Gondor, made up of inner and outer rings that arc out around Mount Mindolluin. Edoras has a ring-wall, a stockade atop a sort of Table Mountain that itself acts like a ring-wall. And a few other examples: The circular tower of Saruman's Orthanc, Sauron's own circular eye, the Ring itself, and Mount Doom, a volcano with a circular opening, being origin and home of the Ring, with Shelob—herself an engorged circle—standing sentinel at the only pass, the Stairs of Cirith Ungol.

Land, argues Schmitt, "contains law within herself, as a reward of labour; she manifests law upon herself, as fixed boundaries; and she sustains law about herself, as a public sign of order" (*NE*, 42). Land and law are tied, insists Schmitt, with the land having a regularity and fecundity that rewards human labor upon the land. Labor rewarded, land manifests law upon itself: there being the boundaries of the crops, partitions of the fields, and above and across the land develops all the public signs of order. Law is, says Schmitt, originally a fence-word, meaning a place to dwell (*NE*, 74–75). The common law of a people is upon the land, the people's shared life, orientated by the rich lawfulness of land. Schmitt: "In particular, *nomos* can be described as a wall, because, like a wall, it, too, is based on sacred orientations. The *nomos* can grow and multiply like land and property: all human *nomoi* are 'nourished' by a single divine *nomos*. . . . It surely is significant that *nomos* can refer also to a scale or succession of notes, i.e., to a musical order" (*NE*, 70–71). History confirms: about the English county of Rutland, Hoskins writes: "Here, in the twelfth-fifteenth centuries, 52 parish churches served fewer than 10,000 people (8991 in 1377). . . . In general, too, the churches of Rutland are large and handsome buildings, some of them superb—out of all proportion to the size of the community they at any time served."[86]

Combining Schmitt and Hoskins, here is Tolkien:

> But in the midst of the land was a mountain tall and steep, and it was named the Meneltarma, the Pillar of Heaven, and upon it was a high place that was hallowed to Eru Ilúvatar. . . . At the

---

86 Hoskins, *The Midland Peasant*, 58, n. 2.

feet of the mountain were built the tombs of the Kings, and hard by upon a hill was Armenelos, fairest of cities, and there stood the tower and the citadel that was raised by Elros son of Eärendil, whom the Valar appointed to be the first King of the Dúnedain. (*S*, 261)

Tolkien roots political *nomos*, the rule of the king appointed by the angels, in the divine *nomos*. The angels mediate divine rule into the *nomos* of the kings, as do the ancestor kings. The political theology of the medieval village, which is, in fact, the political theology of all civilizations, structures Númenor. The two giant statues at Argonath, "the sentinels of Númenor" (*FR*, 383) are a good example of Schmitt's point. "Upon great pedestals founded in the deep waters stood two great kings of stone. . . . The left hand of each was raised palm outwards in gesture of warning" (*FR*, 383). Land and law united. By contrast, the sterility about Mordor, and the lush forests of Isengard destroyed, point to the disorder of the rule of the totalitarians Sauron and Saruman. It is little surprise that Gollum is so fixated upon Bilbo's thievery of his property, or that the theft of the Silmarils brings so much doom, because property is a basic expression of land, law, and common life. For Gollum, the exile, the Ring is a treacherous surrogate, pointing to something lost that is indeed very precious.

Boundaries are basic to fortification and civilization. Tolkien explains at length:

That fantasies which blended the human form with animal and vegetable forms, or gave human faculties to beasts, are ancient is, of course, no evidence for confusion at all. It is, if anything, evidence to the contrary. Fantasy does not blur the sharp outlines of the real world; for it depends on them. As far as our western, European, world is concerned, this "sense of separation" has in fact been attacked and weakened in modern times not by fantasy but by scientific theory. Not by stories of centaurs or werewolves or enchanted bears, but by the hypotheses (or dogmatic guesses) of scientific writers who classed Man not only as "an animal"—that correct classification is ancient—but as "only an animal." There has been a consequent distortion of sentiment. The natural love of men not wholly corrupt for beasts, and the human desire to "get inside the skin" of living things, has run riot. We now get men who love animals more than men; who pity sheep so much that they curse shepherds as wolves; who weep over a slain war-horse and vilify dead soldiers. It is now, not in the days when fairy-stories were begotten, that we get "an absence of the sense of separation." It is a curious result of the application of evolutionary hypothesis concerning Man's animal body to his whole being, that it tends to produce both arrogance and servility. Man has merely succeeded (it seems) in dominating other animals by force and chicane, not by hereditary right. He is a tyrant not a king. A cat may look at a king; but let no cat look at a tyrant![87]

He conveys this idea of demarcation and civilization[88] wonderfully when, after the War of Wrath and Morgoth's defeat by the host of the Valar, Morgoth is pushed through "the Door of the Night beyond the Walls of the World." Eärendil watches "upon the ramparts of the sky" and "a guard is set for ever on those walls" lest Morgoth attempt a return (S, 255).

In brief, Tolkien folds Schmittean themes of war into Distributist ideas of land, solidarity, and home.[89] In so doing, he held onto what is best and most profound about Schmitt, whilst making a vital corrective to that style of thinking. Schmitt thinks war protects ways of life, *ethnoi*. Tolkien took the "King's shilling" and fought for England. Not only was he proud of his regiment but he then launched a literary enterprise to give voice to England. However, to Schmitt's theme of solidarity, Tolkien adds an axiology not only absent in Schmitt, but one Schmitt opposed:[90] home, place, family, community, and craft are estimable when integrated into a Schelerian value hierarchy. This hierarchy refines solidarity and, as our next

---

87 *https://coolcalvary.files.wordpress.com/2018/10/on-fairy-stories1.pdf*, 40.

88 For the idea of the absence of boundaries subverting law and good politics in Ditchling publications, see Douglas Pepler, *The Devil's Devices*, with illustration by Eric Gill (London: The Hampshire House Workshops, 1915), especially 108.

89 These latter themes are basic to the thought of the English conservative, Sir Roger Scruton. Among many works, see *England: An Elegy* (London: Chatto & Windus, 2000), especially chapter 4.

90 Carl Schmitt, *Tyranny of Values* (Candor, NY: Telos Press, 2018).

chapter shows, affirms persons, even in their eccentricity. In Catholic parlance, solidarity needs the supplement of subsidiarity, or personal dignity. The problem of disgust—so very prominent in Tolkien's writing—will help us see the analytical connection between the solidarity of the manring and the interior space within it for personal eccentricity. As such, Tolkien offers a conservative, Catholic, twentieth-century philosophy of war. Gandalf's war aim—defending the Shire—is the symbol of this modern accounting of war.

4

Dignity and the Uruk-hai

T*he War of the Ring*: the original title Tolkien had in mind for the third volume of his now globally famous trilogy. The title does seem appropriate for any part of a book a constant element of which is "the Enemy," as Tolkien so frequently describes the forces of Mordor and their Dark Lord. Tolkien makes an original contribution to thinking about war by melding three different strains of thinking about values and war. The idea of the laws of war, or just war theory, stretch back to the Middle Ages, and is itself a fusion of earlier ideas of worthy combat.[1] The formulation for just war by Thomas Aquinas (d. 1274) remains a benchmark, as does the work of the Spanish Dominican Francisco de Vitoria (d. 1546). Tolkien certainly follows their classical thinking (chapter 5), but he also shares the new theory of war as decision, propounded by Schmitt. As we saw in the last chapter, Tolkien complements Schmitt's thinking with an axiology derived from Scheler. All three of these strains are Catholic. This chapter tracks the similarity between Schmitt and Tolkien on the problem of the decision and adds extra

---

1 Ferguson, *An Essay on the History of Civil Society*, 191–93.

details on the place of Schelerian value theory in Tolkien. The next chapter moves from this new Catholic turn in thinking about decision to the traditional thinking on the subject found in Aquinas and de Vitoria. Stressed in this chapter is the role of disgust and dignity in framing war and, in the next, the role of vengeance. Specifically, in this chapter, I describe Tolkien's position that the friend-enemy distinction tracks the value order of dignity and disgust.

Hobbits, Becoming Political

Hobbits are no strangers to frivolity, and in both *The Hobbit* and *LotR* Hobbits are pushed into seriousness; pushed into understanding that their place in the world is not detached from the balance of power in the world. As their time with the Fellowship unfolds, the Hobbits are forced out of their ordinary way of life—think of the charming scene of confusion when Strider appears not to have heard of "second breakfast" (*FR** 17). The humor of *The Hobbit* is Bilbo's dismay when rudely plucked from the "easy street" of Bag End by the need of the Dwarves for a thief. Hobbits at the beginning and end of *LotR* are a startling contrast. Think only of Sam "in a phantom world of horror" confronting Shelob. Exhausted by the fight but holding the phial of Galadriel and speaking in tongues, "he staggered to his feet and was Samwise the Hobbit, Hamfast's son, again. 'Now come, you filth!' he cried. 'You've hurt my master, you brute, and you'll pay for it'" (*TT*, 712–13). The harm Sam does to Shelob transforms him in the eyes of the orcs. Sam smiles grimly, tells Tolkien, when he overhears Captain Shagrat: "'I'd say there's a large warrior loose, Elf most likely, with an elf-sword anyway'" (*TT*, 722). Sam's transformation captures wonderfully Schmitt's theory of depoliticization.

Political life, Schmitt argues, takes its origin from the friend-enemy distinction. A genuinely political people are ever sensitive to existential threat, to grasping that they might be conquered, and their way of life destroyed.[2] Ignorant of this possibility, a people are

---

2 In a slightly stronger formulation, "a certain opponent in mind" (Schmitt, *Writings on War*, 17).

not a genuine political collective. This state of depoliticization will end in the elimination of such a people or, at best, vassalage. Tying the definition of politics to existential risk in this way, Schmitt *both* builds war into the definition of politics and narrows the scope of war. An enemy is one who threatens a way of life. Threats, disputes, and events that do not rise to this level are not grounds for war. The upshot of Schmitt's definition is that there is more anxiety about war but less of it. This is one reason Schmitt rejects the just war tradition: in this tradition, humanitarian wars—de Vitoria seems to be the first to theorize this possibility—are licit, but, as wars where one group *chooses* to help *another* troubled group, they fail Schmitt's existential requirement.[3]

The spine of *LotR* is the dawning of politics in the Shire. At the start of the book, the Shire is the very definition of "an apolitical riskless sphere" (*CP*, 62). The book begins with mention that the office of the Thain had not been exercised for many years, the mayor a postmaster more than anything else, the yeomanry decrepit, and vague only is the memory of the Shire actually being under the King's law (*FR*, 9–10). A little ways into the book, Gandalf educates Frodo about the risk to the Shire. Frodo is frantic that Gollum told Sauron about Bilbo and the Shire. Censuring Gandalf, he shouts: "I can't understand you. Do you mean to say that you, and the Elves, have let him live on after all those horrible deeds? Now at any rate he is as bad as an Orc, and just an enemy. He deserves death" (*FR*, 58). If *LotR* begins with the dawning of threat in the Shire, it ends with Sam becoming mayor after he and the Hobbits who went to war return. Saruman mocks them as "hobbit-lordlings" (*RK*, 995) to play up the difference between them and the other Hobbits of the Shire. Saruman dispatched, regular folks cheekily name Merry and Pippin *Lordly* but thrill to see them riding "with their mail-shirts so bright and their shields so splendid." By contrast, on their return, Sam and Frodo "went back to ordinary attire" (*RK*, 1002).

---

3 For other reasons why Schmitt rejects the just war tradition, please see my "Catholic Ideas of War: Why Did Carl Schmitt Reject Natural Law?" *Touro Law Journal* 30, no. 1 (2014): 15–76.

After Gandalf relays the story of Gollum and the threat now facing the Shire, Frodo knows he must leave. As Frodo wends his way through the Shire and leaves the place that he loves, he also encounters those who have protected the Shire these many years. Unknown to the Hobbits, they have lived with ever-present threats, protected unawares by rangers of the Dúnedain (*FR*, 59). With the finding of the Ring, the threats are existential, but they were never negligible. Aragorn tells those gathered at the Council of Elrond that he is mocked as "Strider" by: ". . . one fat man who lives within a day's march of foes that would freeze his heart, or lay his little town in ruin, if he were not guarded ceaselessly. Yet we would not have it otherwise. If simple folk are free from care and fear, simple they will be, and we must be secret to keep them so" (*FR*, 242). The Dúnedain—"hunters ever of the servants of the Enemy"—speak of protecting the borders unknown to all (*FR*, 242) and Boromir stresses to what degree Gondor has protected borders unthanked (*FR*, 239). The depoliticization of the Hobbits and men of Bree is put into relief by its opposite: Elrond. This is brilliantly captured by Jackson when he and Gandalf strategize privately about the threat of the Ring, and Elrond recalls his place in the battle against Sauron thousands of years before (*FR** 24).

Throughout *LotR*, the Ring provokes existential wars. The film presents this idea when Saruman stirs the ancient people of the Westfold, the Dunlanders—who think of the Rohirrim as "the robbers of the North" (*TT*, 524)—to kill all of the people in the villages of Rohan and take their ancient lands back from horse riders (*TT** 6). At the Battle of Helm's Deep, Gamling the Old reminds Éomer of the Dunlanders' ancient presence in the Mark: "They hate us, and they are glad; for our doom seems certain to them" (*TT*, 524). Saruman's need for wood to fuel the furnaces of Isengard make him a mortal threat to the Ents: "Our trees and our lives are in great danger," (*TT*, 474) says Treebeard; "Curse him, root and branch" (*TT*, 462) as a "black traitor," crafting a "black evil" of treachery (*TT*, 474). The theme is also evident when Galadriel asks Frodo to look into a sort of prophetic water, the Mirror of Galadriel, and he sees there the destruction of the Shire (FR* 39): images of the Shire burning and Sam in slavery hover in the water. In the book, the "Scouring of the Shire" is the conclusion of RK and is the work of Saruman in the guise of Sharkey (RK, 994–95), hoping to eradicate the life of the Hobbits by the introduction of industrialism.

Ultimately, the revelation of the friend-enemy distinction to Frodo and company is met by the re-establishment of political forms in the Shire (RK, 998). This political transformation is complete when Sam is entrusted by King Elessar with the Star of the Dúnedain (RK, 1071), which represents the crown of the North Kingdom.

Ring and Manring,

Schmitt popularized the idea of "political theology." Exactly what he meant by it is a matter of some debate, but one thing he certainly meant was that any politics adequate to the friend-enemy distinction must concede the theological assumption of the evil of man (CP, 64–65). This explains why the Shire is depoliticized. Some of the classical moral theological sins, the seven deadly sins, are present in Hobbiton but, precisely, not deadly. The Sackville-Baggins lust after Bilbo's lovely home (FR, 67), and he and Frodo are determined the Sackville-Baggins won't drink the last of the Old Winyards, the wonderful wine laid down by Bilbo's father! Still, their envy of Bilbo's house and his standing in the community runs its course harmlessly enough.[4] Murder and serious crime have been unknown in the Shire many a long year, and no Hobbit has ever killed another Hobbit on purpose (RK, 983). Evil is absent from the Shire and so, therefore, is politics: this explains why the Hobbits are a frivolous, playful people.

Likewise Bombadil, one of Tolkien's first, and most beloved, creations. He is so philosophically interesting! Like the Hobbits, he is frivolous and playful and he, also, is outside the political. This point is tricky because he is aware of evil: he knows what the Ring is and to whom it belongs. He also has the power of exorcism (FR,

---

4 Tolkien's portrayal puts me in mind of Aquinas's wry indulgent attitude to human foolishness. For Thomas's account of much vanity as a venial rather than mortal sin, see On Evil, 346.

139). Furthermore, he and Goldberry live inside magical borders, his manring *is* the land, he being the "master of wood, land, and water" (*FR*, 122). Both on account of who Bombadil is, his metaphysical standing, we might say, and his magical borders, for him there is no existential threat. Repeatedly, we are told he has no fear and, magnificently, not even raindrops touch him (*FR*, 127). The Ring has no power over Bombadil, for Tom, as described by Elrond, is "oldest and fatherless," (*FR*, 258) one who existed "before the river and the trees; Tom remembers the first raindrop and the first acorn. He made paths before the Big People" (*FR*, 129). Indeed, in a remarkable episode with Bombadil, that speaks volumes about Frodo's rapid gain in seriousness, Frodo takes exception to Bombadil's playful attitude to the Ring. "He was perhaps a trifle annoyed with Tom for seeming to make so light of what even Gandalf thought so perilously important" (*FR*, 131).

At the Council of Elrond, Erestor asks whether the Ring could be kept safe within the bounds of Bombadil's land. Erestor thinks Bombadil has power over the Ring. Gandalf corrects him: the Ring has no power over Bombadil (*FR*, 259), and indeed, he laughs when holding it (*FR*, 130). "'Say rather that the Ring has no power over him. He is his own master. But he cannot alter the Ring itself, nor break its power over others. And now he is withdrawn into a little land, within bounds that he has set. . . .'" (*FR*, 259). Schmitt's *Political Theology* famously begins, "Sovereign is he who decides on the exception": Bombadil, an enigmatic metaphysical creation of Tolkien's, is existentially free, but he is no sovereign. The Ring poses the question of sovereignty: "One Ring to rule them all, One Ring to find them, One Ring to bring them all and in the darkness bind them, In the Land of Mordor where the Shadows lie." It does so, however, because Eru has made sovereignty and the manring cosmological. The gods about Eru "beheld a sight of surpassing beauty . . . the Secret Fire burnt at the heart of the world." As John Garth points out, in Tolkien's early lexicon of the sacred language of Qenya, this fire is a mystical name for the Holy Ghost.[5] The Ring, animated by the spirit of Sauron, aims to be sovereign over all others, to bind all inside one perverse manring: not protection, but consumption; not for no reason does Shelob, with distended belly, guard the way into Mordor. Sovereign is he or she—but always a person or small group of persons—who monitors the manring and decides when war is necessary for its protection (CP, 27). Such is not Bombadil. Gandalf replies to the Council:

> "But within those bounds nothing seems to dismay him," said Erestor. "Would he not take the Ring and keep it there, for ever harmless?"
>
> "No," said Gandalf, "not willingly. He might do so, if all the free folk of the world begged him, but he would not understand the need. And if he were given the Ring, he would soon forget it, or most likely throw it away. Such things have no hold on his mind. He would be a most unsafe guardian. . . ." (FR, 259)

Gollum is a reverse image of Bombadil. An exile, Gollum has no land. He is, in the magnificent expression of ancient Scottish law, a *landlouper*: one who as a matter of punishment has no fixed place on land; not for no reason Gollum lives *inside* a mountain. He is no part of a manring and thus cannot be an enemy in Schmitt's conception.[6] He is a murderer and hopes to kill Sam and Frodo, but he is no enemy of the Hobbit collective, because no actual threat to any collective. His animosity is all personal hatreds, not political (CP, 28). Gollum is not the enemy of Frodo, just someone who hates him. The object of Gollum's ire is not a collective proper, but a family, the "filthy Bagginses." Frodo offers mercy to Gollum (TT* 3), just as Aragorn does with Wormtongue (TT* 20), because they are merely personal adversaries, whereas both Frodo and Aragorn are intent on utterly destroying the political enemy, Sauron.

---

5 Garth, *Tolkien and the Great War*, 255.

6 "The real friend-enemy grouping is existentially so strong and decisive . . . that grouping is always political which orients itself toward this most extreme possibility. This grouping is therefore always the decisive human grouping, the political entity. If such an entity exists at all, it is always the decisive entity, and it is sovereign in the sense that the decision about the critical situation, even if it is the exception, must always necessarily reside there" (CP, 38).

Decision

Schmitt argues that the problem of the state is the problem of the decision. Any politics, whether of Left or Right, that would presume to remove rulers from making consequential decisions assumes a basic harmony in the world. Such a politics, turned into an "aesthetically balanced harmony," "always finds the way to urbanity" (*PR*, 55–56). It is Whiggery. An example is Fukuyama's elaboration of a liberal democratic bureaucracy which gives equal recognition to all. Industrial capitalism generates this possibility and the end of history—the end of politics—is what he famously states as "the victory of the VCR." Opposing this politics, Schmitt valorizes monarchist thinkers like Bodin, Hobbes, James I of England/VI of Scotland, and the later Catholic monarchists de Bonald, de Maistre, and Donoso Cortés. They are all decisionists. We can add Tolkien to the list.

These monarchists think civilization fragile. History, they contend, does not bend towards justice—there is no pre-established harmony[7]—and it can just as well devolve into primitivism (chapter 6). In Schmitt's telling, decisionists have all asked themselves "the question whether man is a dangerous being or not, a risky or a harmless creature" (*CP*, 58), and answered, risky.[8] The twin political ideas of sovereignty and decisionism (*PT*, 7)[9] address the "risky." Likewise, for Tolkien, history is a *near* stranger to "aesthetically balanced harmony"; it is a contending with risk: the Ring, after all, is "treacherous" (*FR*, 261) and, recall, war begins before Creation is complete. For this reason, when Aragorn, in the old Númenórean style prepares to depart from Arwen, she asks: "Would you then, lord, before your time leave people that live by your word?" (*RK*, 1037). The twin political ideas of the monarchists are present in *LotR*.

---

7 Schmitt, *Writings on War*, 106.

8 This is also the content of Mearsheimer's reply to Fukuyama's classic work of political philosophy (Mearsheimer, *The Tragedy of Great Power Politics*, 30–31).

9 For Schmitt's illustration of decision and the Monroe Doctrine, see Schmitt, *Writings on War*, 87.

There is a marvelous scene in Théoden's Hall. Despite the troubles of Middle-earth, Rohan has been inactive: Théoden's sovereignty suspended on account of his being possessed by Saruman. Gandalf, the newly minted White Wizard, casts out Saruman: for Saruman's sovereignty as the leader of the order of the Istari has itself been suspended; his office as White Wizard passing to Gandalf by the power of Illúvatar. The scene, rendered superbly in the film (*TT** 23), sees Théoden, Gandalf, and Aragorn in tense council. Théoden insists he will not provoke open war with Saruman, but Aragorn counters that open war is already upon Rohan. The king must act, he pleads, and call together the Horse Lords. In a delightful cinematic moment, Gandalf leans into Théoden to counsel Aragorn's suggestion, and puts his hand on the arm of the throne: Théoden glances at Gandalf's hand, cocks his eyebrow, stands in order to distance himself from Gandalf, and declares: "When last I looked, Théoden, not Aragorn, was king of Rohan" (*TT** 23). And yet, Théoden refuses to squarely face the risk to Rohan and makes a decision that infuriates Gandalf: to hole up in Helm's Deep. Here Schmitt's themes are fully on display.

Denethor, Steward of Gondor, provides a second example. Denethor is a figure of vanity. I discussed the central place of vanity in Tolkien's thinking in chapter 1 and do so, again, in chapter 5. In moral theology, the deep structure of vanity is the desire to be seen as no one's inferior. Lord Denethor is a man of ancient lineage (*RK*, 737), and insists upon it. He rages at the idea that a "Ranger of the North" (*RK*, 835), a mere descendant of Isildur, has come back to reclaim the crown. "I will not bow to such a one, last of a ragged house long bereft of lordship and dignity" (*RK*, 836). Pippin observes Denethor's continual efforts to best Gandalf (*RK*, 796): evident in his challenge that he is as wise as Gandalf, the "Grey Fool" (*RK*, 806), in matters of statesmanship. Denethor accuses Gandalf precisely in the matter of sovereignty: "Do I not know thee, Mithrandir? Thy hope is to rule in my stead, to stand behind every throne. . . ." (*RK*, 835). He insists on being a Steward and no "wizard's pupil" (*RK*, 836,

741). In moral theology, vanity is a deadly sin and so it proves in this case, too—a point I return to in later chapters.

Axiology, Framework of the Decision

Decisionism is not dictatorship; it is compatible with, and complements, rule of law. Tolkien sees this clearly: "A Númenórean King was monarch, with the power of unquestioned decision in debate; but he governed the realm with the frame of ancient law, of which he was administrator (and interpreter) but not the maker" (*Letters*, 324 #245). Let's tease out this point.

Typical of the laws of war are questions like: Is the pursuit of empire grounds for war? What things can be held as property? Is legal jurisdiction necessary for war? Can the innocent be plundered in a just war? Can enemy combatants be killed even after capture?

The answer to any of these questions relies on a much larger intellectual vision of morals and politics. If, when assessing the moral standing of an action, the *consequences* of an act—for example, whether the act enhances the security of a nation—are of paramount importance, then perhaps torture is moral. This style of moral assessment is consequentialism, and its most famous advocates are the English philosopher-reformers, Bentham and Mill. A consideration of consequences is seldom alien to any adjudication of a moral problem (ST I-II, q. 95, a. 3), but, amongst moralists, at stake is the primacy of this consideration. For example, if, in assessing an action, most prominent is whether the act fosters character, then torture is far less likely to be moral. Aristotle, for example, thinks character development primary. Intrinsicalists, like Aurel Kolnai, think there are some acts that are intrinsically evil: acts which may not be done no matter the circumstances or consequences. These acts may never be done even if, for example, doing the act would certainly enhance the security of a nation. Torture is wrong, what moralists call a *per se* evil. Broad ethical commitments like the three just stated determine which wars are justified and what sorts of things one can do to an enemy.

The traditional laws of war sit ill with the fashionable theory today that morality is subjective: justice in war is relative to the historical, geographical, and cultural development of various peoples (Hume and Schmitt). Does Tolkien's famous description of the trilogy as a mythology for England (S, xiii) strike a nationalist chord, making the book's ethical sensibility militantly English? What are we to make of Tolkien's own utterly self-conscious rejection of what appears most Western—that there are few echoes of Roman civilization in Middle-earth,[10] never mind the period of the European Enlightenment?

In the twentieth century, people started to write books about the West. There was Spengler's famous 1918 *The Decline of the West* and Kolnai's 1938 *War against the West*. Attacks on the World Trade Center in New York in 2001 prompted fresh inquiry into the West. Prominent was Benedict XVI, who wondered: Does moral consensus exist?

Benedict is not only asking whether people basically agree about morality, he sharpens his question. Western rationality, he contends, is an enormous boon to humanity, generating technologies of communication, engineering, and medicine; our lives are richer for all these things. But Western rationality has also eaten away at moral consensus, and in no small part because this rationality contemns the world's religions, religions that largely order the societies of the world to this day. Modernity, or better the Second Enlightenment (preface), Benedict says, "has shaken the moral consciousness in a way completely unknown to the cultures that existed previously."[11] This has happened because moral evidence is not like scientific

---

10 Ordway observes that Tolkien, like one of his favorite writers, William Morris, took a dim view of ancient Rome. She contends that Tolkien's controversial depiction of Orcs as "a grim dark band" is a reference to Romans, and so not racism. Orcs are slavers and imagined as Roman legions, she argues. Tolkien disliked imperialism: it was part of his anarchism that people should not go about bossing others around. She proposes that Tolkien may have equated ancient Romans with Italian fascists since his son fighting in Africa in WW2 mostly contended with Italian troops (Ordway, *Tolkien's Modern Reading*, 178–82). It is also worth noting that the popes of the twentieth century have cautioned against an overestimation of the Ancients (please see McAleer and Rosenthal, *The Wisdom of Our Ancestors*).

11 Ratzinger, *Christianity and the Crisis of Cultures*, 30.

evidence, and people are skeptical about what is not "demonstrated experimentally." In the absence of moral evidence, Western rationality has modeled ethical decision-making on the calculative method that has borne so much rich fruit in scientific and technological areas: nothing is right or wrong, but actions are assessed on a calculation of consequences. Consequentialism reigns, therefore.

In truth, Benedict argues, our contemporary ethics rests on a mutilated rationality: a rationality that has lost its basic orientation on account of severing the connection with "the basic memory of mankind."[12] What is this basic memory? There is a long tradition in Western philosophy that argues that ordinary moral consciousness, or what Latin jurists called the *ius gentium*, the law of peoples, is a trustworthy guide to right morals. The *ius gentium* is the idea that all people have a commonsense grasp of moral foundations and basically agree about the values essential for a vibrant community (ST I-II, q. 95, a. 4). Kolnai argues that this moral consensus stems from our shared emotional life, that our sentiments are the root of moral community. *LotR* offers evidence for this claim, especially respecting disgust, anger, and pity. In the next chapter, I discuss Tolkien's views on anger and pity, and how they relate to vengeance and punishment. Here, I want to demonstrate Tolkien's extensive reliance on disgust as a moral emotion and how it sets bearings for the conduct of war.

Disgust

Consensus—feeling-with—as the key to moral life has a venerable history. De Vitoria argued that cannibalism is condemned in the *ius gentium* because it provokes disgust. Along with thinkers like Scheler and Kolnai, de Vitoria argues that a moral community is built around a shared emotional life that tracks hierarchies of value; these hierarchies, though complex, are rigorously objective. Can we

---

12 Ratzinger, *Values in a Time of Upheaval*, 27.

share the confidence of these thinkers that these "great fundamental structures of values"[13] exist and can be known?

LotR shows that these "fundamental structures" of moral insight have global appeal. Worldwide earnings for the film trilogy stand at around US$3 billion. How can such a deeply moral and political film have global success unless its moral and political principles are readily comprehensible and *appealing*? What are those principles?

Consider one of the earliest combat film scenes. Aragorn, king-in-waiting, fights a captain of the Uruk-hai after the Uruk-hai captured Merry and Pippin and mortally wounded Boromir. The captain, a real bruiser, after Aragorn has left his knife in the Uruk-hai's thigh, pulls out the blade and licks his own blood off the blade with real relish. Aragorn, well aware now that defeat also means his body will be outraged, finally manages to victoriously conclude the combat (FR* 45). As Aragorn dispatches the cannibal the music soars and decency, for a moment, at least, wins out.

A thought-experiment: imagine a film audience in Malaysia, a predominantly Muslim country. The scene described ending, can you imagine someone in the Malaysian audience turning to his neighbor and saying: "Excuse me, I don't understand. I really wanted the Uruk-hai to win that fight. I thought he was the hero. I thought the cannibal seemed so trustworthy, loyal, and kind-hearted." I suggest that such a reaction is inconceivable. Ordinary moral consciousness the world over easily "reads" the moral structure of the scene. The scene expresses a moral consensus.

Let me illustrate this point more fully. In the film version of *The Two Towers* there is a brilliantly crafted exorcism scene. The basic event is in the book (*TT*, 503–5) but Jackson adds a lot of dramatic heft. Gandalf confronts Wormtongue, the treacherous advisor to the king of the Rohirrim, Théoden, whom we see seated on a throne, a man broken and befuddled. Casting Wormtongue aside in a sort of "get behind me, Satan" moment, Gandalf advances to the throne.

---

13 Ratzinger, *Values in a Time of Upheaval*, 41.

King Théoden is possessed by the rogue White Wizard: exorcism here will be no mean achievement, for Théoden is held in the grip of Saruman, the cunning but proud leader of the Istari, the order of wizards or angels sent by Illúvatar to help the good of Middle-earth (*S*, 299). Revealing himself to Saruman and the assembled court of Théoden as the true White Wizard, Gandalf casts Saruman out of Théoden King, as Tolkien likes to style him. The scene ends wonderfully with the corruption of possession finally falling off Théoden, and he returns to kingly stature (*TT*** 20). The moral structure of this scene is a near-perfect match to a description of values that Kolnai offers as proof of moral consensus:

> ... highly general dimensions of right-doing and wrong-doing, which I would quote here in the language of values rather than of obligations: that benevolence is good and malice, bad; that veracity is right and mendacity, wrong; and similarly with the contrast-pairs of courage and cowardice, self-control and intemperance, respect for others and arrogant self-assertion, yet on the other hand self-respect and servile self-surrender, adulation or pliancy, dignity and meretricious cynicism, magnanimity and cruelty, chastity and lust, self-control and intemperance, honesty and dishonesty, fidelity and treachery, loyalty and treason.... what we are facing here is a consensual perspective of feelings, insights, views and codifications (*EVR*, 154).

Wormtongue exudes dishonesty, treachery, and mendacity. He lusts after Théoden's niece Éowyn and, at every turn, exhibits a cynical pliancy to maintain his position as counsellor. He has given himself in servile self-surrender to Saruman, debasing himself utterly.

Tolkien's description of Wormtongue at the end of the trilogy reinforces the role of moral consensus. In an episode of the Scouring of the Shire, Wormtongue's debasement through Saruman has intensified. Tolkien describes him: "'Worm! Worm!' Saruman called; and out of a nearby hut came Wormtongue, crawling, almost like a dog. 'To the road again, Worm!' said Saruman. 'These fine fellows and lordlings are turning us adrift again. Come along!'"(*RK*, 995).

Contrasting with Wormtongue is Gandalf, a rock of good, self-mastery, magnanimity, and dignity. His relationship to these values is confirmed when, at the end of the exorcism scene, he restores them to Théoden, who had lost them through Wormtongue's treachery. Tolkien expresses this idea conceptually, too: "In Faerie one can indeed conceive of an ogre who possesses a castle hideous as a nightmare (for the evil of the ogre wills it so), but one cannot conceive of a house built with a good purpose—an inn, a hostel for travellers, the hall of a virtuous and noble king—that is yet sickeningly ugly."[14]

Enough has been said to show that values structure these scenes and make them readily comprehensible to us and on an international scale. A magnificent image of value perception, and from an unlikely source, is offered in *The Two Towers*. Gollum, variously known as Stinker (according to Sam) or "the poor treacherous creature" (according to Frodo), is leading Frodo to Shelob's Lair to be eaten. Climbing Cirith Ungol in an attempt to pass secretly into Mordor, the Hobbits rest and fall asleep.

> Peace was in both their faces. Gollum looked at them. A strange expression passed over his lean hungry face. The gleam faded from his eyes, and they went dim and grey, old and tired. A spasm of pain seemed to twist him, and he turned away, peering back up towards the pass, shaking his head, as if engaged in some interior debate. Then he came back, and slowly putting out a trembling hand, very cautiously he touched Frodo's knee—but almost the touch was a caress. (*TT*, 699)

Of course, soon he guides them to the lair. Fully on display here is Scheler's idea of the *Ordo Amoris*, acts deferring to "the mysterious laws of the interresonance of love and hate." Gollum hears the appeal of the Music of the Ainur, but fails, and Sam bears some moral responsibility, too (chapter 6). The value order is the archetype for the struggle at the center of *LotR*, wherein Sauron, as a spirit of malice, contends for control of Middle-earth against the Fellowship of the Ring. Sauron is a corrupted will cleaving to the disvalues of

---

14 https://coolcalvary.files.wordpress.com/2018/10/on-fairy-stories1.pdf, 32.

hate, high-mindedness,[15] sacrilege, and disgusting things. All the servants of Morgoth, Sauron included, pursue the other races "with hatred" (S, 259), whilst the Fellowship expresses a manifold of loves, loyal to the values of simplicity, home, craft, eccentricity, patience, liberty, gallantry, and sacrificial love.

It is sometimes thought that Tolkien is heavy-handed with his portrait of Sauron and the forces of Mordor; that he paints them too darkly, all nuance of moral struggle and ambiguity missing, and some have even gone so far as to suppose racism. This is to fail to see something crucial, a profound structural moral principle at work in *LotR*. Tolkien, again and again, relies on the idea of disgust when trying to capture the moral tone of Mordor.

In 1929, Kolnai wrote a seminal work on disgust in which he argued that disgust is not merely a "yuck" reaction, but a source of basic knowledge about the world and, especially, about moral order. I think Tolkien agrees. Kolnai's analysis of disgust influenced Salvador Dali, Georges Bataille, and Jean Paul Sartre, to name some. Kolnai did not agree that everything physically disgusting is morally disgusting, but he did insist that sometimes this is true, and when true, genuine moral disvalues in the world are disclosed to us. That is, disgust is an objective insight into values, not merely a document of some subjective, personal, or cultural likes and dislikes. Disgust expresses, therefore, one of the deep layers of moral consensus. It echoes "the Invisible Order" (Scheler).

Kolnai observes that disgust is only ever a reaction to biological material. A stone cannot be disgusting unless modeled in some organic fashion. When rummaging the funeral pyre of the Orcs and Uruk-hai slain by the Horse-lords of Rohan, Gimli finds a snapped knife: "'It was an Orc-weapon,' he said, holding it gingerly, and looking with disgust at the carved handle; it had been shaped like a hideous head with squinting eyes and leering mouth" (*TT*, 478). The disgust reaction is possible because here an inorganic material

---

15 See Kolnai's essay on high-mindedness in the volume of his essays, *Politics, Values, and National Socialism*.

144

is shaped as something organic. The disgusting is not an experience primarily of death, but it is linked. Putrefaction provokes a strong disgust reaction, for disgust centers on "life in the wrong place." It is exaggerated living growth, for example, a tumor protruding from the body—think here of the astonishing Orc general we see at the Siege of Gondor (*RK** 36), slain by Aragorn (*RK** 53)—the buzzing of a swarm of flies, and rapidly squirming maggots in putrefying flesh. Consider poor Gollum:

> Gollum blinked, hooding the malice of his eyes with their heavy pale lids. A very miserable creature he looked, dripping and dank, smelling of fish (he still clutched one in his hand); his sparse locks were hanging like rank weed over his bony brows, his nose was sniveling. (*TT*, 674)

The disgusting, says Kolnai, in some way reaches out to us, having something like a proboscis that searches us out and seeks to attach itself. Consider how Frodo experiences Mordor:

> Nothing lived, not even the leprous growths that feed on rottenness. The gasping pools were choked with ash and crawling muds, sickly white and grey, as if the mountains had vomited the filth of their entrails upon the lands about ... a land defiled, diseased beyond all healing—unless the Great Sea should enter in and wash it with oblivion. (*TT*, 617)

Here, already, the land reflects that the Ring would reach out to bind and blight. A bit the same: Rivendell quakes and shudders in horror when Gandalf uses the language of Mordor at the Council of Elrond (*FR** 27).

We keep a distance from the disgusting, trying to rid ourselves of its sticky, clinging intimacy. Think of the way we remove a dead animal, perhaps prodding it first to make sure it is dead, then using a shovel to quickly get it into a bag, all the time wearing gloves. Think of the odd comic habit of people dealing with mice in the home when they put their trousers into their socks lest the mice run up their legs. Revealing in this regard is a scene with Gandalf. Guessing the true identity of Bilbo's ring, Gandalf, in Bilbo's home, keeps it at a distance. Having Frodo set it in an envelope (*FR** 7), Gandalf seeks to avoid defilement, as he tries to keep the disgusting things that issue from Sauron at a distance from himself and Frodo.

This need to keep the disgusting at a distance explains the vomit reaction to what disgusts. It is this phenomenon of *closing in on the self* that disgust exudes that explains the look on Aragorn's face when he sees the captain of the Uruk-hai pull the blade from his leg and lick off his own blood. "I will lick you next," communicates the disgusting servant of Saruman's lust for domination. Kolnai speaks of disgust, as it were, grinning and smirking, leering at us, seeking intimacy. Frodo, close to collapse in the valley of Minas Morgul, gains a second wind when he imagines Gondor broken. Looking at the once great city of Minas Ithil, now only populated by the ghosts of men—"a shapeless fear lived within the ruined walls" (*TT*, 677)—Frodo, conversing with Faramir, ponders:

> Would you have me come to Gondor with this Thing, the Thing that drove your brother mad with desire? What spell would it work in Minas Tirith? Shall there be two cities of Minas Morgul, grinning at each other across a dead land filled with rottenness?" (*TT*, 677)

Ultimately, the problem of disgust raises the question of personalism. A basic interest of twentieth-century Catholic thought, personalism is the philosophical effort to capture the ontological and psychological depth of the human person. Kolnai's *On Disgust* is a classic example of this effort.[16] Persons are centers of eccentricity, expressive of a unique, privileged perspective, including a certain liberty or aloofness from the rest of the world. The disgusting—marked by dissolution, swarm, and liquefaction—is hostile to the restraint and distinctness that marks personhood. The Orcs are cannibals: Sam wonders, "'Orcs drink, don't they?' 'Yes, they drink,' said Frodo. 'But do not let us speak of that. Such drink is not for us'" (*TT*, 696).

---

16 Aurel Kolnai, *On Disgust* (Chicago: Open Court, 2004), 73–74.

Kolnai writes:

> ... civilization signifies and demands—mastery over nature and self-mastery of mankind, noble distance, objectivity, nobility, obligingness, tolerance, uprightness, readiness to come to an understanding and to community with what is alien, refusal to give the precedence to the drives for validation and struggle, acceptance of the multiplicity of values and needs. (*PVNS*, 50–51)

In light of Kolnai's idea of "noble distance"—it tracks Przywara's "posture of distance"—it is no surprise that Tolkien depicts the agents of Sauron and Saruman, agents of totalitarian ambition, as disgusting, seeking to cancel personhood and liberty: "the maggot-folk of Mordor" (*TT*, 687). In Tolkien's mind, the friend-enemy distinction—which decisionism monitors—tracks the value order of dignity and disgust.

Dignity, Considered Phenomenoligally

In a fantastic image of a searchlight atop a bastion of Sauron's empire, Tolkien links the inspecting gaze of the regime and disgust. Frodo is cowering from a light:

> Not the imprisoned moonlight welling through the marble walls of Minas Ithil long ago, Tower of the Moon, fair and radiant in the hollows of the hills. Paler indeed than the moon ailing in some slow eclipse was the light of it now, wavering and blowing like a noisome exhalation of decay, a corpse-light, a light that illuminated nothing. In the walls and tower windows showed, like countless black holes looking inward into emptiness; but the topmost course of the tower revolved slowly, first one way and then another, a huge ghostly head leering into the night. (*TT*, 688)

The "corpse-light" "leering into the night" is a brilliant image of the Ring's effort to defeat Distributism, and its correlate, personalism. The disgust hinges on the effort to cancel the borders of the manring,

and such encroachments on sacred space provoke war. In consequence, disgust also encroaches on personal dignity.

Tolkien's "corpse-light" "leering into the night" describes the
phenomenology of disgust; the very language matches Kolnai as he
speaks of the disgusting as that which leers and smirks at you, being
an uninvited intimacy, reaching across, cloying to you. Phenomenology shows that the disgusting intrudes on our persons. Kolnai:

> Every disgusting reaction contains an element of plain resis-
> tance, and this is first of all the vehement *rejection of pre-
> sumption* . . . [and] the object itself requires, in order to be
> disgusting, that a proximizing tendency be represented in its
> so-being, a moment of nearness which also carries with it a
> tendency to encroach within the orbit of experience of the
> perceiving (knowing) subject.[17]

Disgust is evidence that persons are aloof from the world, they
have a reserve, a height, an unbendedness or intangibility. In Kant's
language, an autonomy. This is why unwanted touching is paradig-
matic of consent violations on college campuses, at work, and in the
doctor's office. The distance constitutive of personhood is what is
meant by human dignity.

In response to someone's dignity, I, as it were, bow before them,
I acknowledge their sovereignty. Acknowledging their sovereignty
is the same as my affirming the leading attribute of our humanity, a
discerning consciousness. Bowing, a person is set at a height, and it
is only at a height that:

> I am able to make comparisons, estimate distances, and pene-
> trate spatial structures as I could not otherwise do. I no longer
> merely represent an *automatic* focus of vison but embody a
> privileged and nameable focus of visual perception and thus,
> in a sense, an enhanced *centrality of consciousness*. In some
> respect and some measure, I have also gained a certain *distance*
> from the earth and a relative *independence* from it.[18]

17 *On Disgust*, 65.

18 Aurel Kolnai, "The Concept of Hierarchy," in Aurel Kolnai, *Ethics, Value, & Reality* (New Brunswick, NJ: Transaction, 2008), 176.

Distance is basic to discerning consciousness. It is our worth and our nature. This is what is meant by human dignity. Kolnai:

> . . . the qualities of distinctness, delimitation, and distance; of something that conveys the idea of being intangible, invulnerable, inaccessible to destructive or corruptive or subversive interference. Dignity is thus comparable, metaphorically, to something like "tempered steel."[19]

Such formulations are not new or peculiar to Catholicism. When David Hume speaks of modesty, he characterizes it as "the dread of intrusion."[20] Adam Smith speaks the same way.[21] Dignity is a taboo. You cannot touch the taboo and you cannot touch persons, uninvited, or even inadvertently. Of the idea of the person, Kolnai: "There forms around it the atmosphere of a qualitative, mysterious and transcendent dignity."[22] A nice example of taboo as a symbol of the dignity of a person is Aragorn's warning outside the doors of Théoden's Hall.

> Slowly Aragorn unbuckled his belt and himself set his sword upright against the wall. "Here I set it," he said; "but I command you not to touch it, nor permit any other to lay hand on it. In this elvish sheath dwells the Blade that was Broken and has been made again. Telchar first wrought it in the deeps of time. Death shall come to any man that draws Elendil's sword save Elendil's heir." The guard stepped back and looked with amazement on Aragorn. (*TT*, 500)

---

19 Aurel Kolnai, "Dignity," in *Politics, Values, & National Socialism* (New Brunswick, NJ: Transaction, 2013), 230.

20 David Hume, *An Inquiry concerning the Principles of Morals* (Oxford: Oxford University Press, 2004), 140–41.

21 "On the other hand, what noble propriety and grace do we feel in the conduct of those who, in their own case, exert that recollection and self-command which constitute the dignity of every passion, and which bring it down to what others can enter into! We are disgusted with that clamorous grief, which, without any delicacy, calls upon our compassion with sighs and tears and importunate lamentations. But we reverence that reserved, that silent and majestic sorrow, which discovers itself only in the swelling of the eyes, in the quivering of the lips and cheeks, and in the distant, but affecting, coldness of the whole behaviour" (Smith, *The Theory of Moral Sentiments*, I.i.5.3, 24).

22 Aurel Kolnai, "Human Dignity Today," in *Politics, Values, & National Socialism*, 219.

This phenomenon repeats in Gimli's reaction to the change in Aragorn when confronted by Éomer of the Horse-lords:

> Aragorn threw back his cloak. The elven-sheath glittered as he grasped it, and the bright blade of Andúril shone like a sudden flame as he swept it out. "Elendil!" he cried. "I am Aragorn, son of Arathorn...." Gimli and Legolas looked at their companion in amazement, for they had not seen him in this mood before. He seemed to have grown in stature while Éomer had shrunk; and in his living face they caught a brief vision of the power and majesty of the kings of stone.... Éomer stepped back and a look of awe was in his face. (*TT*, 423)

A final example is Gandalf growing enormous in reaction to Bilbo's impertinence:

> Gandalf's eyes flashed. "It will be my turn to get angry soon," he said. "If you say that again, I shall. Then you will see Gandalf the Grey uncloaked." He took a step towards the hobbit, and he seemed to grow tall and menacing; his shadow filled the little room. Bilbo backed away to the wall.... (*FR*, 33)

To summarize: from phenomenology, we learn that disgust is the most primordial evaluative structure of the psyche. It is aversive to disvalue, but, positively, it shows that being human includes an inherent property of desiring not to be wantonly meddled with; this is the value structure original to human nature that the idea of human dignity expresses. The idea is confirmed by Przywara's analogical metaphysics, expressed in his idea of the "posture of distance."

Dignity, Considered Metaphyically

Przywara argues that the core of Thomism is the idea of secondary cause. There is an analogy of being throughout the cosmos: substances are like God in being true causes, but unlike, because not utterly self-animating. Persons are a special type of secondary cause, an extravagant type, having lordship over self. This explains persons' eccentricities, a phenomenon Tolkien thoroughly enjoyed. Sam's dad, the Gaffer, is a disapproving observer of the foibles of others; Tolkien relished them. He relays one astonishing story of a contemporary, a Mr. Shorthouse from Birmingham: "He seemed to fancy himself as a reincarnation of some renaissance Italian, and dressed the part" (*Letters*, 348 # 257). Human dignity picks out this inherent property of self-shaping. This is why the Thomistic jurist Francisco de Vitoria argued against those denying the humanity of the peoples of the New World, that the indigenous were truly human: the complexity of their cities was evidence of rational mastery of self. Having dignity, the inhabitants were not to be meddled with, de Vitoria insisted. This idea is the core of Gandalf's insight into Sauron's malice (*FR*, 48).

Linking the idea of human dignity to the concept of secondary cause has a potent implication. Consider this military ethics example from de Vitoria, designed to show that our moral significance is not derived exclusively from our being a part of a common good. A city is under siege and the besiegers offer a deal. Rather than raze the city to the ground, the attackers will leave the city alone if the city picks one innocent resident and kills him (her, or child). The common good appears to require the city indeed pick someone and dispatch that innocent. De Vitoria argues this would be a tyrannical act, for no person is simply a part of a whole. De Vitoria rejects a common political analogy: a person is to the common good, as an arm is to the body. Instead, he reasons: "For a [bodily] member cannot suffer injury, since it does not have its own proper good to which it has a right. But a man can suffer an injury, since a man has a proper good to which he has a right. . . . But an innocent person is his very own good and alone he suffers, and therefore it is not lawful to kill him." Standing in a line of Catholic reasoning that includes Scotus and Molina, de Vitoria argues that subsidiarity is the recognition that "an innocent person is his very own good." The person is the lowest level of self-ordering good, to be amplified by subsidiarity, when needed.[23]

---

23 Francisco de Vitoria, *On Homicide* (Milwaukee, WI: Marquette University Press, 1997), 185–87.

That persons are secondary causes of an extravagant kind, having the dignity, and burden, to shape themselves is vividly on display in the false creation of the Dwarves by Aulë.

Eru speaks to him gently about this false creation and Aulë laments that "in my impatience I have fallen into folly." One of the aratar, Aulë could "create" Dwarves, but only as automata. God probes: "Why dost thou attempt a thing which thou knowest is beyond thy power and thy authority?" Aulë knows he cannot make dignified persons but "he was unwilling to await the fulfilment of the designs of Ilúvatar." God quizzes him: "the creatures of thy hand and mind can live only by that being, moving when thou thinkest to move them, and if thy thought be elsewhere, standing idle. Is that thy desire?" Critically, Aulë confesses: "I did not desire such lordship. I desired things other than I am, to love and to teach them." Critical, because as we are about to see in chapter 5, that possession is the mark of Melkor, he does not desire things "other than I am." Possession runs counter to subsidiarity, and Eru gives Aulë a dramatic lesson on this point. In a fit of remorse, Aulë picks up his hammer to smash his Dwarves, and they flinch. Eru asks: "Dost thou not see that these things have now a life of their own, and speak with their own voices? Else they would not have flinched from they blow, nor from any command of thy will." The capacity of the Dwarves to now operate free of the control of the will of their creator is the gift of dignity from Eru, a principle of their creation. Just as the guards at Théoden's Hall step away from Aragorn and his sword, and just as Bilbo steps away from Gandalf, his dignity fully revealed, so the Dwarves, their dignity born, flinch before Aulë. In all these cases, we have a "posture of distance" (Przywara), the experience of "nobility of distance" (Kolnai).

Another lesson is still to be taught. Taking us back to chapter 1, Eru had compassion for Aulë "because of his humility," but still he demands that the Dwarves be put to sleep until the Elves—"the children of my adoption and the children of my choice"—should stir and move about Arda. This order of appearance conforms to Eru's design but also blocks that Aulë's "impatience should be rewarded"

(S, 43–44). Wrongdoing demands punishment. We now move from the new turn in Catholic thinking about war to the traditional found in Aquinas and de Vitoria, rooted in the theme of avenging wrongs. In this chapter, we saw Tolkien's position that the friend-enemy distinction tracks the value order of dignity and disgust. It is time to consider how war, in Tolkien, tracks the value of vengeance and disvalue of possession.

5

Possession and Ringwraiths

To date, the argument that Tolkien is a philosopher of war comprises: 1) beauty as an antidote to apocalypticism; 2) his meditation on the strategic place of flora in war; 3) the role of land and husbandry in orienting the refinement of civilization worth fighting for; and 4) that the beautiful sets forth distance, a phenomenon critical to both decision and dignity. The Ring cancels dignity. Explaining its effect on Frodo, Tolkien: "the breaking of his mind and will under demonic pressure" (*Letters*, 327 #246). The biographies of Tolkien document how real to his mind was the conflict between good and evil, and recount his vivid sense that evil was the work of the Devil.[1] Morgoth, "the Dark Enemy of the World" (*S*, 31), is Tolkien's Satan (*Letters*, 202 #156)—described as "the Diabolus" (*Letters*, 191 #153)—and Lord Sauron is a demon in Morgoth's service (*S*, 17, 27, 49–50).

This fifth chapter explores how war and theology combine in complex and stunning ways in Tolkien. Specifically, Tolkien's treatment of war juggles Christian virtues like humility and mercy, as

---

1 White, *J. R. R. Tolkien*, 143, and George Sayer, "Recollections of J. R. R. Tolkien," in *Tolkien: A Celebration*, ed. Joseph Pearce (San Francisco: Ignatius, 2001), 8.

well as just war theory. Tolkien read Aquinas.[2] For a Catholic intellectual as steeped in war, personally and imaginatively, as Tolkien, it is unsurprising that just war theory features in the legendarium. However, Aquinas's theory of homicide invokes vengeance and punishment. Mercy and vengeance hardly seem reconcilable. We already have a clue as to how they fit together: dignity. One thing I want to show in this chapter is how the Ring neatly conveys Aquinas's theory of diabolical possession. Contradicting dignity, the Ring's taking possession of others warrants punishment by war.

Let us watch Tolkien juggle.

Humility

Aulë's humility saves the god from the wrath of Eru. Though of great power, Aulë understood modesty, that God's goodness will not permit the creation of automata "persons." In his "bones," he understood that possession is incompatible with dignity. Tolkien's aesthetics is an exposition of modesty. As we saw from the battle with the Balrog, Gandalf is an illustration, and it is striking to see him counsel humility when laying out the grand strategy of the Allies.

Gandalf is its architect, and he borrows it from St. Paul: *not many of you were wise according to worldly standards . . . but God chose what is foolish in the world to shame the wise, God chose what is weak in the world to shame the strong* (1 Cor. 1:26–27). This passage is a commonplace in medieval philosophical texts, especially amongst Franciscans. They were more skeptical than other religious orders about the worth of Greek science and philosophy for understanding the real, inner significance of the world.[3] This text from Paul is one of the great touchstones for that skepticism (e.g., St. Bonaventure). Gandalf, at least before his transformation into the pope-like White Wizard, is Franciscan-like.

---

2 For Tolkien's reliance on Aquinas's hylomorphism, see J. R. R. Tolkien, *The Nature of Middle-earth*, 171–72.

3 Tolkien was sympathetic to mystical "reads" of reality (Garth, *Tolkien and the Great War*, 251).

At different times, Gandalf explains the basic strategy of the war and sometimes must defend it. To Gandalf's mind *the foolishness of God is wiser than men* (1 Cor. 1:25), and the use of Frodo—and Gollum, even—is a case of *God chose what is low and despised in the world, even things that are not, to bring to nothing things that are, so that no human being might boast in the presence of God* (1 Cor. 1:28–29). Citing Isaiah, Paul speaks of the intention of God: *I will destroy the wisdom of the wise* (1 Cor. 1:19). At the Council of Elrond, the fundamental strategy unfolds. I must quote at length:

> "Thus we return once more to the destroying of the Ring," said Erestor, "and yet we come no nearer. What strength have we for the finding of the Fire in which it was made? That is the path of despair. Of folly I would say, if the long wisdom of Elrond did not forbid me."
>
> "Despair, or folly?" said Gandalf. "It is not despair, for despair is only for those who see the end beyond all doubt. We do not. It is wisdom to recognize necessity, when all other courses have been weighed, though as folly it may appear to those who cling to false hope. Well, let folly be our cloak, a veil before the eyes of the Enemy! For he is very wise, and weighs all things to a nicety in the scales of his malice. But the only measure that he knows is desire, desire for power; and so he judges all hearts. Into his heart the thought will not enter that any will refuse it, that having the Ring we may seek to destroy it. If we seek this, we shall put him out of reckoning."
>
> "At least for a while," said Elrond, "The road must be trod, but it will be very hard. And neither strength nor wisdom will carry us far upon it. This quest may be attempted by the weak with as much hope as the strong. Yet such is oft the course of deeds that move the wheels of the world: small hands do them because they must, while the eyes of the great are elsewhere." (*FR*, 262)

Boromir (*FR*, 390) and Denethor both accuse Gandalf of foolishness. Sending Frodo with the Ring into the lands of the enemy strikes these noble and powerful men as foolishness. Approaching the Steward of Gondor, Gandalf warns Pippin not to confuse his like with Théoden, King of Rohan:

Be careful of your words, Master Peregrin! This is no time for hobbit pertness. Théoden is a kindly old man. Denethor is of another sort, proud and subtle, a man of far greater lineage and power, though he is not called a king . Do not tell him more than you need, and leave quiet the matter of Frodo's errand. (*RK*, 737)

Finally debating strategy with Denethor, the Pauline theme dominates:

"You are wise, maybe, Mithrandir, yet with all your subtleties you have not all wisdom. Counsels may be found that are neither the webs of wizards nor the haste of fools. I have in this matter more lore and wisdom then you deem."

"What then is your wisdom?" said Gandalf.

"Enough to perceive that there are two follies to avoid. To use this thing is perilous. At this hour, to send it in the hands of a witless halfling in to the land of the Enemy himself, as you have done, and this son of mine, is madness."

"And the Lord Denethor what would he have done?"

"Neither. But most surely not for any argument would he have set this thing at a hazard beyond all but a fool's hope, risking our utter ruin, if the Enemy should recover what he lost. Nay, it should have been kept, hidden, hidden dark and deep." (*RK*, 795)

The ideal of humility is one of the great Christian legacies to world culture. Another is rule of law. Aquinas's just war theory is a part of his jurisprudence.

Law

In his *Summa theologica* II-II, Question 64, Aquinas established the basic framework for Catholic thinking about homicide: addressing the problems of types of killings, who can licitly kill, for what reasons, and on what authority. Indeed, he bequeathed the basic laws of homicide to the West, since a quick look at Blackstone's famous commentary on English Common Law shows the framework largely unchanged after five hundred years.[4]

Aquinas's solution to the moral questions raised by killing is rooted in natural law, an innovation of medieval scholasticism. His solution views persons as both social and autonomous. For this reason, there are public and private goods that need tending, and given the reality of sin, sometimes protecting. Aquinas thus distinguishes public authority from private authority, and argues that the care of the common good requires public authority to have a privileged use of force. In Aquinas's time, there were many social bodies that counted as public authorities—kings and queens, dukes and barons, abbots and town councils, to name some.[5] This changed in the drive of kings and queens to become absolute monarchs in the sixteenth and seventeenth centuries. Today is, oftentimes, no different: the state has authority to kill; private citizens do not. For example, the state has the authority to conduct war and police operations as part of its duty of care for the common good.

Aquinas argues that the norm of security is that force may repel force. The state's use of lethal force always assumes, therefore, a prior injustice, and, as a response to that injustice, it must be proportionate to the prior harm. For this reason, Aquinas also believed that the public authority to kill extended to capital punishment. This authority is not unlimited, however. Lethal authority only extends to those guilty under the laws of war or those found guilty by a court of law. Gandalf bitterly rebukes Denethor as he prepares a pyre for himself and Faramir:

> "Authority is not given to you, Steward of Gondor, to order the hour of your death," answered Gandalf. "And only the heathen kings, under the domination of the Dark Power, did thus, slaying themselves in pride and despair, murdering their kin to ease their own death." (RK, 835)

---

4 For a fuller discussion, please see my *To Kill Another: Homicide and Natural Law* (London: Routledge, 2012).

5 On the scope of "the right of jurisdiction" in the feudal model, including war and capital punishment, see Adam Smith, *Lectures on Jurisprudence*, 127–32.

Sauron is a tyrant because he is a renegade from the authority of Ilúvatar (S, 27), and so kills on private authority. Gollum also kills on private authority, killing Déagol, and is punished with exile by the Riverfolk (FR, 52). He nurses resentment, hoping to vengefully kill "Bagginses" for taking his precious.

> Now we can eat fish in peace. No, not in peace, precious. For Precious is lost; yes, lost. Dirty hobbits, nasty hobbits. Gone and left us, *Gollum*; and Precious is gone. Only poor Sméagol all alone. No Precious. Nasty Men, they'll take it, steal my Precious. Thieves. We hates them. Fissh, nice fissh. Makes us strong. Makes eyes bright, fingers tight, yes. Throttle them, precious. Throttle them all, yes, if we gets chances. (*TT*, 671)

Nonetheless, it is noticeable to what degree others in *LotR* kill on public authority. Gandalf marshals forces for war because he is the gods' representative. The Ents also go into "conclave" (*TT*, 470) to decide what action is to be taken against Saruman; that decision is "the last march of the Ents" (*TT*, 475). A fabulous part in the books runs:

> "You have looked in that accursed stone of wizardry!" exclaimed Gimli with fear and astonishment in his face. "Did you say aught to—him? Even Gandalf feared that encounter."
>
> "You forget to whom you speak," said Aragorn sternly, and his eyes glinted. "What do you fear I should say to him? Did I not openly proclaim my title before the doors of Edoras? Nay, Gimli," he said in a softer voice, and the grimness left his face, and he looked like one who has laboured in sleepless pain for many nights. "Nay, my friends, I am the lawful master of the Stone. . . ." (*RK*, 763)

The Fellowship gathers under Lord Elrond's stewardship and is comprised of representatives of the great Lords of Middle-earth, who, as is clear in the books, come to the meeting at Rivendell with diplomatic corps. In *The Fellowship of the Ring*, Legolas is present, but mostly it is the Elf diplomat Erestor who speaks. We meet some of the great Lords themselves later. The princes of the West gather after the Siege of Gondor to deliberate the final confrontation with Sauron. Prince Imrahil is named as amongst the great princes, but to emphasize the elevation of the persons at council, Legolas and Gimli are not invited (*RK*, 860).

Subsequent to Aquinas, in the 1530s, de Vitoria made important contributions to the natural law tradition on questions of homicide. For example, he addressed a problem that seems to challenge the coherence of Aquinas's basic division between killing on public and private authority: Can a private citizen kill a tyrant? To maintain Aquinas's distinction, de Vitoria argued that if the tyrant is a legitimate sovereign, then the answer is "no." Matters are different, however, if the tyrant is a usurper: then the answer is "yes." Interestingly, the individual who kills the tyrant does not act on private authority, however, but on public; for in the case of usurpation, open war exists between the usurper and the republic. By de Vitoria's lights, therefore, any person of the free peoples of the West could kill Sauron or Saruman, as both are usurpers. Following de Vitoria, then, we should think of the Council of Elrond as a strategy meeting, not some formalization of permission for an attack on Sauron. Of course, for Tolkien, the Council is also about the return to legitimacy, the return of the King of Gondor. It heralds order and establishment (chapter 6).

Aquinas's rules of war, briefly stated: only a properly constituted public authority can wage war, with proper cause, that is, to "avenge wrongs," and with right intention, to "advance the good." In short, war, rightly ordered, serves "to deliver the needy from the hands of sinners."[6] How exactly do these norms relate to natural law? Expressed theologically, natural law is a participation in Eternal Law, the life of Christ.[7] Expressed intuitively, the first formal principle of natural law, that one do good and avoid evil,[8] is derived from the axiom that

---

6 Aquinas, *Summa theologica*, II-II, q. 40.

7 Thomas Aquinas, *Treatise on Law* (Washington, DC: Regnery, 2001), 38–39.

8 Aquinas, *Treatise on Law*, 59–60.

the good is diffusive.[9] Catholic jurists have long held that persons are ordered to advancing the good, and war may well deliver the needy and serve the common good.

Vengeance

De Vitoria begins his defense of war by noting Aquinas's application to the famous passage of St. Paul, that a public authority is "a revenger to execute wrath upon him that doeth evil" (PW, 297). He lists four reasons for war: (1) revenge for injury received; (2) defense of people and property; (3) recovery of property; and (4) to establish peace and security (PW, 319). All four rationales are found in Tolkien.

For Aquinas, (1) just war is a punishment: it is rooted in anger for an injury received and pursued for the sake of just vengeance.

Aragorn gives voice to the idea. After the Uruk-hai take Merry and Pippin, he swears: "'With hope or without hope, we will follow the trail of our enemies. And woe to them, if we prove the swifter!'" (*TT*, 410). Chasing the band of Uruk-hai that has Merry and Pippin, Gimli, Legolas, and Aragorn keep up a remarkable pace. After days of pursuit, one morning Legolas notices the sky red at dawn and declares, "red sun rises, blood has been spilt this night" (*TT** 10). They later learn from the Horse Master Éomer that riders of Rohan stormed the Uruk-hai camp at night and "left none alive." In his 1272 *De malo*, Aquinas reasons: "For it is evidently virtuous for one to seek vengeance according to the proper ordination of justice, as, for example, when one seeks vengeance for the correction of sin without violating what the law prescribes. And this is to be angry at sin."[10] Éomer's work of vengeance was total.

Aquinas's theory of war is the bedrock of the West's belief that war can be conducted in a civilized manner. War, rightly waged, can express God's justice, a punishment for havoc. Aragorn and Éomer

---

9 Please see my *Ecstatic Morality and Sexual Politics: A Catholic and Antitotalitarian Theory of the Body*, 23–27.

10 Aquinas, *On Evil*, 374.

speak openly of war as vengeance. Dying from wounds at the Battle of the Pelennor Fields, Théoden makes Éomer king. Éomer's grief at the passing of his king is compounded when he sees his sister laying on the battlefield. "He stood a moment as a man who is pierced in the midst of a cry by an arrow through his heart; and then his face went deathly white, and a cold fury rose in him. . . . Over the field rang his clear voice calling: 'Death! Ride, ride to ruin and the world's ending!'" His forces move forward with him to confront the enemy anew: "Death they cried with one voice loud and terrible" (*RK*, 825–26). He meets Aragorn in the midst of the battle. "And they clasped hand in hand. 'Nor indeed more timely,' said Éomer. 'You come none too soon, my friend. Much loss and sorrow has befallen us.' 'Then let us avenge it, ere we speak of it!' said Aragorn, and they rode back to battle together" (*RK*, 830). The battle concludes, and Tolkien writes:

> And in that hour the great Battle of the field of Gondor was over; and not one living foe was left within the circuit of the Rammas. All were slain save those who fled to die, or to drown in the red foam of the River. Few ever came eastward to Morgul or Mordor; and to the land of the Haradrim came only a tale from far off; a rumor of the wrath and terror of Gondor. (*RK*, 830)

Tolkien's work, and especially *The Silmarillion*, is laced with images of punishment and accounts of wars of wrath. The good and the bad heartily engage in them; the gods, too: "But at the last the might of Valinor came up out of the West . . . for the host of the Valar were arrayed in forms young and fair and terrible . . . and the uncounted legions of the Orcs perished like straw in a great fire, or were swept like shrivelled leaves before a burning wind. Few remained to trouble the world for long years after" (*S*, 251). Treebeard is a good example, also. Once angered enough about the destruction of the trees, Tree-beard savors revenge, embracing a war of annihilation against his enemies.[11] Gandalf warns Gimli:

---

11 This echoes the clear warning Fangorn gives the Elven King of the Galadhrim: "I know mine, and you know yours; let neither side molest what is the other's" (J. R. R. Tolkien, *Unfinished Tales* [Ballantine], 173).

Certainly the forest of Fangorn is perilous—not least to those that are too ready with their axes; and Fangorn himself, he is perilous too; yet he is wise and kindly nonetheless. But now his long wrath is brimming over, and all the forest is filled with it. The coming of the hobbits and the tidings that they brought have spilled it: it will soon be running like a flood; but its tide is turned against Saruman and the axes of Isengard. (*TT*, 488)

For Aquinas, (2) protection of the innocent and property might require killing those who harm them, or perhaps even threaten to harm them.

Tolkien certainly shares this conviction. Éomer wonders what doom Aragorn brings out of the North. Aragorn puts his point starkly: "'The doom of choice,' said Aragorn. 'You may say this to Théoden son of Thengel, open war lies before him, with Sauron or against him. None may live now as they have lived, and few shall keep what they call their own'" (*TT*, 423). Sauron's utter destruction is an animating principle of the war because innocent people must suffer if Sauron is permitted continued existence. This basic moral legitimacy for war pervades Tolkien's pages and explains the portrayal of Gimli and Legolas having a relish for combat. It is likely that Tolkien follows Kolnai in the conviction that the willingness to defend the innocent is basic to the integrity of moral order as such. A staple of moral theology, the theory of intrinsic evils is the claim that there are acts that may never licitly be done, no matter the circumstances, and no matter the pragmatic pressures to perform them. That the innocent cannot be intentionally and directly killed is a well-known example. Moral theology is here profound, insists Kolnai, for it is from intrinsicalism that ethical life takes its "primordial basis of moral orientation." Far from fundamentally immoral, war can be a guardian of moral order. Tolkien clearly thought so.

For Aquinas, (3) war for the restoration of property is licit.

This is a large part of *The Silmarillion*, and, of course, this principle drives the assault upon Smaug in *The Hobbit*. The Elvish king Thingol asks the Dwarves to set his Silmaril into the Nauglamir, a necklace made by the Dwarves long ago. The Dwarves "lust to possess" both necklace and jewel, and "they dissembled their mind" working on the jewelry only to steal it once completed. Thingol is slain and the Dwarves steal away but "they were pursued to the death." Beren leads at the battle of Sarn Athrad and returns the jewelry to the Elves. When the Silmaril in the Nauglamir is worn by Lúthien after the battle of Sarn Athrad, there, on Middle-earth, was "the vision of greatest beauty and glory that has ever been outside the realm of Valinor." In consequence, no place in "the Land of the Dead that Live" has been "since so fair, so fruitful, or so filled with light" (S, 235).

This episode is a fine example of the moral theological insight that vanity is a deadly sin. The Dwarves' lust for beautifully crafted things keeps on generating death: only two Dwarves escape the wrath of the Elves at Sarn Athrad, and they go on to claim to those they meet that the Dwarves were all killed because the Elvenking wanted to cheat them of their reward for working on the jewelry. This lie stokes the wrath of the Dwarves and "long they sat taking thought for vengeance" (S, 232–33). Jackson dwells on this very point at the start of his film version of *The Hobbit*. The beauties of Erebor are ravaged by dragon fire and the surviving Dwarves nurse their resentment of Smaug for years: *The Hobbit* is the tale of how they plot to kill the dragon and get their property back.

And now, at greater length, Aquinas (4) argues war is permitted to secure peace.

Security

It is a longstanding Catholic idea that war is for the sake of peace. It goes back to Augustine, at least—though not to Plato, who argues the inverse (Laws, 803d). Aquinas and de Vitoria argue that because war is a punishment, wars can be offensive, and not only defensive. On the one hand, de Vitoria says, "there can be no vengeance where there has not first been a culpable offence" (*PW*, 303), but, on the other, he also reasons that wars sometimes must be started to preserve the peace: that defense sometimes requires offensive war to secure peace. "Without security, all the other good things together cannot make for happiness. When enemies upset the tranquility of the commonwealth, therefore, it is lawful to take vengeance upon them" (*PW*, 305).

Théoden accuses Saruman of being a peace-breaker and vows punishment, for "we will have peace," he tells Saruman, "when you and all your works have perished" (*TT*, 566). He invokes classic just war reasoning:

> Even if your war on me was just—as it was not, for were you ten times as wise you would have no right to rule me and mine for your own profit as you desired—even so, what will you say of your torches in Westfold and the children that lie dead there? And they hewed Háma's body before the gates of the Hornburg, after he was dead. (*TT*, 566)

Théoden accuses Saruman of four things, each of which singly is a ground for war: usurpation of authority over a people to which he has no right; destruction of property; killing of the innocent; and unnatural acts.[12]

In the *Summa theologica*, in the part sometimes called *Treatise on Law*, Aquinas distinguishes natural law from human law (ST, q. 91, article 3). Human law is that law that issues from the world's monarchs, parliaments, and legislative bodies, both national and international, as well as custom. This civil law is a necessary supplement to natural law, for the latter concerns only the general principles of a rational and virtuous life. Human law concerns itself with particular matters and can express national mores. Punishment is part of natural law, but what precise punishments are set against particular violations of the common good, is, Aquinas argues, the work of human law. The violations happen in specific circumstances and, for punishment to be balanced, awareness of circumstances is crucial: natural law, therefore, permits punishment, but it does not

---

12 On this last point, see de Vitoria's fascinating discussion of cannibalism and the refusal of the right to burial as grounds for war (*PW*, 209–12, 225). Interestingly, even the Dunlendings, primitive men and enemies of Rohan, seek to justify their hatred of the Rohirrim by claiming that Helm Hammerhand was a snow-troll and cannibal (*RK*, 1041).,

mandate definite punishments. For example, Plato is a witness to the idea that purification is more basic to legal order than punishment.

The civil laws that mandate punishment channel wrath. Aquinas again: "Therefore, we should say regarding the question at issue that anger will be good and virtuous and called zealous if it be a desire for vengeance insofar as it is really righteous. But anger is a sin if it should belong to a vengeance apparently and falsely righteous."[13] Virtuous wrath is distinguished from false revenge because the latter is disproportionate to the injury, exercised by someone without proper authority, and, stemming from hatred and envy, it ignores "the obligations of justice."[14] A fine illustration of Aquinas's point appears at the end of *LotR*. The Hobbits return victorious to the Shire. However,

> . . . it was one of the saddest hours in their lives. The great chimney rose up before them; and as they drew near the old village across the Water, through rows of new mean houses along each side of the road, they saw the new mill in all its frowning and dirty ugliness: a great brick building straddling the stream, which it fouled with a steaming and stinking out-flow. (*RK*, 993)

The Shire is now disgusting—the work of Saruman, they come to discover. Confronting Saruman at last, some of the Hobbits want to kill him. Frodo counsels: "It is useless to meet revenge with revenge: it will heal nothing." This seems contrary to Aquinas, but note what happens next. Ordered to leave, Saruman prepares to go, but, in a flash, lunges at Frodo with a knife. The blade snaps on Frodo's mithril mail-coat and Sam moves to kill Saruman. "'No, Sam!' said Frodo. 'Do not kill him even now. For he has not hurt me. And in any case I do not wish him to be slain in this evil mood. He was great once, of a noble kind that we should not dare to raise our hands against'" (*RK*, 996).

---

13 *On Evil*, 378.
14 *On Evil*, 378, 382, 385.

Thomas's distinction between righteous and false vengeance leaps from the page. The three conditions are present. Sam is not to harm Saruman for the basic condition of punishment is not present: a prior wrong. Of course, Saruman has done plenty wrong, but not in this specific circumstance: Frodo is unharmed. Furthermore, the punishment would spring from hatred—"this evil mood." Nor is there proper authority to harm him, for, intriguingly, and to be discussed more in chapter 6, "we should not dare to raise our hands" against someone of his "noble kind."

Contrasting is the encounter between the shield-maiden Éowyn and one of the Black Riders, the Black Captain, Lord of the Nazgûl. Théoden is lying on the battlefield when the Lord of the Nazgûl approaches, intent on outraging the dying king. The king's knights are strewn dead around him, save Éowyn. "Begone," she warns the wraith lord, "if you be not deathless! For living or dark undead, I will smite you, if you touch him" (*RK*, 823). Though Merry is beside her, the Black Captain "heeded him no more than a worm in the mud." Éowyn kills the foul dragon-like creature—"it stank"—upon which the Black Captain sits, but "out of the wreck rose the Black Rider, tall and threatening, towering above her. With a cry of hatred that stung the very ears like venom he let fall his mace" (*RK*, 824). Merry slashes the wraith king behind the knee, the mace blow misses, and Éowyn successfully drives her sword into him though "the sword broke sparkling into many shards" (*RK*, 824).

Éowyn's sword sparkling as it delivers the death blow is meant to convey the justice of that kill. The value tones in this battlefield encounter ratify the killing. Frodo gives voice to Tolkien's thought that a different constellation of value tones befits mercy.

Mercy

Aquinas's contributions to the theory of war are immense, but he also identified mercy as the leading trait of God. Aquinas held that mercy is basic to the entire metaphysical order; it is the inner core of reality (ST I, q. 21, a. 3, ad 2).[15] It is natural to wonder how Tolkien's interest in war fits into his broader moral theological outlook, and what role the themes of mercy and forgiveness play in his philosophy of war.

There are a number of places in *LotR* where mercy, or a related quality, like clemency, figures. The most obvious example from the film version is when Gandalf, shortly before confronting the Balrog in the mines of Moria, tutors Frodo in pity for Gollum (*FR** 34). The passage is oft cited, and justly so: it is a wonderful moment. Frodo: "What a pity that Bilbo did not stab that vile creature, when he had a chance!" Gandalf replies: "Pity? It was Pity that stayed his hand. Pity, and Mercy: not to strike without need. And he has been well rewarded, Frodo. Be sure that he took so little hurt from the evil, and escaped in the end, because he began his ownership of the Ring so. With Pity." In the book (*FR*, 58), this exchange is in the second chapter, which Tolkien tells us was the seed for the entire work (he says he wrote it some years before 1939). Interestingly, in the same chapter, Tolkien also presents pity as a temptation. Gandalf explains to Frodo that, were he (Gandalf) to take the Ring, he would become a Dark Lord: "Yet the way of the Ring to my heart is by pity, pity for weakness and the desire of strength to do good" (*FR*, 69).

Despite this strong identification of pity and good, pity is not straightforwardly good, and no hint of pity or mercy is offered Sauron. Indeed, Sauron's utter destruction is an animating principle of the war. At its conclusion, the Towers of the Teeth collapse and "the Captains of the West" see "a vast soaring darkness." Tolkien writes: "Enormous it reared above the world, and stretched out towards them a vast threatening hand, terrible but impotent: for even as it leaned over them, a great wind took it, and it was all blown away, and passed; and then a hush fell. The Captains bowed their heads . . ." (*RK*, 928). Interestingly, this recalls Frodo's reaction to the destruction of Saruman. The Captains of the West know what

---

15 Cf. St. Bonaventure, *A Journey into the Mind of God*, especially the seventh chapter.

Sauron is, and they also acknowledge the judgment of the Valar who have sent the wind to scatter Sauron's "spirit of malice."

One wants to know: What is it about Gollum, missing in Sauron, that warrants pity? Isn't mercy a blanket requirement covering every malefactor? What distinctions amongst malefactors is Tolkien making? Is he right that mercy is conditional on certain attributes being present, and these missing, a person is just out of luck? After all, who hasn't heard a priest during a sermon speaking of infinite love? Why did that priestly idea not resonate with the Catholic Tolkien?

These questions go to a deeper problem: How do the values of war and forgiveness relate? There are many who think they don't relate at all. In political terms, and generally speaking, people who are liberal say war is abhorrent. They feel uncomfortable around soldiers and don't understand their interest in things like weaponry and tactics, nor the culture that helped shape them. Oddly, many of these same people also love *LotR*. This is strange, because Tolkien could not make it clearer that he admires the martial. Interestingly, nor could the film version. One could not claim that Peter Jackson made an anti-war movie, or even hinted at such in the film's sensibility. Some of the most loveable characters are, it is undeniable, enthusiastic about war. Gimli and Legolas relish combat and even Treebeard, once angered enough about the destruction of the trees, savors revenge, embracing a war of annihilation against his enemies.

Humanitarians who love the film do not appear to find these characters repellent, far from it. They adore Treebeard as an expression of nature but seem oblivious to a passage like this, where Legolas speaks with him:

> "Strange it may seem," said Legolas, "but while Gimli lives I shall not come to Fangorn alone. His axe is not for tress, but for Orc-necks, O Fangorn, Master of Fangorn's Wood. Forty-two he hewed in the battle."
> "Hoo! Come now!" said Treebeard. "That is a better story!" (*TT*, 571)

I suspect such an oddity has an explanation: there is a moral consensus—fashionable to deny, perhaps—that the martial is a value and not a disvalue.

If wars can be just, presumably this is because not everything can be forgiven: or even if something could possibly be forgiven, there is no obligation to do so; otherwise, it would seem war could never be licit. If you think forgiveness an obligation, something you *must* do, then war cannot be just. The response to evil and injury would always be forgiveness. There certainly is a contemporary humanitarian sensibility that is moving in this direction. Evil must be "understood," one must seek out "root causes," identify ways in which one's own behavior may have contributed to the evil, provoked it. Reconciliation of difference, based on mutual understanding, is called for, rather than war. This attitude strikes some as basically right, but for other folk it is pushing condoning far too far.

Much will have to be said, but the reconciliation of these values will hinge on what Tolkien thinks about the obligatory nature of forgiveness. It is at least possible to ask, even for a Christian, whether forgiveness is always required. Might it be that sometimes forgiveness is a proper response to a moral problem and, other times, war? Again, moral consensus is sure to answer "yes." I think Tolkien basically agrees with Kolnai. We will follow our usual method: first, details from Kolnai, then numerous applications to Tolkien.

Kolnai argues that the constituent parts of an action, and the distinctions governing how the parts relate to the norms of action, are many. He argues that human acts are not all equally localizable under a simple rational rubric, as suggested by utilitarianism, for example. Rather, acts carry a value "tone." Kolnai calls this tone "moral emphasis" (*EVR*, 100): objects of the will's choice are laden with values and sometimes exhibit "a tone of warning, urging, vetoing, and commanding." The most imperious tones attach to negative rather than positive precepts. Moral demands intrude upon our daily lives most forcefully as prohibitions, "do not kill," "do not steal," and so on. Negative claims of justice, in other words, make their presence felt;

they have strong emphasis (*EVR*, 105). They impose the strictest duties.

By contrast, a positive precept like "defend the widow and protect the lowly" certainly does make a claim upon us, but less forcefully than "do not kill," and this is evident from our daily practice. Positive precepts stem from higher and more admirable values but they also have less emphasis (*EVR*, 106). To fail in these duties diminishes our moral standing but does not (straightforwardly)[16] make us morally corrupt.

Consider Kolnai's claim that, at best, forgiveness is a quasi-obligation (*EVR*, 223, 221). Someone might argue that, for a Christian, forgiveness is an obligation. Perhaps even a non-Christian might think forgiveness an obligation. Certainly, the contemporary humanitarian wants to replace judgment and condemnation with "understanding." The humanitarian impulse displayed here justly stems from the insight that forgiveness is a very high value, one we should all want to exhibit. However, no matter that it is a high value, forgiveness is also of weak emphasis. By contrast, thinks Kolnai, a somewhat lower value, justice, has strong emphasis.

By way of illustration: imagine one saw the wife of a slain man putting flowers on the grave of her husband's killer. Approaching her we ask, "What are you doing?" We learn the flowers are a token of her forgiveness. On learning this, I think all of us would know we were in the presence of a remarkable person, a remarkable value-realization. Yet, we could well imagine speaking with another woman in the same situation who tells us she will never forgive her husband's killer. We would, I imagine, still be impressed: the woman's sense of justice would register with us. We would not, I think, be nearly as impressed by her as we are with the first woman but nor, in any way whatsoever,

---

16 Kolnai is likely right that over time a constant failure to live up to the positive precepts will diminish our capacity to do even the strictest duties. See his essay, "Are There degrees of Ethical Universality?" in *Exploring the World of Human Practice: Readings in and about the Philosophy of Aurel Kolnai*, ed. Zoltán Balázs and Francis Dunlop (Budapest: CEU Press, 2004), 83–94. For Kolnai's point, see Albert Camus's *The Fall*.

would we think her a corrupt moral personality. That is, both values appeal, but in a definite hierarchy.

From this phenomenology of moral experience, Kolnai concludes that the reason we do not censure the second woman for not forgiving is that there is no obligation to forgive. We would be aghast if neither woman felt an injustice had been done. A definite obligation to affirm the value of justice does exist, and to fail to affirm this value is a serious moral failing. But to fail to forgive is not itself a moral failing, at least not a failing of anything like the same degree. Put simply: to murder is a lot more immoral than failing to forgive. The most Kolnai is willing to say is that if someone beseeches forgiveness, and if that person has demonstrated a change of heart, then a quasi-obligation to forgive surely exists. But only a quasi-obligation exists, no more.

Kolnai's insight is structurally present in *LotR*. The epic runs along two parallel lines, the story of justice—the warriors Aragorn, Gimli, and Legolas—and the story of pity and mercy—Frodo and Gollum. Note that Gandalf is a guide to both! It is impossible to deny that war is an ordinary part of life for much of Middle-earth. For this reason, war is viewed as expected, and so it is a craft for which one might train. In an age like our own, when so many go to college and study the liberal arts, it is easy to forget that training for war was one of the traditional mechanical arts in medieval times, along with weaving, tailoring, commerce, and agriculture. Tolkien knows this, of course, and a warrior class is clearly imagined, and sometimes in unlikely places.

Gandalf, connected with ideas of wisdom and divinity (*TT*, 484), educates Frodo on the importance of mercy (a lesson well-learnt by the time Frodo actually meets Gollum). Even though Frodo is something like a meek Christlike figure, it must not be forgotten that he is a weird version of "special ops," sneaking behind enemy lines whilst the conventional forces square off against Sauron's hordes. "As furtively as scouts within the campment of their enemies, they crept down on to the road, and stole along its westward edge under the stony bank, grey as the stones themselves, and soft-footed as hunting cats" (*TT*, 686). Like James Bond, who is not well-known for his mercy, Frodo will destroy Sauron utterly. We must conclude that, for Tolkien, mercy is a high, perhaps the highest, value, but one of weak emphasis, such that a special ops Frodo will show mercy to some, but not to others. To some, Frodo is a suffering servant Christ-like figure, but Frodo is not consistently a font of mercy.

Indeed, Frodo's sense of forgiveness is rather odd. Sauron is destroyed and Sam looks painfully at the maimed hand of Frodo. Sam knows Gollum took one of Frodo's fingers, and he expresses the wish that Gollum have taken his whole hand rather than maimed his master. Frodo reminds Sam that the quest would have failed but for Gollum, and so exhorts Sam to forgive Gollum all his mischief: "The Quest would have been in vain, even at the bitter end. So let us forgive him!" (*RK*, 926). Here, forgiveness seems to stem from a rather pragmatic "all's well that ends well." Though a conservation at a culminating point of the story, the exhortation to forgive is barely moral at all.

Forgiveness is one of the tone-setting values, *one* of the leading structural principles of Tolkien's social vision. The manring, and its concomitant values, is another. Friendship and culture might flourish within the manring, but the solidarity of the manring requires solidification of the enclosure; defense requires wars of wrath. David Hume, for one, doesn't see the need for this at all. Ruined cities will flourish again and, novelty ranking as high as ever, people will come together "to show their wit or their breeding; their taste in conversation or living, in clothes or furniture." To answer moral reversal and betrayal with vanity and luxury, to claim that the operations of wealth creation and the goods that flow from this creation satisfy, is Hume's answer. In Hume's own time, Adam Ferguson lambasted him for discounting the moral quality of war: Ferguson believed Hume minimized the seriousness of the need for moral repair in his suggestion that vanity would be a fix; some offenses require the martial.[17] Tolkien thinks Ferguson is right.

---

17 Ferguson, *An Essay on the History of Civil Society*, 242–43.

Punishment

Treebeard's joy of battle in *LotR* is, in fact, Treebeard's return to form. In *The Silmarillion*, when the Dwarf army was shattered by Beren in retribution for the plundering of Doriath, some who would escape were pursued by Ents, the Shepherds of the Trees, "and they drove the Dwarves into the shadowy woods of Ered Lindon: whence, it is said, came never one to climb the high passes that led to their homes" (*S*, 235). The Ents seem to channel de Vitoria: "The simple rout of the enemy is not enough to cancel out the shame and dishonor incurred by the commonwealth; this must be done by the imposition of severe penalties and punishments. Amongst other things, a prince is required to defend and preserve the honor and authority of the commonwealth" (*PW*, 306). It is licit, argues de Vitoria, to kill all the enemy combatants even once victory is gained and "the matter is beyond danger," because war is not merely about defense of self and property, but vengeance. Capital punishment, he adds, is enacted after danger has passed, and, by analogy, dealing with foreign enemies in the same fashion is permitted (*PW*, 320). Treebeard's wrath is announced early in Tolkien's lore. Yvanna, a member of "The Exalted," thus one of the first eight angelic beings created by Ilúvatar (*S*, 19), had long since warned those who would work in the smithy and be in need of wood, that "there shall walk a power in the forests whose wrath they will arouse at their peril" (*S*, 46). Recalling this warning, Gandalf says of Treebeard, "his long slow wrath is brimming over" (*TT*, 488).

For such a profound work, delving into the deepest layers of collective experience, *LotR* is strange in not having a courtroom scene. The Middle Ages incubated ideas about "due process," the nature of trial, evidence, double jeopardy, *mens rea*, and the division of legal powers, insisting that no single person may act as judge, jury and executioner.[18] Certainly, Tolkien makes it a mark of Sauron's

---

18 Francisco de Vitoria, *On Homicide*, 156–59. Cf. my *To Kill Another*, chapter 3, as well as "Witness for the Self: *Miranda v. Arizona*'s Political Theology," *Touro Law Review* 36, no. 4 (2021): 1079–95.

empire that "the spirit of malice" indulges in arbitrary imprisonment, slavery, deportation, mutilation, and physical and mental torture. Tolkien does not shy from varied forms of graphic punishment. The *lex talionis*—a system of justice wherein the value of body parts are compared to one another as a form of restitution, and which dominated Anglo-Saxon law in the early Middle Ages—is prominent. Beren loses a hand for his theft of the Silmarils, Sauron's tyranny costs a finger, and Gollum finally exacts his revenge biting off Frodo's finger as restitution for knowingly keeping his Precious.[19]

Gollum's fratricide is punished with exile. Capital punishment does not figure in *LotR*, as it does so graphically in *Game of Thrones*, but Tolkien hints at it, certainly. Théoden promises Saruman he shall hang from the gibbet for the crime of killing the children of the Westfold (*TT*, 566). It might be thought Frodo's refusal to allow the Hobbits to kill Saruman at the end of *LotR* for his scouring of the Shire is Tolkien demurring from the practice. I talk about this more in chapter 6, but from what has been said in this chapter, the likely reason is that the Hobbits may not kill Saruman because they have no authority to do so. Frodo exiles Saruman from the Shire. To the modern ear, exile sounds like a significantly preferable alternative to capital punishment. However, in ancient law it was catastrophic, as we see Tolkien portray when Gollum is exiled by the Riverfolk, to disastrous effect on his psyche. In exile, a person lost all identity, home, and rights. In the Bible, Cain's protest to God is that his exile means that anyone who happens upon Cain could kill him. Though Socrates, once condemned to death, could escape Athens, he refuses to do so, for death is preferable to exile. In old Scottish law, the exile is called *landlouper*, one who runs across the land, because having no place of rest on land. Gollum realizes this figure of the *landlouper* in dramatic fashion: he has no rest on land but only inside the mountain, on an island in the middle of its subterranean lake, a moat, the only manring left to him.

---

19 On law and body parts, see the fantastic book by Bill Miller, *An Eye for an Eye* (Cambridge: Cambridge University Press, 2007).

Poor Gollum is a figure of another unusual punishment. There is an extremely interesting use of law and punishment in the episode of Gollum and the Forbidden Pool, Henneth Annûn. The medieval tradition of law laid the foundation of modern law and strongly affirmed legal culpability for voluntary acts. Adam Smith identifies a curiosity in a much older tradition of law, the piacular. In Roman Law, one can be liable for punishment even if not actually guilty of voluntary wrongdoing. Smith's account:

> As, in the ancient heathen religion, that holy ground which had been consecrated to some god, was not to be trod upon but upon solemn and necessary occasions, and the man who had even ignorantly violated it, became piacular from that moment, and, until proper atonement should be made, incurred the vengeance of that powerful and invisible being to whom it had been set apart.[20]

Tolkien's application of the idea is more archaic than Smith's. Smith uses it to develop the claim that the human person *is* the sacred ground upon which trespass makes one piacular. Tolkien takes the pool of water at Henneth Annûn as the holy ground of heathen understanding (*TT*, 670–71, 674).

Hints of the medieval are present in Frodo's reasoning about Gollum's trespass at Henneth Annûn. Certainly, when Frodo stops Faramir from exercising lawful punishment, it is far too much to say that Tolkien is gesturing towards the contemporary Catholic, or humanitarian, sensibility that public authority must defend the common good and also offer the offender opportunity for rehabilitation. Gollum is spared to live another day, but not on account of hope for the restoration of his personal integrity. Frodo appeals to Faramir: "'the creature is wretched and hungry,' said Frodo, 'and unaware of his danger'" (*TT*, 670). This last "unaware of his danger" seems to point to the medieval condition for punishment: a prior understanding of the law.

---

20 Smith, *The Theory of Moral Sentiments*, 107.

But even here, ideas strange to modern sensibility predominate. Faramir agrees to take Gollum captive rather than execute him. Walking up to Gollum, who is eating a fish, "Frodo shivered, listening with pity and disgust," and it flickers across his mind to push Faramir to enact the law and order Gollum's execution. His disgust at Gollum is overcome not by humanitarianism but a more primary relationship: "But no, Gollum had a claim on him now. The servant has a claim on the master for service, even service in fear" (*TT*, 672). Gollum, after some fashion, is now inside a manring. Schmitt argues (*CP*, 52) that the core of the manring, of all political relationships, is the principle *protego ergo obligo*: after some fashion, Gollum is aware of his inclusion. Obscuring the threat of capture, Frodo has Gollum follow him. Amidst all the confusion of his scrambled psyche, Gollum nonetheless grasps that Frodo has betrayed the manring:

> Gollum crawled along close to the brink for a little way, snuffling and suspicious. Presently he stopped and raised his head. "Something's there!" he said. "Not a hobbit." Suddenly he turned back. A green light was flickering in his bulging eyes. "Masster, masster!" he hissed. "Wicked! Tricksy! False!" He spat and stretched out his long arms with white snapping fingers. (*TT*, 672)

Even Gollum can grasp that value guarded by the manring. Sauron is offered no mercy because completely indifferent to his trespass on the dignity vouchsafed by the manring. What disvalues does this augur?

Reprimitivism

What is *LotR* about? Tolkien insists in the Preface to *LotR* that the answer is "nothing." He points out, for example, that the germ of the entire work, "The Shadow of the Past," the second chapter, was composed well before WW2. Tolkien disliked allegory, mentioned the point many times, and insisted *LotR* was not about WW2. If it is about anything at all, he states, it is his research into languages. Nonetheless, all stories that are coherent, and powerful, must confront and use ideas. In the Milton Waldman letter, Tolkien proposes a number of profound themes that his work addresses. Christopher Tolkien felt metaphysical and theological motivations became dominant in his father's thinking. Amongst possible ideas, I have proposed war as a unifying theme, one having many parts: vanity, patience, land, property, vengeance, and forgiveness, to name only some. War allowed Tolkien to think about Scheler's "hostile modern spirit." This spirit is reprimitivism.

LotR is about totalitarianism not because of when it was written, but because it is about the struggle of civilization against reprimitivism. Totalitarianism, argues Kolnai, is "a critical answer to an already existing civilization," (*PVNS*, 45) and *LotR* is about the place of war in answering this convulsive criticism.

Kolnai defines a "Christian Conservative" as an anti-totalitarian, and it is easy to see how Tolkien fits the bill. Tolkien famously referred to himself as an anarchist (or in favor of an unconstitutional monarchy) in a 1943 letter to Christopher. We see it in this depiction: "The Shire at this time had hardly any 'government.' Families for the most part managed their own affairs" (*FR*, 9). Tolkien is quite different from the militant leftist anarchist of popular imagination, of course, but he certainly is as horrified as any such anarchist reading Kolnai's description of totalitarian state power. There are definite continuities between Sauron and Saruman and Kolnai's description of totalitarianism's technique of government:

> They [Nazism and Communism] both imply one-part rule, severe dictatorship with deified "leaders" as personal figureheads, a régime of terror in permanence exercised by the secret police, State omnipotence encroaching upon all domains of life including the most intimate ones, the reducing of law and morality to mere functions of state-power and of the government's will, the tendency to suppress such social inequality as is not inherent in the gradation of political power proper, and lastly, the substitution for transcendent religion of political ideology and the self-worship of Society as informed by an exclusive and militant will implying a pretension on the

government's part to "represent" that will entirely, taken in its massive self-identity one and indivisible. (*PL*, 106)

Sauron and Saruman high in their towers are good examples of glorified leaders. The Ringwraiths are Sauron's Praetorian Guard, and Saruman has the Uruk-hai. It is interesting that it is the Ringwraiths who first instill terror into the Hobbits (*FR** 13). The Ringwraiths are also the instrument of "State omnipotence." Gollum screeches: "'Wraiths!' he wailed. 'Wraiths on wings! The Precious is their master. They see everything, everything. Nothing can hide from them. Curse the White Face! And they tell Him everything. He sees. He knows" (*TT*, 616). All objective morality is cast down before Sauron's will to domination. Frodo experiences the Dark Lord's will:

> It was more than the drag of the Ring that made him cower and stoop as he walked. The Eye: that horrible growing sense of a hostile will that strove with great power to pierce all shadows of cloud, and earth, and flesh, and to see you: to pin you under its deadly gaze, naked, immovable. (*TT*, 616)

An equality of hideousness defines the Orcs, their aggressively militant life knows only officers—and the Orc general is the very embodiment of the disgusting (*RK** 36)—but no aristocracy, wealth, artisans, scholars, dandies (Bilbo!) or yeoman farmers. All these things must be levelled. The Ring lusts for a "massive self-identity one and indivisible," and the cost is civilization.

"One Ring to rule them all" is the motto of primitivism. The Ring is a principle of domination, stimulating, in Augustine's phrase, the *libido dominandi*. In his *City of God*, Augustine argues that domination takes the character of fratricide. Think only of the fratricidal dynamics between Gollum and Bilbo, Gollum and Frodo, Sméagol and Déagol, Gollum and Sméagol even, Boromir and Faramir, Boromir and Aragorn, Gandalf and Saruman, and even the Orcs and Uruk-hai. Augustine's basic claim is that politics always engages the problem of homicide. Aquinas, in his questions on war and killing, echoes this, as does Schmitt with his friend-enemy distinction. Fratricide is murder *inside* a manring: as such, it always subverts civilization. One of Tolkien's great, dark themes is civilization temporarily staving off defeat (*RK*, 949–50). Glories are possible, but defeat and collapse stalk civilizational efforts (*S*, 90). Think only of the Elves leaving Middle-earth (*FR*, 42). The Ring aims at primitivism because it always seeks to subvert a manring, the border of civilization and the eccentricity it makes possible.

Possession

The theme of fratricide and subversion do not belong to Augustine alone. The Ring's most famous forbearer is Plato's Ring of Gyges. In the *Republic*, Plato recalls an old Greek tale. A simple man finds a ring that gives him the power of invisibility. Promptly, he steals into the palace, sleeps with the queen, kills the king, and sets himself up as a tyrant. The Ring of Gyges subverts legitimate authority. About Sauron, we are told: "For he is very wise, and weighs all things to a nicety in the scales of his malice. But the only measure that he knows is desire, desire for power; and so he judges all hearts" (*FR*, 262). Plato's story is a device to put flesh on the thesis that people are only good because afraid of the consequences of getting caught doing wrong. It also poses a challenge: Is it possible to imagine that someone with great power might still do good? Tolkien takes up the challenge. Contrasting with the Ring of Power are the three ancient Elf rings. Not made by Sauron, and never idle, about them Elrond says: "But they were not made as weapons of war or conquest: that is not their power. Those who made them did not desire strength or domination or hoarded wealth, but understanding, making, and healing, and to preserve all things unstained" (*FR*, 262). These Rings help build and preserve civilization.

The Ring of Gyges stirs the lust of a simple man and prompts him to kill and subvert. Tolkien takes up this theme and expands on the character of *libido*. The Ring, we are told, utilizes malice already present, exacerbates it dramatically, but does hold to the channel already presented by some aspect of the bearer's character. In a brilliant scene from the film, Galadriel tells us she would become a Dark

Queen were she to wear the Ring (*FR**39). The scene also recalls to mind that in *The Silmarillion* she participated in a rebellion against the Valar in the hope of having her own kingdom (*S*, 83–84, 127). In a somewhat similar way, Gandalf tells us that should he take the Ring he would become a cruel tyrant, the Ring twisting and manipulating his pity and desire to do good (*FR*, 60). At the opposite end of the spectrum is Gollum. That he ends up living inside a mountain is hardly a surprise because before he even killed to get the Ring, Sméagol was in the process of abandoning the world.

> He was interested in roots and beginnings; he dived into deep pools; he burrowed under trees and growing plants; he tunneled into green mounds; and he ceased to look up at the hill-tops, or the leaves on trees, or the flowers opening in the air; his head and his eyes were downward. (*FR*, 52)

And thus, with the taking of the Ring:

> He was very pleased with his discovery and he concealed it; and he used it to find out secrets, and he put his knowledge to crooked and malicious uses. He became sharp-eyed and keen-eared for all that was hurtful. The ring had given him power according to his stature. (*FR*, 52)

The classic definition of evil holds that it is the privation of being: it always has a target, to remove what is good from the world. The Ring acts akin to demonic possession (*FR*, 56, 59): "It was not Gollum, Frodo, but the Ring itself that decided things. The Ring left *him* ... it had devoured him. It could make no further use of him: he was too small and mean" (*FR*, 54). In most films, the devil inhabits the victim's body and slowly eats away at her. This is certainly the popular opinion about how demonic possession works. Tolkien had read St. Thomas Aquinas, however. Utilizing Aristotle's work on dreams, St. Thomas argues that a demon controls his victim *by watching him* and *talking to him*. The demon learns by observation what emotion predominates in a person, then persuades him to act by an appeal to that emotion. That appeal is made in words and images.[21] This is why Sauron, Lord of the One Ring, is an eye, watching (FR, 392; RK, 804) and speaking (FR* 15).

Sauron is not really Master of the Ring (FR, 261). He made the Ring, but he is an emissary of Melkor, and the Ring reflects the appetites of its deepest origin. We meet Melkor on the second page of The Silmarillion. Evil enters creation when "desire grew hot within him to bring into being things of his own" (S, 16). The Ring thus toys with people's interest in possessions. Sméagol must have the Ring as soon as he sees it. It becomes his Precious once he has murdered Déagol. In The Hobbit, Bilbo plays the role of a thief for the Dwarves, but to Gollum he really is a thief, taking his Precious: "Thief, thief! Baggins! We hates it forever!" (FR, 12).

Bilbo, despite his goodness, later struggles to relinquish the Ring. He calls it "my own. My precious" (FR, 33). Gandalf tries to clarify the problem for Bilbo but he gets annoyed when Gandalf raises the matter (FR, 47): "you are always badgering me about my ring" (FR, 33). Bilbo insists to Gandalf that even if Gollum once had the ring, "it's not his now, but mine. And I shall keep it, I say" (FR, 33 & 47). He is unaware that the ring is, in fact, the Ring. Gandalf explains its character to Frodo. "It is far more powerful than I ever dared to think at first, so powerful that in the end it would utterly overcome anyone of mortal race who possessed it. It would possess him" (FR, 45).

Jackson has a fantastic scene where Bilbo darts at an astonished Frodo to try to claw back the Ring. The gesture is so out of character and his whole face twists, his eyes popping, gargoyle-like (FR* 29). Isildur's bane, which makes Aragorn feel accursed, is the doom that follows from Isildur's incapacity to destroy the Ring when he had the chance (FR* 28). Frodo later repeats Isildur's failure, and Gollum inadvertently completes the Quest for him: Gollum overwhelms Frodo's desire to possess the Ring but falls into the fires of Mount Doom.

---

21 On Evil, 156.

Kolnai describes totalitarianism's true believer thusly: "a dull, unawoken and prejudiced being, lacking the civilized traits of human autonomy, rationality, versatility and world-openness" (*PVNS*, 45). This description is a good approximation to orc life and fits nicely with the suggestion of the films, in which Jackson intriguingly proposes that the Ring possesses victims by hypnosis. It suspends a person's character.

Scheler identifies four basic value categories, each of which includes a myriad of discrete values. The value categories form a hierarchy and, in order from highest to lowest, they are spiritual and personal, intellectual and cultural, vital, and pleasurable or pragmatic (*NS*, 72). Human beings work (pragmatic), have family and national connections (vital), enjoy hobbies, games, and reading (intellectual), and praise (holy). Persons relate to one another via these four basic categories of value, but a person only pronouncedly appears "wherever we meet with *signs* or *traces* of its spiritual activity, in a work of art, for instance, or in the felt unity of a voluntary action;" "we immediately encounter in this an active individual self" (*NS*, 242). Persons have a unique, perduring, disclosing standing (*NS*, 60). Should a civilization's symbol or organization invert the rankings, occluding persons' disclosive standing, such a civilization must be reformed. Much of Scheler's writing puts this ranking to work, identifying philosophical and political ideals that engage in value reversal. Scheler compares this reversal to the idea of hypnotic usurpation (*NS*, 39–44). This image captures nicely the person falling away from disclosive standing. In *The Nature of Sympathy*, Scheler, working from psychological studies on hypnotism, speaks of "the ecstatic habit of surrendering in passively riveted attention." Scheler puts the point formally:

> Psychologically, however, we must regard it as a more general characteristic of the hypnotic state, that in it the intellectual centre of all cognitive activity is put out of action, whereas the organic reflex system is stirred into increased activity, and this in respect of its most ancient functions and modes of operation; the "seat" of the hypnotic subject's own intellectual activity

is so *usurped* by that of the hypnotist that his organic and motor centres also come under the latter's intellectual authority, employment and control. (NS, 21)

To put his point vividly, he retells an account of a squirrel observed in the jungle to actually move towards the open jaws of a snake. Why?

... the squirrel's instinct for self-preservation has succumbed to an ecstatic participation in the object of the snake's own appetitive nisus, namely "swallowing." The squirrel identifies in feeling with the snake, and thereupon spontaneously establishes corporeal "identity" with it, by disappearing down its throat. (NS, 21–22)

Scheler's idea of hypnotic usurpation captures well the action of the Ring. The idea is fully on display in the Jackson film, in which Frodo is drawn towards a Nazgûl (*TT** 57 & 60). He not only exposes himself to the creature but moves, as though drugged, towards its clawed feet: standing before it he somnolently prepares to put the Ring on his finger and so seal his fate. Sam pulls him away in disbelief, but Frodo lashes out, putting Sting to Sam's throat. Usurpation of will is at the core of Melkor's evil. Having slain the two trees, darkness falls: "In that hour was made a Darkness that seemed not lack but a thing with being of its own: for it was indeed made by malice out of Light, and it had power to pierce the eye, and to enter heart and mind, and strangle the very will" (S, 76). It is a phenomenon as far from Eru as can be imagined. As we saw in chapter 4, it is why Eru corrects Aulë's false creation of the Dwarves as automata.

The Orcs move herdlike, exhibiting little personality, more akin to a swarm than discrete persons exhibiting self-mastery. Boromir, to his horror, awakens from the Ring's control—"a madness took me" (FR, 390)—and can hardly believe he has tried to harm Frodo. The memory of his attack on Frodo torments his last minutes alive (FR* 45). Frodo escapes from Boromir by putting on the Ring. The Ring on, the Eye comes searching, feeling its way to Frodo's location. Tolkien includes this marvelous metaphysical passage. Frodo, crouching on the ground:

> He heard himself crying out: *Never, never! Or was it: Verily I come, I come to you?* He could not tell. Then as a flash from some other point of power there came to his mind another thought: *Take it off! Take it off! Fool, take it off! Take off the Ring!* The two powers strove in him. For a moment, perfectly balanced between their piercing points, he writhed, tormented. Suddenly he was aware of himself again. Frodo, neither the Voice nor the Ring: free to choose, and with one remaining instant in which to do so. He took the ring off his finger. (*FR*, 392)

Frodo, with help from Gandalf, staves off the usurpation this time. Like Bilbo, Frodo has a resilience against the Ring—recall Elrond's admiration of this (*FR** 24)—and Frodo reasserts himself. Typically, however, the Ring cancels personal identity: for example, changing Boromir into someone he can barely recognize. The Ring rids its hosts of personality and collapses manrings: always, it aims at sameness, an ego tribalism. Kolnai picks out identity as the metaphysical heart of totalitarianism:

> The metaphysical core of the concept of social Totality is the concept of Identity; and the postulate of Identity, again, is implicit in man's pretension to metaphysical sovereignty, his aspiration to be God; for if I admit any entitative "otherness" of mind and will on a footing with myself, if I am aware of any human consciousness and purpose distinct from my own, if I recognize any valid law and authority over and above my will—and not an efflux and manifestation thereof—I cannot be God. (*PL*, 33)

The effort to collapse the gulf between the Creator and the created, Morgoth's effort to collapse the gulf between himself and Eru, to find the Secret Fire, is, says Tolkien himself, the great metaphysical and moral theme of the work (*S*, xiii). Morgoth, prime Gnostic, seeks to eradicate the *analogia entis*.

Fascism

Like Aquinas's devils, the Ring looks to accentuate a destructive trait. At the Council of Elrond, Boromir is desperate to employ the Ring in the defense of Gondor. He is startled by the folly of Gandalf's plan (*FR** 27). When he attacks Frodo at Amon Hen, he returns to the theme:

> "It is by our own folly that the Enemy will defeat us," cried Boromir. "How it angers me! Fool! Obstinate fool! Running willfully to death and ruining our cause. If any mortals have claim to the Ring, it is the men of Númenor, and not Halflings. It is not yours save by unhappy chance. It might have been mine. It should be mine. Give it to me!" (*FR*, 390)

Boromir might be thought proud here, but his actual grievance is with Gandalf's war strategy; he has always wanted to use the extraordinary weapon to meet an extraordinary need. At Elrond's Council, he argues:

> "I do not understand all this," he said. "Saruman is a traitor, but did he not have a glimpse of wisdom? Why should we not think that the Great Ring has come into our hands to serve us in the very hour of need? Wielding it the Free Lords of the Free may surely defeat the Enemy. That is what he most fears, I deem.
>
> "The Men of Gondor are valiant, and they will never submit; but they may be beaten down. Valour needs first strength, and then a weapon. Let the Ring be your weapon, if it has such power as you say. Take it and go forth to victory!" (*FR*, 261)

Boromir's energy is an almost perfect match to an attitude Kolnai identifies in the Nazis:

> But Nazism, devoid of patience and wisdom, bent on prompt success, and mesmerized with the idea of taking mankind on the rebound, borrowed its soul from that very experience of an unstable historical situation calling for "activism" and evoking a trance of "dynamism," whose progressive and revolutionary

meaning it irrationalized into the sublimely meaningless concept of a "crisis in permanence": the hour of great deeds, the cosmic Walpurgis-night, its own law and purpose and the object of a morbid mystical worship. (*PL*, 115)

Just as the Shire is a Tolkien ideal, so Gandalf, part priest and part warrior—like Aragorn—is another. Boromir is no ideal, but he is not a stand-in for the Nazi, either. Boromir's rashness is for the sake of Gondor, for the sake of civilization. Tolkien loathed Hitler and saw him as a corrupter of Germany's great legacy to the West (*Letters*, 55 #45). With the role of Germany in the twentieth century, it is easy to forget that British military planning on the runup to the Great War assumed France and Russia would be the enemy. That they would be the country's allies dawned on planners slowly.[22] Tolkien was a Francophobe, and far preferred the Germanic and Nordic. There are plenty who think Tolkien a fascist,[23] and, with his sympathy for Franco, why is obvious, yet still mistaken. Perhaps some make the association without really understanding Nazism and, because allergic to conservatism, quickly collapse Toryism into fascism. You see this in Michael Moorcock, for example.[24]

A quick recap of what we have seen so far that undermines the fascist charge, before we take a different tack on this question. In chapter 1, we saw that Tolkien's aesthetics relies on a sober philosophy of history of incomplete knowledge, restraint, and patience. By contrast, we saw Italian fascism embraced acceleration. Fascism is a form of Gnosticism—it is not a philosophy of persons deferring to the cosmos—and so is Marxism. Unsurprisingly, then, we also saw that the New Left embraces acceleration. The Shire is a picture of ancestral order. By contrast, in his study of Nazism a few years after WW2, Camus says "Hitler was history in its purest form." Hitler was an arch convulsionist, because, as explained by Hans Frank on

---

22 John Gooch, *The Plans of War: The General Staff and British Military Strategy, c. 1900–1916* (London: Routledge, 2017), 15.

23 https://www.spectator.co.uk/article/why-is-bilbo-baggins-a-fascist-favourite-/.

24 https://www.newstatesman.com/culture/2015/07/michael-moorcock-i-think-tolkien-was-crypto-fascist.

trial at Nuremberg, Hitler had a "hatred of form."[25] In chapter 2, we saw that Mackinder's geopolitics made plain to British Toryism that the national pastime of gardening—an exercise in form—was also strategic, flora critical to defensive lines. Certainly, I take it as demonstrated that there is a close affinity between Tolkien and Schmitt. Though I made this connection in chapter 3, the burden of that chapter was to show how Tolkien critically modifies Schmitt's manring—an ancient insight into human community, as explained by the anti-Nazi Huizinga—with a value architecture derived from the German Catholic Tory, Max Scheler. Thus, in chapter 4, I laid great stress on Bilbo, the eccentric Hobbit. I have argued that at the core of Tolkien's Tory philosophy of war is dignity. Using Scheler, chapter 5 has shown that the Ring works by hypnosis, a suppression of personality by usurping an individual's control center.

We can make a fresh approach to this long argument. Kolnai is probably the most philosophically acute observer of fascism. Living in Austria, he commented on its rise in Europe in real time, and published a massive and meticulous study of Hitlerism in 1937, *The War Against the West*.[26] He identifies the Nazi manring as a "tribal egotism." He complemented his gigantic study in a 1950 essay. In my opinion, "Three Riders of the Apocalypse" is one of the richest essays in twentieth-century political thought. The following is a long quote, but its quality justifies my including it: it is, I think, one of the most graphic descriptions of the aims of Hitlerism and, I do not think it can be avoided, it captures *something* of Tolkien's own post-liberalism.

Kolnai argues that Nazism aimed to save Germany from Bolshevism, and also:

> To abolish the liberal and democratic framework of bourgeois society itself, which provides Socialist subversion with a thriving-ground ... reaching out into a vaster historical perspective,

---

25 Camus, *The Rebel*, 179.

26 Please see my discussion, "Nazi Sexual Politics: Kolnai on the Threat of Re-Primitivism," in *Aurel Kolnai's* The War Against the West *Reconsidered*, ed. Wolfgang Bialas (London: Routledge, 2019), 156–66.

to undo the work of the French Revolution, together with the mental atmosphere of rationalism, enlightenment and progress which bred forth that revolution ... to turn back to, and to revive, autochthonous national traditions, with more stress laid on their political exploitation than on their historic genuineness and therefore a tendency to interpret them in a narrow, aggressive, as it were "tribal" and deliberately mythical sense ... negating, over and above liberalism and rationalism, Christian civilization as such (the breeding-ground of Modernity and Progress) as well as the Faith which has informed it, together with some if not most of its subsoil in Greco-Roman antiquity; and groping back, in its quest for "rejuvenating" anti-modern traditions, across the Prussian glory of yesterday and the more brutal aspects of the German Middle Ages towards the barbarous world of Teutonic heathendom—not without a side-glance, in my opinion at any rate, at Hindu racialism and caste religion. (*PL*, 111)

As seen, *LotR* is an effort to think of a world different from "the liberal and democratic framework of bourgeois society," "the mental atmosphere of rationalism," the leading philosophies of history belonging to Enlightenment, to downplay the West's Greco-Roman inheritance, and, in the mind of some critics, to justify a "a side-glance at racialism." I have tried to show that Tolkien's post-liberal Toryism requires distinctions be made and careful nuance respected.

Tolkien's proposal is a Tory one, not fascist, despite some overlap in the nationalist complaint about the erosion of identity under the pressures of the Industrial Enlightenment.[27] Kolnai identifies tribal egoism as a core metaphysical principle of Nazism. In this chapter, we saw that the Ring is a false adornment that opens a channel to demonic possession, making all an appendage of Melkor's ego. Its hypnotic quality robs others of their own eccentric ego function. Aulë can honestly confess to Eru, "I desired things other than I am," but Melkor never could. This critical difference sits at the

---

27 You can also find such a nationalist critique in Tolkien's contemporary, Wittgenstein. See J. C. Nyíri, "Wittgenstein's Later Work in relation to Conservatism," in *Wittgenstein and His Times*, ed. Brian McGuinness (Chicago: University of Chicago Press, 1982), 14–68, especially 51–52.

heart of the wars of the legendarium. I have proposed that Tolkien is an ancestral thinker. His is a myth of patience, the settled order of the gardener, not apocalypticism. Tolkien is intent on preserving the West's Christian heritage, which, as Benedict XVI points out, includes a "purified" Greco-Roman inheritance. And, as Ferguson pointed out at the height of the Scottish Enlightenment in a searing condemnation of the slave civilization of Athens and Rome, that inheritance desperately needed purifying.[28] Tolkien's emphasis on a Nordic or Anglo-Saxon ethos is, in fact, not nihilism but an affirmation of a hierarchy of civilizational values,[29] and, in Bilbo and the Shire, there is not exactly a dismissal of bourgeois values—Bilbo loves doilies, fancy waistcoats, and exceptional wines and tobacco—so much as curtailment of their *primacy*.[30] This is why I think the Shire a match for Scheler's Distributism. I think Holly Ordway's study on Tolkien's appreciation of modern literature has upended much in Tolkien studies. Yes, Tolkien was dead set against the myth of modernity, but could find elements of value in Enlightenment rationality. We saw that Tolkien loved motor cars and even offered a cautious welcome to brutalist architecture. Gandalf's war strategy is not irrationalism, either: it expresses skepticism that the *obvious* deliverances of pragmatic rationality are necessarily superior to other options. Rationality has its own perversions.[31]

However, we are not done yet. There is another possible concern. Tolkien's is an aesthetic resistance to modernity's philosophy of history. In a famous 1935 essay, the philosopher of history Walter Benjamin argues that fascism translates politics into an aesthetics

---

28 Ferguson, *An Essay on the History of Civil Society*, 176–77; cf. Smith, *Lectures on Jurisprudence*, 176–81.

29 It can be read comparably to Adam Smith's interest in English law as a legacy of natural moral sentiment prior to accretions of Canon and Civil Law, which overlaid those sentiments with legal fictions. See Smith, *Lectures on Jurisprudence*, 98.

30 You can find a similar sensibility in the hard-left Lacanian psycho-analytical social theorist Slavoy Žižek. Amongst many places, see https://www.project-syndicate.org/commentary/ukraine-russian-occupation-or-western-neoliberal-colonization-by-slavoj-zizek-2022-08.

31 Cf. Benedict XVI, *Regensburg Address* (Lecture given in the Aula Magna of the University of Regensburg, Germany, Sept. 15, 2006), https://www.vatican.va/content/benedict-xvi/en/speeches/2006/september/documents/hf_ben-xvi_spe_20060912_university-regensburg.html.

because, though a mass political movement, it has no interest in challenging inherited property inequities. It offers the populace a participation in an aesthetic economy lest the real economy of the corporate barons be assaulted. Marxism aims to politicize art, whilst, as a sop, fascism develops politics as a liturgy. Participating in liturgy, the masses get to express themselves but make no headway in gaining more property rights. The ultimate liturgical art is war, argues Benjamin. Evoking Clausewitz on absolute war, Benjamin: "Only war makes it possible to mobilize all of today's technical resources while maintaining the property system."[32] You readily see the problem. I have claimed Tolkien is a philosopher of war and a liturgist. Has Benjamin "sealed the deal" on Tolkien, the fascist? Not only has he not closed the deal, but the argument is already answered. Of course, much of the power of Benjamin's argument is lost if one does not think property relations basic to human relations: if you think persons relate to one another foundationally through "the mysterious laws of the interresonance of love and hate." There is another problem. Putting war in the register of aesthetics does not entail fascism. Thinkers from ancient Greece to the Scottish Enlightenment have done so. The mass political movement of fascism is inextricable from the Industrial Enlightenment. Who does Benjamin turn to for his charge against fascism? Our old friend Marinetti. Benjamin cites his manifesto on the Italian war in Ethiopia: "War is beautiful because it initiates the dreamt-of metallization of the human body. War is beautiful because it enriches a flowering meadow with the fiery orchids of machine guns." Fascist aesthetics is about convulsion, not cosmos. As Kolnai insightfully notes, fascism thrills to a "cosmic Walpurgis-night."

In the introduction, I argued that Aragorn's battle standard offers a lesson in patience—that it teaches deference to the time signature of things other than us, the stars and trees. The Standard of Elendil, the symbol of the House of Anárion, is a restrainer of

---

32 Walter Benjamin, "The Work of Art in the Age of Mechanical Reproduction," 19–20, https://web.mit.edu/allanmc/www/benjamin.pdf.

apocalypticism. In our final chapter, we return to where we started, aesthetics. Tolkien's philosophy of war hinges on whether there is a good type of vanity, i.e., whether we can parse vanity and find an adornment—a clarity and comeliness, as Aquinas puts it—that builds up persons rather than a decoration that puts them down. Specifically, the topic of our closing chapter is hierarchy, which will help us tease out the connection between Hume's "refined taste in monarchies" and Tolkien's monarchy as a restrainer of reprimitivism.

6

Civilization and Arwen's Battle Standard

How do the works of civilization adorn us without tripping the corrosion of vanity? After all, civilization is all about dressing up, style, flair, and attending to beauty. But how to indulge beauty without provoking its malign twin? There is *something* about civilization caught by the old phrase: "If you've got it, flaunt it." Maybe this is what the Puritans saw clearly? If so, Tolkien's Middle-earth as a cosmos of restrained shimmer is a nonstarter. Note how the Dwarves have some singular failings in this regard. The Dwarves lust for the Nauglamir; they glory in their own creation. Their vanity brings upon them an Elvish war of wrath (S, 235). They fare no better with the Balrog. When building the city of Khazad-dûm, their lust for mithril leads the Dwarves to mine so deep that they disturb the Balrog slumbering in the mountain foundation of Moria (FR* 34). In both cases, utter destruction follows upon vanity. The Dwarves amply illustrate that beauty is tricky, how vanity provokes war. Yet, their mithril shirt saves Frodo.

Mithril

Frodo must carry the Ring of Power back to the place it was made, the only place it can be destroyed. Knowing that the struggle between Frodo and Sauron will be bitter indeed, Frodo is given a gift to assist him in his quest by his Uncle Bilbo. Having once fought a dragon to help Dwarves regain stolen treasure, Bilbo was given in reward a mithril shirt. Mithril is not only the apple of every Dwarf's eye—it being a precious metal of great beauty and enormous value—but, made into a shirt, it is a chainmail vest resistant to all blades and arrows. Even after Frodo is speared in the chest by a cave troll, to the amazement of all, he lives. It is this event that reveals to his companions that he has such a shirt, for Frodo had always kept it hidden beneath his regular clothes (*FR** 35). To keep hidden an object the worth of a kingdom (*FR** 34) is a symbol, a counter to the reigning idea of vanity.[1] Close to the fires of Mount Doom, and close to destroying the Ring, Frodo is captured by Lord Sauron's orcs. Robbing Frodo of his clothes, the orcs discover the shirt and, fighting each other to the death for possession of it (*RK*, 885), they allow Frodo to slip away to their utter ruin; for he then completes his mission and destroys the Ring. Mithril is thus instrumental in destroying Sauron but, once again, because vanity proves deadly.

Aquinas describes vanity as a pincer. In his presentation of the deadly sins, vanity ranks immediately below pride and is the first enumerated sin: pride is the source of all sin and not, strictly speaking, one of the seven deadly sins, but all of them at root. Thomas distills the deep structure of vanity as the desire to make manifest one's superiority over others *or, at the very least,* never to be seen as another's inferior.[2] He argues that vanity has a double structure: it boasts, to vaunt the self over others, and, failing in this strategy,

1 A symbol, because the argument is not that Bilbo would not have sported his fancy shirt if he'd known its value. Gandalf chuckles that he never told Bilbo just how much the shirt is worth. However, it does seem more likely that Frodo would have been more immune to its charms, even though he could not ultimately resist the Ring.

2 Aquinas, *On Evil*, 349.

or perhaps simultaneously, works to diminish other people in the eyes of their neighbors; to bring them down a notch, to match our lower standing. It is this pincer movement that explains why most of us are ensnared by vanity. How does Tolkien's account of beauty escape encirclement in the pincer movement of vanity? Specifically, assuming I am right, how does Tolkien's philosophy of war as a better aesthetics than Gnostic variants dodge the vaunting of the self and shimmy away from sham egalitarianism?

Before answering, two preliminaries: first, where do we see the pincer in the legendarium; and second, where do we see it in modernity's philosophy of history, which, I have argued, is the special target of Tolkien's resistance art?

We can partially distinguish the moral corruption of Saruman and Sauron by thinking of the pincer movement. Saruman tends towards vaunting, Sauron towards belittling. Partially, because the pincers fold into one another; it is a blended moral phenomenon.

Amusingly, Gandalf adopts the Hobbit fashion for smoking a pipe, and it unbalances Saruman. Secretly, Saruman adopts the fashion himself, but publicly he mocks Gandalf for it. He mocks him because Saruman is anxious about Gandalf's stature and influence. For this reason, he "was ever ready to gainsay him or to make little of his counsels."[3] This double structure of vanity is fully on display at the White Council of 1251. Gandalf has proposed an attack on Sauron in Dol Guldur. Predictably, Saruman denounces the idea. As his idea is pooh-poohed, Gandalf sits saying nothing, only "smoking prodigiously." "Both the silence and the smoke seemed to annoy Saruman, and before the Council dispersed he said to Gandalf: 'When weighty matters are in debate, Mithrandir, I wonder a little that you should play with your toys of fire and smoke, while others are in earnest speech.'" Belittling Gandalf as a lover of toys, Saruman puffs himself up as one of "earnest speech." To which Gandalf replies that pipe-weed "gives patience, to listen to error without anger" and

---

3 J. R. R. Tolkien, *Unfinished Tales* (Ballantine), 364–65.

then, blowing rings of smoke, leaves Saruman in high anxiety that his own designs on the Rings of Power have been found out.[4]

Melkor illustrates the second strategy. Tolkien explains that the Elves are Morgoth's particular object of hatred because Ilúvatar made them the most talented creators of Middle-earth (*S*, xiv). For this reason, the Enemy makes the Orcs by twisting and inverting captured Elves: he subtracts the beauty, wisdom, and grace of Ilúvatar's Elves to flaunt his creative power in the face of Ilúvatar (*S*, 50): "for he sought therein to increase the power and glory of the part assigned to himself" and "the melodies which had been heard before foundered in a sea of turbulent sound" (*S*, 16). Creatively, Melkor refuses to be bested by Eru. He makes things "for himself, to be their Lord" (*Letters*, 195 #153). This is why uniformization is the mark of the Ring's reprimitivism. We saw in the previous chapter that wearing the Ring makes each a worse person. Galadriel even predicts that were she to wear the Ring all would despair. The Dark Lord makes others low that he might be glorified, a contest over creativity that is, says Tolkien, fundamental to the book (*Letters*, 188 #153).

Tolkien does not dislike everything about modernity, but he does reject its Gnostic philosophy of history. He agrees with Benjamin that the aesthetics of fascism generates absolute war, but his argument is of far wider scope than Benjamin's. Tolkien believes that fascism and communism, as well as liberalism, all trade on a convulsiveness undermining personhood by tearing us from the cosmos. We have seen Tolkien's worry about Gnostic apocalypticism repeat in thinkers as varied as Benedict XVI, Camus, and Voegelin. Nor is Tolkien's belief that the Gnostic philosophy of history is a three-headed monster idiosyncratic. It is a Tory staple. Commenting on the East and West blocs of the Cold War, Kolnai writes:

> However, these worlds manifest, to a great extent, a significant substance in common: that is, their adherence to technicism, "materialist" utilitarianism and the thematic cult of progress. In this respect, their dominant traits are not very different from

4 J. R. R. Tolkien, *Unfinished Tales* (Ballantine), 366–67.

those of the former fascist world, or of what survives of it.
(*PVNS*, 214)

However, in making this fusion, Tolkien sets himself a difficult task. His focus is aesthetics but, seemingly, vanity is a potent
tool against equalitarianism. Doesn't the pincer of vanity (liberalism) feud against the pincer of faux egalitarianism (communism)?
Worse, vanity appears to be alive and well in the Shire. It is the fancy
Hobbits, he tells us, who still live in holes in the ground, and Bilbo
is a landed gent. Following Distributism, the Shire is built around
freehold. As Adam Smith points out, it was the feudal institution of
freehold that sparked a revolution in ornamentation.[5] Property and
home must needs raise the issue of vanity, decoration, and hierarchy.
Bilbo is quite fastidious about his home furnishings! Indeed, he is
a dandy: he has whole *rooms* devoted to his clothes (*H*, 1). It is a
delicate issue for Tolkien because clothing can demonstrate openness
to distinctive, hierarchical, and diverse values. Kolnai speaks of "the
garments of civilization" contrasting with the "uniformization" of
totalitarianism: the monochromatic black and grey of Sauron's forces
stands as a symbol of the primitivism Sauron's rule entails. Tolkien's
rejection of vanity might appear to invite precisely the *Theyocracy*
he is against (think Mao jacket). It is for this very reason that the
Scottish Whigs celebrated commerce against the unnaturalness of
the eighteenth-century spartan Calvinists, whom Hume dubs the
"severe moralists." Bilbo, with his racks of clothes, would be miserable
in Sparta. Tolkien—a self-described "little Lord Fauntleroy"—too![6]

To show that the pincers are not feuding, Scheler takes on Hume.
Whiggery devolves into the spiritual vampire, a reprimitivism. Vanity
is so morally problematic, argues Scheler, because inherent in it is
a reversal of value: the high value of personal discrimination is for-
saken for lower generic values of assimilation (*NS*, 39–44). Fashion!

---

5 Smith, *Lectures on Jurisprudence*, 261–63.

6 When attending reunions for the boys of the prestigious Birmingham school, King Edward's,
Tolkien was remembered for "my taste in coloured socks" (*Letters*, 70 #58). Tolkien struggled for
money his whole life but would die a millionaire—in the seventies a rare feat: one of the first things
he did when the money from *LotR* rolled in was buy himself a pair of handmade brogues.

Perceptively, Scheler observes that vanity trips the abandonment of the self. Our eccentricities as persons are hollowed out as we latch on to what is fashionable, and a spiritual vampire replaces the human person. Ever sensitive to how he is received by others, the vain man lives as a merely social self, his personal, individual self left untended. The spiritual vampire, writes Scheler, "does not fasten on a single individual, but always on one after another, so as to live a life of his own in their experiences, and fill the void within" (*NS*, 43). Hume celebrates vanity as refinement, but Scheler predicts thralldom and uniformization. It is telling that the Whig Fukuyama concedes this point, speaking of scientific commerce as "an increasing homogenization of all human societies."[7] The decoration of fashion folds back into equalitarianism and makes no moral advance on Sparta, therefore.

A High Bar

Schmitt celebrates the nineteenth-century Church and delights in the fact that so often in the period "the Catholic church turned out to be the rock on which romantic vanity . . . was shattered" (*PR*, 49). The Church's guide through the snares of vanity was Aquinas. Demonstrated so far is that vanity propels modernity's three riders of the apocalypse. Wars are fought over decoration, contends Tolkien, so how can Arwen's battle standard—a clarity and comeliness—jump the Thomistic bar?

Aquinas's treatment of vanity is complex, and Tolkien's use follows the weaving contours of Thomas's assessment closely. In *De malo*, Aquinas writes:

> And one of the things that human beings naturally desire is excellence. For it is natural for both human beings and everything to seek in desired goods the perfection that consists of a certain excellence. Therefore, the will will indeed be morally right and belong to loftiness of spirit if it seeks excellence in accord with the rule of reason informed by God. (*De malo*, 328)

7 Fukuyama, *The End of History*, xiv.

Pride, understood as "loftiness of spirit," is natural, as humans seek excellence. The reason? "Every good naturally desired is a likeness of God's goodness," because God is generosity and generosity always aims to ennoble, aiming, as Scheler would put it, to enhance the value of the beloved.[8]

Thomas cites various Roman authors who, unsurprisingly, dwell on the naturalness of vanity. He also cites an argument that, since humans want to know the truth, they also want the truth about themselves known.[9] Thomas promptly dispatches this argument: to know the truth is to perfect the intellect and humans naturally desire to perfect their appetites: "But to desire that others know one's goodness is not a desire for one's own perfection." Here, Thomas appears to set his face against vanity as the Scots understood it: a concern for how one is viewed in the eyes of the spectator.

Consider again the exorcism scene in the film version of *The Two Towers*. Prior, Gandalf, the Grey Wizard, is resurrected as the White Wizard. In the scene, he purges from King Théoden the defrocked White Wizard, Saruman. Besides an exorcism, the scene is also the transition from humility to glory for Gandalf: a transition from a St. Francis-style figure of mendicant poverty to a pope. Does Tolkien invoke Roman virtue and depart from Thomas? Peter Jackson's reading (*TT**15) defers wonderfully to Thomas's fuller analysis of vanity.

Thomas argues that vanity, underwritten by the right norms, is good. These norms are truth, the common good, and care of the self. To desire that one is known by others to be good can be a laudable desire: if manifesting one's goodness redounds to the glory of God; if it works for the good of one's neighbor; and if one is strengthened in virtue and encouraged to persevere. Indeed, in language akin to Hume's, Thomas argues that manifesting glory helps neighbors,

---

8 Cf. Martin D'Arcy, SJ, *The Mind and Heart of Love: A Study in Eros and Agape* (Providence, RI: Cluny, 2019).

9 *On Evil*, 341.

"who, perceiving one's goodness, are drawn to imitate it."[10] The moral purity of Gandalf is revealed in splendor to others. It is beheld so that the faint hearts of the people of Rohan, King Théoden's people, might take courage to face down the war that is upon them. Another good example is when Galadriel shares her greatness with Frodo, exhibiting her gift of foresight (FR, 355). Overwhelming in the moment, it is nonetheless meant to strengthen his resolve as the Ring-bearer, for he sees—at least in the film version—the destruction of the Shire; he sees Sam and all he loves driven into slavery or destroyed.

The Shire is an exemplar of Scheler's variant of Distributism. The estate both delivers decoration and is an institutional curtailment of vanity. The estate breaks the grip of totalizing identity, for every estate is a center of privilege, articulating values peculiar to each. An estate is far removed from primitivism, for estates are culturally productive. The estate blocks uniformization by a conversion of vanity to place and belonging. Beautiful things abound in Middle-earth—beginning with the adornment wrought by the Ainur (S, 15)—but they decorate as expressions of fixed identities (Letters, 196 #154), of estates. Tolkien's different peoples have diverse creative talents—evident in Gimli's "give me your name, horse-master, and I will give you mine" (TT, 422)—and make prominent a highly modified division of labor.

Monarchy is another institution that clips the wings of vanity. His is a Tory proposal for stable identity based on estates deferring to an order of transcendental value tones, and with the martial as a sentinel to protect the works of civilization. The apex institution structured by that order is monarchy. This is where Tolkien's quip about an anarchist order[11] with a monarch who cares mostly about the cut of his Vizier's trousers comes in.

---

10 On Evil, 343.

11 Tolkien's interest in anarchism was, I think, quite genuine. In a cheeky wartime letter about WW2, he writes: "There is only one bright spot and that is the growing habit of disgruntled men of dynamiting factories and power-stations; I hope that, encouraged now as 'patriotism,' may remain a habit! But it won't do any good, if it is not universal" (Letters, 64 #52).

I contend that Tolkien is a postliberal. Postliberalism is a big church, and a definition of what counts is not easy, but defending monarchy certainly qualifies. Right governance and monarchy are paired in Tolkien because monarchy gets aesthetics right: its aloofness and upwards gesture forces our mind towards what transcends and measures, the hierarchy of value tones. The steadfastness of monarchy is a time signature—like that of trees and stars—where time is slow and sober. Its "posture of distance," its fixed rites, have a restraining function on Futurism and its politics. The Standard of Elendil twins monarchy and cosmos, a core symbol of Tolkien's "cosmogonical drama" arresting apocalypticism.[12] It is the focus on this cosmic measure that makes Tolkien's philosophy of war analytically rich, and the burden of this chapter is to show how the livery of the House of Anárion is a decoration that affirms the dignity of persons, a good vanity, if you will. At the end, there is a twist: Sam, after a fashion, is the embodiment of the Standard of Elendil. Sam is *LotR*'s "chief hero," as Tolkien says, because, expert in flora, he is a *katechon*, a restrainer of apocalypse.

Value Hierarchy

Tolkien's ideal monarch—Charles III, perhaps?[13]—is a rich symbol. In Voegelin, person-affirming symbols stretch between cosmos and differentiation. They exhibit the human condition, an "In-Between of imperfection and perfection, time and timelessness, mortality and immortality."[14] History is the chronicle of the human effort at order: imposed to stabilize, political symbolizations reply to metaphysical precariousness.[15] These "saving tales" include: the king as compass, king and pope as two swords, Puritan commoners as Saints of God (*NSP*, 146–47), and the workers of the General Strike

---

12 Cf. Schmitt, *Land and Sea*, 17–18.

13 He certainly would have appreciated Charles III's connection to Charles II and The King's Oak (Garth, *The Worlds of J. R. R. Tolkien*, 115).

14 https://voegelinview.com/testing-the-truth-of-the-in-between/.

15 Voegelin, *Israel and Revelation*, ix; cf. Voegelin, *New Science of Politics*, 134.

(Sorel). Though Tolkien imagines priest kings in Númenor, Tolkien's letters give a more intimate symbol: amusingly, he gives a depiction somewhat like the British monarchy: "Give me a king whose chief interest in life is stamps, railways, or race-horses; and who has the power to sack his Vizier ... if he does not like the cut of his trousers" (*Letters*, 64 #52).

A vizier sacked for the cut of his jib is a ludic, playful symbol, but the work it does is potent. Symbols manage anxiety, they are "the sedatives that keep it down."[16] Tolkien offers a "saving tale," too. Voegelin contends that the West's great political choice is between the Christian "saving tale,"[17] proposing trust in the cosmos, or symbols of Gnostic certitude[18]—the Mechanism (Fukuyama's liberalism), Party (communism), or Führer (fascism). Tolkien explains that Gandalf has no more certitude about the meaning and development of history than does "a living theologian" (*Letters*, 203 #156). Tolkien's position is clear. He explains that his own work is a species of a genus: "The Christian joy, the Gloria, is of the same kind; but it is preeminently (infinitely, if our capacity were not finite) high and joyous. But this story is supreme; and it is true. Art has been verified. God is the Lord, of angels, and of men—and of elves. Legend and History have met and fused."[19] The human is positioned between the transitory and the lasting—"the ephemeral lowliness of man to the everlastingness of the gods"[20]—so the trick is to find a way to minimize the anxiety of existence, to balance the "horror of losing, with the passing of existence, the slender foothold in the partnership of being."[21] Establishment serves.

---

16 Voegelin, "Anxiety and Reason," 61.

17 For Voegelin, Christianity is not just a "saving tale" but: "So not an ordinary myth, but a saving tale saved from death." He accords merely the same status to the myth of Socrates as articulated by Plato (Voegelin, "Structures of Consciousness," in *Collected Works of Eric Voegelin*, vol. 33, 368).

18 Voegelin, *The Ecumenic Age*, 19.

19 J. R. R. Tolkien, *On Fairy Tales*, 35.

20 Voegelin, *Israel and Revelation*, 4.

21 Voegelin, *Israel and Revelation*, 5.

The year *The Hobbit* appeared, the pope proposed natural law as that "slender foothold." Invoking a realist, objective, and universal moral theory, Pius XI:

> Some restraint is necessary for man considered either as an individual or in society. Even the barbaric peoples had this inner check in the natural law written by God in the heart of every man. And where this natural law was held in higher esteem, ancient nations rose to a grandeur that still fascinates—more than it should—certain superficial students of human history.[22]

What is this restraint that helps us escape the acquisitive lusts of the Dwarves without being submerged in the uniformization of the Orcs? To counter uniformization—the false belief that "the removal of formal distinctions between categories of men will appear to supply, in itself alone, the substance of human dignity" (*PVNS*, 217)—Tolkien proposes hierarchy.

> Now they laid Boromir in the middle of the boat that was to bear him away. The grey hood and elven-cloak they folded and placed beneath his head. They combed his long dark hair and arrayed it upon his shoulders. The golden belt of Lórien gleamed about his waist. His helm they set beside him, and across his lap they laid the cloven horn and hilts and shards of his sword; beneath his feet they put the swords of his enemies. (*TT*, 406–7)

Tolkien is a monarchist because he appreciates that there is no moral order without the restraint of establishment.

Tolkien employs ideas of hierarchy and privilege throughout *LotR*. The heroes and villains of the myth are rather like the statues of saints you see round the walls of churches. Each has a defining object in hand, or a particular look, that conveys values or disvalues. To consider a few:

Legolas the Elf: bow: spiritual, and graceful.

Gimli the Dwarf: axe: earthy, and industrious.

---

22 Pius XI, *Divini Redemptoris* (1937), para. 21.

Gandalf the Wizard: staff: wisdom, and power (and fireworks!).

Strider "of the race of Men": sword: kingly, and guardian of the peace.

Boromir "of the race of Men": horn: knightly, and standard bearer.

Éomer the horse-master: horse: plains, and good cheer of the hall.

Sam the gardener: cooking implements and herbs: domestic, and loyal.

Frodo the "elf-friend": book: student of lore, and "Ring bearer."

Sméagol: gait and shape: exile, and possessive.

Wormtongue: black hair against sallow, wet skin: rhetorical, and conniving.

Tolkien's characterization of his heroes and villains shows that the world is saturated with discrete moral and aesthetic values, personal and communal. I have only to write the word "peach" and readers immediately have the value in mind: you might recall the taste, but may just as well remember the scent off a perfume, a bar of soap, or its hint in the smell of a rose.[23] Values are part of the furniture of the world, and the qualities of objects and persons are constellations of values. The idea of reality as value saturation was made famous by Scheler. Tolkien was like-minded. Writing to his son, Christopher, who was fighting in WW2, Tolkien recommended writing, as it had served him well in WW1: "I sense amongst all your pains (some merely physical) the desire to express your *feeling* about good, evil, fair, foul in some way: to rationalize it, and prevent it just festering. In my case it generated Morgoth and the History of the Gnomes" (*Letters*, 78 #66).

From highest to lowest, Scheler observes a hierarchy of values: spiritual and personal, intellectual and cultural, vital, and pleasurable or pragmatic. For example, consider Charles III's car, a vintage Aston Martin. The car has pragmatic values (it gets him places in comfort); vital values (being a sports car); cultural value (Aston Martins,

---

23 For an elaboration of value tones, please see McAleer and Rosenthal, *The Wisdom of Our Ancestors*, chapter 3.

featured in fashion shoots and movies, are iconic); and personal values, too (the ownership, care, and reverence for the vehicle tells us much about the person of Charles III). It is of a piece with his regard for heritage, and the serious-minded quality of British men's fashion reflects his thinky persona. To this example, one could literally add tens of thousands more, the theory comprehending all objects and our relations to them. Though tweaked in various ways, Scheler's theory became a staple of Catholic moral reflection in the twentieth century. It was tremendously influential: Kolnai, Saint John Paul II, and Edith Stein (St. Theresa Benedicta of the Cross) all developed value ethics from his work that circulate widely in Catholic circles today.

Put more formally, Kolnai describes value theory as the claim that values are an "autonomous, impersonal code of objective norms," universals discerned as qualities inherent in persons, objects, and actions, "bowing to the intrinsic evidence of Moral Cognition." In other words, values compel our attention. Scheler speaks of "the beautiful structure of the world of values" and Tolkien agrees: "We should look at green again, and be startled anew (but not blinded) by blue and yellow and red. We should meet the centaur and the dragon, and then perhaps suddenly behold, like ancient shepherds, sheep, and dogs, and horses—and wolves"[24] Here is a comparable idea in Ruskin, a writer Tolkien admired.[25] Describing the particular beauty of English country towns, Ruskin:

> They are not so often merely warm scarlet as they are warm purple—a more beautiful colour still: and they owe this colour to a mingling with the vermilion of the deep grayish or purple hue of our fine Welsh slates on the more respectable roofs, made more blue still by the colour of intervening atmosphere. If you examine one of these Welsh slates freshly broken, you will find its purple colour clear and vivid . . .[26]

---

24 J. R. R. Tolkien, *On Fairy Tales*, 146.
25 Ordway, *Tolkien's Modern Reading*, 303.
26 John Ruskin, *Unto This Last and Other Writings* (London: Penguin, 1985), 119.

The members of the Fellowship depict Scheler's value rankings. One could spend all day documenting what values in the hierarchy attach to each character, but here are some. Legolas exhibits all the ranks. After the loss of Gandalf, Lorien gives sanctuary to the Fellowship. Legolas's grief foregrounds a piercing lament for Gandalf sung by the Elves (*FR** 38). His spiritual air is evident in his weapon, the bow and arrow befits the way he surfs through the world, whereas Gimli's axe, needing to be hefted, captures perfectly his fireplug vitality, twinned as it is with the earthiness of a Dwarf's love of minerals. As an Elf, singing and lore, grace and beauty, define Legolas: intellectual and cultural values. He is ethereal, his step so light he walks on the surface of snow where others' legs sink into drifts. His agility, speed, and magnificent eyesight are playfully captured by Peter Jackson: he casts much of his movement as a snowboarder—think of the great scene (*RK** 54) where he slides down the trunk of a Haradrim elephant, a Mûmakil, firing arrows into his enemies: the vital values. Legolas is strikingly happy. Highly gifted, he exudes calm, and, in battle, positive relish: Scheler's hedonic or pleasure values. Closely aligned with Scheler, Kolnai could be speaking of Legolas in this passage:

> In my own surmise, nobleness is not so much a special value modality besides vital, moral and aesthetic value as the mark of a specially intimate *compenetration* between a concrete being (notably, a person) and some salient modality of vital, aesthetical, intellectual or moral values. We would call a man "noble" whom we could not as it were *imagine* to act or behave in any situation otherwise than with intensity, grace, genius, originality, grandeur, justice, generosity or high-mindedness. (*EVR*, 181)

Gandalf, like Legolas, matches this description of nobility. Despite being Istari, Radagast, perhaps like Bombadil, is too eccentric to quite match the value cluster of nobility. Radagast the Brown is portrayed by Jackson as hermit-like, something of a dotty St. Francis type, his messy clothing a home for animals; his knowledge is of nature, less of lore. He cuts a nervous figure, gaining insight from the vital values of Middle-earth, rather than books of lore, like the scholarly Gandalf. Tolkien casts him as a naïf manipulated unknowingly by Saruman (S, 302).

Gandalf typifies the intellectual and cultural, and others do so, as well. Obviously, Elrond, but also Aragorn, whose sophistication becomes evident once the guise of Strider is pierced. We are left in no doubt as to Denethor's intellectuality, and equally, Frodo's. Unlike most Hobbits, Frodo is bookish (in the film this is stressed in the first shot of Frodo). His aristocratic (FR, 3) lineage contains more than one unusual Hobbit (FR, 22–23) and he has absorbed values atypical of a Hobbit. Hearing him sing, Goldberry compliments him: "I had not heard that folk of the Shire were so sweet tongued. But I see you are an elf-friend; the light in your eyes and the ring in your voice tells it" (FR, 122). Faramir is also puzzled by Frodo: "there is something strange about you, Frodo, an elvish air, maybe" (TT, 653).

Tolkien, Value Theorist

Consider this important, somewhat long, reflection on LotR:

The story is cast in terms of a good side, and a bad side, beauty against ruthless ugliness, tyranny against kinship, moderated freedom with consent against compulsion that has long lost any object save mere power, and so on; but both sides in some degree, conservative or destructive, want a measure of control. But if you have, as it were taken "a vow of poverty," renounced control, and take your delight in things for themselves without reference to yourself, watching, observing, and to some extent knowing, then the question of the rights and wrongs of power and control might become utterly meaningless to you, and the means of power quite valueless. It is a natural pacifist view ... but the view of Rivendell seems to be that it is an excellent thing to have represented, but that there are in fact things with which it cannot cope. (Letters, 178–79 #144)

The Elves and Hobbits share this contemplative attitude towards value tones, "delight in things for themselves." This appears to be the role of Tom Bombadil: he's in the book to recall this "vow of poverty," the antithesis of the Machine. Tolkien explains that the Elves are close to him, being artists. As he puts it, their focus is "Zoology and Botany not Cattle-breeding or Agriculture" (*Letters*, 192 #153). For Tolkien, Elvish craft traces the contours of values structuring nature, and most especially the values exhibited by wood; and Hobbits tend to the seeds of the garden, potencies of color, texture, movement, dimension, structure, and scent. The vow of poverty, as Tolkien uses the expression, is an abandonment of the power to manipulate objects contrary to their nature; it is an obedient attitude to establishment (the return of the king!). It is, to follow Kolnai, a bow to the sovereignty of objects (*EVR*, 38).[27]

As Tolkien puts it, "in the view of Rivendell," contemplation of value tones is not sufficient to ward off the likes of a Melkor. War is a critical component of safeguarding civilization, but, as argued throughout these pages, war is not unconnected with veneration of value tones. Inquiring into "the height of values," Scheler observes that values that are less transitory, less dependent, and less relative, rank higher—the stars and trees. Love is a high value—as art, from pop songs to opera, testifies—because it is absurd to say, "I love you, for now." It is part of the value essence of love to be *sub specie quadam aeterni* (*FE*, 91–92). This idea is conveyed in the patient and sorrowful love of Arwen and Aragorn. It would be a value confusion to expect to be literally loved at your place of work, which is merely expressive of a lower value, a bond of common interests. Work is a place of dependency, therefore, whereas marriage is how two become one flesh. This logic is universal. For example, a bespoke wedding dress is a value higher than the bolt of fabric from which it was made, as the former is less relative than the partibility of the bolt from which it was cut (*FE*, 93). Tolkien introduces the same idea when saying that the introduction of the Elven-strain into the line of men was "part of a Divine Plan for the ennoblement of the Human Race" (*Letters*, 194 #153). At its core, value theory aims to safeguard the

---

27 Cf. "Reality, once self-evident, and therefore not conceptually experienced, but which can now only be reached by an effort of the individual mind—this is what is contained in a true poetic metaphor" (Barfield, *Poetic Diction*, 88).

standing of persons. It is hierarchy that prevents reductive—and primitivizing—characterizations of persons.

I have touched upon this important passage previously, but now note that it is organized around value hierarchy:

> I think that questions about "purpose" are only really useful when they refer to the conscious purposes or objects of human beings, or to the uses of things they design and make. As for "other things" their value resides in themselves: they ARE, they would exist even if we did not. If we go up the scale of being to "other living things," such as, say, some small plant, it presents shape and organization: a "pattern" recognizable (with variation) in its kin and offspring; and that is deeply interesting, because these things are "other" and we did not make them, and they seem to proceed from a fountain of invention incalculably richer than our own. (*Letters*, 399 #310)

This reflection is built around a scale of value. Intellectual value kicks it off with Tolkien's talk of conscious purpose. His example of things where "their value resides in themselves" is a plant, vital value. Then, in the negative, he cites hedonic values, i.e., the manner in which even a small plant defies our pragmatic grasp of its possibilities. As letter #310 closes, Tolkien invokes the holy, sheer praise, "to be moved by it to praise and thanks." Our experience of the world culminates in the *Gloria*: "We praise you, we call you holy, we worship you, we proclaim your glory, we thank you for the greatness of your splendor."

Tolkien makes subtle use of ranking in a philosophical discussion of pity. A letter from Peter Hastings, the manager of a Catholic bookshop in Oxford named after Cardinal Newman, queries why one of the trolls, William, shows pity to Frodo. In *The Hobbit*, Tolkien has William use the expression *poor little blighter* about Frodo. Tolkien concedes to Hastings that, had he written *The Hobbit* twenty years later, once "my world" had taken on fuller shape, he would not have used the expression, and, a subtle point, he would not have named a troll *William*. The name is charming for a troll, suggesting he is merely a silly billy, but it connotes altogether too much personhood. Tolkien goes on to explain that William's hesitation in gobbling up

Frodo had no more *intentionality* behind it than a beast of prey "lazily patting a creature it could eat, but does not want to, since it is not hungry." William is a misnaming not merely of a troll but the value hierarchy. You can't name things ranking so low on the hierarchy as a troll *William*.

Tolkien then observes that the same must be said of the behaviors of many persons: "Or indeed than there is in many of men's actions, whose real roots are in satiety, sloth, or a purely non-moral natural softness, though they may dignify them by 'pity's' name" (*Letters*, 191 #153). The first thing to note is that no one—and certainly not a writer as gifted as Tolkien—ever uses a formulation like "non-moral natural softness." You'll not find that expression in *LotR*! This is a phrase right out of a moral theology manual or a philosophy book. It is a staple of value theory to distinguish non-moral from moral values. Tolkien is making this very point. I may exhibit something very like pity not because I act morally towards the frail and damaged but because my constitution is such that I am always gentle around all, no matter the situation, or even provocation. That I naturally move through the world with a light touch, not imposing myself and being second to everything, does not mean I have acted morally, ever. In moral theology there is a handy Latin distinction between the *actus hominis* and the *actus humani*. There are acts done by a human and then there are intentional, volitional actions performed with full moral clarity.[28] For the experienced driver, changing gears in a car is a case of the former, and being a Good Samaritan, or relishing the niceties of torture, a case of the latter. Note also that Tolkien keys the ranking to the idea of dignity, exactly as you find in Scheler or Kolnai. Denoting something "pity" is to over-dignify a behavior if it is a mere *actus hominis*, which will be true of many of the genial acts of those whom we'd identify, tagging them as exhibiting, philosophically, a non-moral natural softness. This is often the moral content of those persons who think of themselves as kind. I propose that this example shows that Tolkien knew about, and felt

---

28 Cf. Karol Wojtyła, *Person and Community* (New York: Peter Lang, 1993), 96.

comfortable using, value theory. Regular folk don't drop this kind of reasoning into their letters.

Tolkien gives an example of the sovereignty of the object. In *The Mariner's Wife*, Elves visit Númenor in a ship bedecked with flowers. They give a sapling to Aldarion. Note the value tones: "To Aldarion they gave a sapling tree, whose bark was snow-white, and its stem straight, strong and pliant as it were of steel." Aldarion thanks them, adding, the "wood of such a tree must be precious indeed." The Elves do not know: "'Maybe; we know not,' said they.'None has ever been hewn. It bears cool leaves in summer, and flowers in winter.'"[29] The Elves express the sovereignty of the object. Aldarion, planting a new tree for each he cuts down for his ships, might be thought to do so, as well, but people aren't convinced: "yet to many beside Erendis it seemed that he had little love for trees in themselves, caring for them rather as timber that would serve his designs."[30] When his relationships with his wife and father collapse, in a rage, Aldarion has his house destroyed, his garden uprooted, and its trees felled for his boats, save the gift from the Elves. "The white Elven-tree alone he spared; and when the woodcutters were gone he looked at it, standing amid the desolation, and he saw for the first time that it was in itself beautiful."[31] Finally, amidst the maelstrom of his mood, the willful Aldarion bows to the sovereignty of the tree. This experience is what Owen Barfield, whom Tolkien admired, calls *poetic diction*.[32]

Privilege, Illustrated

Kolnai adds significantly to Scheler's theory when arguing that recognition of and support for values requires privilege, establishment. Kolnai thinks a simple intuition of moral value is possible; however, in the normal course of things, values make their appeal in and through manifold emotional ties expressed in social institutions:

29 J. R. R. Tolkien, *Unfinished Tales* (Ballantine), 198.

30 J. R. R. Tolkien, *Unfinished Tales* (Ballantine), 199.

31 J. R. R. Tolkien, *Unfinished Tales* (Ballantine), 211.

32 Barfield, *Poetic Diction*, 86–88.

hearth and home, the village with its civic hall and church, farms, schools, guilds, workshops, and such. *Privilege* is Kolnai's word for Scheler's estates: there are myriad centers of privilege spanning the liberal and mechanical arts. A car mechanic's family-owned garage is as much a value-bearing site as a lord's country estate. Of course, bad government can eradicate estates and make social forms that run counter to the appeal of moral sentiments. Kolnai does not think there is some one-to-one relationship, say, that aristocratic privilege assures that aristocrats are gallant. Indeed, Morgoth, the highest-born, "abuses of his highest privilege" (*Letters*, 195 #153). However, Kolnai does believe that aristocratic privilege *encourages* gallantry and knightly behavior. As we'll see below, Sam learns some such from Frodo and the Elves, and Frodo learns it more completely from Gandalf, who himself was tutored by Nienna. Huizinga argues that the great narratives of knightly life did in fact transform the behavior of medieval warriors for the better.[33] Moral insight is, in any rich sense, social, and vulnerable, should privilege be destroyed. This is why Sam—in the film version—can assure Frodo that some things are worth fighting for.

Already touched on, the encounter between Frodo and Saruman at the close of the trilogy includes the idea of privilege. Saruman has made an attempt on Frodo's life. It failed only on account of the mithril chain mail Frodo wears, and the Hobbits want to kill Saruman. Frodo commands them not to because Hobbits must not assault Istari: "He was great once, of a noble kind that we should not dare to raise our hands against" (*RK*, 996). Frodo is keenly aware that privilege cements social order; that reverence is due the angelic status of Saruman, despite his great fall. Gandalf taught Frodo about the role of hierarchy in Middle-earth. In the seminal chapter "The Shadow of the Past," there is a nice comic scene where Frodo in his anxiety pushes Gandalf on the extent of his knowledge of the Ring. One senses Gandalf's pride is bruised by Frodo's pushiness: "Gandalf looked at Frodo, and his eyes glinted. 'I knew much and

---

33 Huizinga, *Homo Ludens*, 95–96, 179–80.

I have learned much,' he answered. 'But I am not going to give an account of all my doings to *you*. The history of Elendil and Isildur and the One Ring is known to all the Wise'" (*FR*, 55). Gandalf insists on the gulf that separates a Hobbit from the office of an Istari, not least one two thousand years old! The point is found later (*TT*, 567) and it repeats an earlier lesson Gandalf gave to Bilbo (*FR*, 33).

In "The Concept of Hierarchy," Kolnai offers a fascinating example for why these supporting institutions of moral life must be institutions of privilege. Imagine, he asks, climbing a hill. On the flat, before climbing, various aspects of the landscape stand out. Even a little elevation, however, adds richness to what one sees. In particular, with the climb underway, one can come to see behind the buildings and copses that previously had blocked one's sight. The phenomenology of height suggests, says Kolnai, that civilizational values are only acquired atop elevated positions. Authors as diverse as Cicero and the writer of *Beowulf* attest that height is an attribute of public authority and, of course, we speak of being elevated to the bench, and of judges handing down decisions. Egalitarianism is, of course, a value. But it is most definitely a low value, tending in fact towards disvalue—for it tends to restrict our very capacity to recognize value, rejecting, as it does, raised positions.

Consider what Gandalf says to Pippin about Denethor, Steward of Gondor, lodged high in the Citadel above the White City. By way of a warning, he says:

> He is not as other men of this time, Pippin, and whatever be his descent from father to son, by some chance the blood of Westernesse runs nearly true in him; as it does in his other son, Faramir, and yet not in Boromir whom he loved best. He has long sight. He can perceive, if he bends his will thither, much of what is passing in the minds of men, even of those that dwell far of. It is difficult to deceive him, and dangerous to try." (*RK*, 742–43)

Tolkien links height, status, and wisdom, just as Kolnai would expect. Entering the Citadel, Pippin experiences awe, and sees: "at the far end upon a dais of many steps was set a high throne ... but the throne was empty. At the foot of the dais, upon the lowest step which was broad and deep, there was a stone chair, black and unadorned, and on it sat an old man gazing at his lap" (*RK*, 738). Tolkien gives us Pippin's sense of Denethor:"Denethor looked indeed much more like a wizard than Gandalf did, more kingly, beautiful, and power-ful; and older. Yet by a sense other than sight Pippin perceived that Gandalf had the greater power and the deeper wisdom, and a majesty that was veiled. And he was older, far older" (*RK*, 740).

Vantage Points

Towers and authority abound in Tolkien. Arwen and Aragorn wed in the High City, the uppermost part of the White City (*RK*, 951). It is fitting for Aragorn, who is "so lofty a figure, in descent and office" (*Letters*, 323 #244). As Gandalf prepares to take his leave, he walks Aragorn to the Place of the Kings, a spot above the White City, high up on Mount Mindolluin (*RK*, 949). Jackson superbly portrays the point in the fight scene between Gandalf and Saruman; they fight for suprem-acy atop the tower of Orthanc (*FR*** 12). In the book, when Aragorn and Éomer first meet, there is a tussle for authority that Tolkien describes in images of the shifting heights of the warriors (*TT*, 423). Cinemati-cally, a great job is done with Theoden's Hall. The camera shows Edoras atop a craggy mountain and the riders—Gandalf, Aragorn, Gimli, and Legolas—are seen always on a climb, even through the town of Edoras, as they approach closer to the king's hall (*TT*** 20). Most stunning of all is the long climb by the Fellowship through Caras Galadhon: up and up through the tress they go, and when they first catch sight of Gal-adriel and Celeborn they are coming down steps from even further up. Evoking Kolnai's brilliant image of the mountain and sight, Galadriel speaks of her sight, knowing that one of their number has fallen, though the travellers are yet to tell her anything (*FR*** 38). All these characters are "persons of high estate and breeding" (*Letters*, 324 #245).

The races of Middle-earth are each markers of privilege, vantage points on the expanse of the value order. The Dúnedain are a good example. Guardians of the Hobbits and other simple folk, the dwin-dling descendants of the Númenóreans are now Rangers. They are a race, part of a bloodline, with long life (*RK*, 950, 1102; *S*, 261) and have Aragorn at their head. The bloodline peculiar to the Dúnedain gives them a distinctive access to the world, knowing "the languages of beasts and birds," a vantage point for special entry into the order of things. This is one of the things privilege accomplishes, thinks Kolnai. Each of the races has some particular knowledge and inhabit the world differently on account of it. Critically, Sam Gamgee is a gardener—a sort of echo of Yavanna—but he is not unique amongst Hobbits in his intimacy with things that grow in gardens: "a well-ordered and well-farmed countryside was their favorite haunt" (*FR*, 1). Legolas has remarkable eyesight and a love and understanding of trees. Consider the very beautiful exchange between Legolas and Gimli. Legolas, a Woodland Elf, has an affinity with trees, Gimli minerals. They make a pact that after the war each shall try to learn about what the other loves. The pact is made after Legolas is moved by the poetry of an enthused Gimli. He has seen the caves at Helm's Deep and speaks of the "everlasting music of water that tinkles into pools" and hopes to "tend these glades of flowering stone" (*TT*, 534–35). The poetry of Gimli opens a plane of values that previously had been closed to Legolas.

Vantage points or privilege comprise a manifold of memberships and belonging that break up power, and estates create diverse identities, fostering personalism (*PL*, 47). Kolnai writes:

> Privilege means the social projection, the institutional recognition, the traditional embodiment of the essentially insurmountable dividedness [amongst persons] . . . the fact that a few or rather, very many men in different ways transcend the "common level" of mankind, as though that in man which points beyond man took shape in them, in this or that limited respect, so that through their instrumentality others reach beyond their own immediate possession or proper nature, and enrich themselves by a contact with higher values primarily alien from them and not properly theirs, according to the mode of Participation." (*PL*, 22)

The Fellowship's encounter with Galadriel is a fine match for this passage. Galadriel is ancient, much older than Lord Elrond. In *The Silmarillion*, she is present at the great migration of the Elves into the West. She is a ring-bearer, steward of the Ring of Adamant, a ring of guardianship (*S*, 298). At the marvelous gift-giving scene on their departure from Lórien, she bestows discrete values on members of the Fellowship. Touched with the comic, Gimli falls hard for the great and ancient queen. The ancient feud between Dwarves and Elves falls away entire, so astonished is he by her beauty. This is the first seed for his coming to grasp the aesthetic values of the Elves. It also intensifies his gallantry: Gimli now fights as much *for her* as from fellowship and loathing of orcs. Her privilege is also her service to Middle-earth and, as Gimli comes under her spell, so her values matter to him and he participates afresh in the guardianship of Middle-earth, her mission. Sam, "little gardener and lover of trees" (*FR*, 366), is given a share in her guardianship, also, for he receives earth from Galadriel's orchard, and she promises him: "there will be few gardens in Middle-earth that will bloom like your garden" (*FR*, 366). In all cases, something of her grandeur and lineage rubs off on them: the values she bears ennoble them; she raises them up.

By contrast, a common feature of those who do evil in *LotR* is departure from their privileged positions, privileged manrings. Sauron is, originally, Maia, and Saruman, Istari. The Istari, as befits angels, range across the land. Gandalf is the "Grey Pilgrim," "an old land-rover."[34] Saruman's subtle entry into evil is symbolized by the change in the manner of life typical of his manring. Of the Istari, Tolkien says: "Long they had journeyed far and wide among Elves and Men, and held converse also with beast and with birds; and the peoples" (*S*, 300). However, Saruman takes up residence in Orthanc Tower, "and took counsel with none save himself" (*S*, 302). Treebeard points out that, though once a common sight in the Forest of Fangorn, not for long years has Saruman been out walking (*TT*,

---

34 J. R. R. Tolkien, *Unfinished Tales* (Ballantine), 365, 409.

462). Gandalf is quite otherwise. The Council of the Wise forms to combat the growing Shadow:

> Galadriel indeed had wished that Mithrandir [Gandalf] should be the head of the Council, and Saruman begrudged them that, for his pride and desire of mastery was grown great; but Mithrandir refused the office, since he would have no ties and no allegiance, save to those who sent him, and he would abide in no place nor be subject to any summons. But Saruman now began to study the lore of the Rings of Power, their making and their history. (S, 300)

More ancient yet is Melkor, Master of Sauron. Most favored of the Holy Ones,[35] the Ainur, who listened as Ilúvatar spun the world out of music, Melkor "had gone often alone into the void places . . . but being alone he had begun to conceive thoughts of his own unlike those of his brethren" (S, 16). Morgoth is exiled by Manwë, a faithful Ainur, who "shut him beyond the World" (S, 260). Gandalf reveals to Saruman that he is no longer the White Wizard, saying, "I cast you from the order and from the Council" (TT, 569).

Livery and Flora

> And it came to pass that in the hour of defeat Aragorn came up from the sea and unfurled the standard of Arwen in the battle of the Fields of Pelennor, and in that day he was first hailed as king. (RK, 1036)

Carl Schmitt has made prominent once more St. Paul's figure of the *katechon*, the sovereign holding back apocalyptic disorder.[36] Arwen and Aragorn are such. Arwen crafts the Standard of Elendil, "and in hope she made for him a great and kingly standard" (RK, 1036). It breaks out above the field of battle:

---

35 He is coeval and equipotent with Manwë, who remains loyal to Eru (*Letters*, 283 #211).
36 Schmitt, *Land and Sea*, 17–18.

> There flowered a White Tree, and that was for Gondor; but
> Seven Stars were about it, and a high crown above it, the signs
> of Elendil that no lord had borne for years beyond count. And
> the stars flamed in the sunlight, for they were wrought of gems
> by Arwen daughter of Elrond; and the crown was bright in the
> morning, for it was wrought of mithril and gold. (RK, 829)

Battle standard shimmering, hope is renewed "and the joy and
wonder of the City was a music of trumpets and a ringing of bells."
Renewed war inspired by beauty and hope of the return of good
rule with the reestablishment of the kings of the House of Anárion.
Why the hope? Arwen's luxurious standard affirms Aragorn's rule
as one measured by cosmos, flora, and livery. Rule obedient to the
value hierarchy.

Arwen's standard bespeaks nobility, a constellation of moral and
aesthetic values, embodied in privilege, and makes prominent the
desirability of distance and independence; it teaches the importance
of being dominant, or at least, being self-contained and not put upon.
This is why the Horse-lords, seeing the standard, "the mirth of the
Rohirrim was a torrent of laughter and a flashing of swords." Kolnai:

> Civilization signifies and demands—mastery over nature and
> self-mastery of mankind, noble distance, objectivity, nobility,
> obligingness, tolerance, uprightness, readiness to come to an
> understanding and to community with what is alien, refusal
> to give the precedence to the drives for validation and struggle,
> acceptance of the multiplicity of values and needs.[37]

In our world, civilization, "noble distance" from raw appetite, is
housed in the offices of the peerage, the bench, ambassadorial staffs,
officers on Quarterdeck and NCOs, curators, management and
stewardship, trustees, football coaches and captains, and artisans
and their tools, to name a tiny fraction. Kolnai makes an additional
point, one that strongly figures in Tolkien. Kolnai was Austro-Hun-
garian, a Jewish convert to Catholicism. Fleeing the Nazis, he settled
in England and loved a particular English expression: "I knows a

---

37 Kolnai, *Politics, Values, and National Socialism*, 50–51.

gentleman when I sees im." Simultaneously, the expression speaks to moral consensus, as well as privilege, that establishment is tone-set-ting. The idea is expressed by Tolkien, depicting "the half republic half aristocracy of the Shire" (*Letters*, 241 #183). It is an implication of the consensus expressed in "I knows a gentleman when I sees im" that value-bearing sites of privilege sit atop a broader reservoir of value leadenness. Ultimately, this point touches on why Sam is, as Tolkien says, the real hero of *LotR*: he embodies "the half republic half aristocracy of the Shire."

Kolnai's point is that offices are structured by discrete val-ue-tones and whilst a simple intuition of each is possible, in the normal course of things, values make their appeal in and through establishment. Moral perception is relatively rudimentary without the mediation of the ties expressed in associations: hearth and home, the village, with its civic hall and church, farms, schools, guilds and unions, workshops, and on and on. In an interesting way, this returns us to the Whigs. Kolnai thought the eighteenth-century Scottish development of the idea of the moral spectator a critical improve-ment in moral analysis. The standards of institutions are a spectator over the people, but, equally, all have expectations of others, and "the people" monitor their governing institutions.[38] Wondering about the origins of genius, Hume argues that the individuals celebrated in history books emerge from a spirit of genius pervading a people and essential to this common spirit are conditions fostering law, mastery of mechanical arts, learning, and commerce. As Hume puts it, "Can we expect, that a government will be well modelled by a people, who know not how to make a spinning-wheel, or to employ a loom to advantage?"[39] Establishment relies on, consolidates, and refines the original value experience and dignity of a people. Put another way, establishment is the *vox populi*, one already attuned to value hierarchy.[40]

38 Smith, *Lectures on Jurisprudence*, 282–87.

39 Hume, "Of the Refinement in the Arts," in *Essays Moral, Political and Literary*, 273.

40 Smith, *Lectures on Jurisprudence*, 19, 335–38.

The Shire is illustrative. It is an autonomous, agricultural region of self-sufficient communities, where beer-drinking and pipe-smoking are primary activities, and though the king's law is acknowledged, the king also seems far away. Far away, ideally because fretting over his Vizier's tailoring, but more to the point, because moral consensus is part of Tolkien's interest in the potential of anarchism. Sam is the exemplar; he is the bridge between vital value tones and holy beauty. Tolkien: "I think the simple 'rustic' love of Sam and his Rosie (nowhere elaborated) is absolutely essential to the study of his (the chief hero's) character, and to the theme of the relation of ordinary life (breathing, eating, working, begetting) and quests, sacrifice, causes, and the 'longing for Elves,' and sheer beauty" (*Letters*, 161 #131). Keeping up Frodo's spirits at the nadir of their trial, Sam: "'And then we can have some rest and some sleep,' said Sam. He laughed grimly. 'And I mean just that, Mr. Frodo. I mean plain ordinary rest, and sleep, and waking up to a morning's work in the garden. I'm afraid that's all I'm hoping for all the time" (*TT*, 697). Sam *is* the adage, "I knows a gentleman when I sees im," and he well captures Kolnai's contention: "the nobleness *of* society depends, not merely on the nobleness (in the widest sense of the word) of its *leading* members but also on the nobleness of its members in general, as a whole, and the possibilities it affords for the unfolding of the nobleness virtually present in its average, I would venture to say in its *humblest* members."

The principals in *Lord of the Rings* are all aristocrats, except Sam. Gandalf is an angel, Galadriel and Elrond are of ancient lineage, Gimli and Legolas are highborn, Boromir is the son of the Steward of Gondor, Aragon is a king, Bilbo, and the rest of the Hobbits in the story, are members of families linked to The Thain. As the story unfolds, Sam rises in stature, and others fail: the highborn Boromir falls: caught in the madness of desire for the Ring, he betrays the Fellowship. Others, like the Hobbits Merry and Pippin, are mostly silly fellows. Galadriel, though a hero in *Lord of the Rings*, has had to reestablish her standing over many ages. Saruman, another angel, falls, utterly. Tolkien agrees with Kolnai: hierarchy does not guarantee noble acts, but it does encourage them. Sam loves Elves, he admires them. Low born he might be, but at a critical moment he *lives up to* the ideal of the knight, ably taught him by Aragorn. At the critical moment, it is establishment, the livery of the House of Anárion, that helps Sam save Frodo, and Middle Earth. Indeed, towards the end of the book, moments before his death, Saruman inadvertently observes the Hobbits have come back from the war as knights.

Sam does what only three others are ever known to have done: once holding the Ring, he gives it back freely. As Frodo starts to fail, slowly destroyed by demonic possession, it is Sam who literally carries him to the fires of Mount Doom so the Ring can be consumed in the flames. Frodo spent and prostrate, Sam could take the Precious as his own. He does not, because schooled by higher things, including gardening. Tolkien explains the ontology of a plant thusly: "a helpless passive sufferer" (*Letters*, 239 #183). About trees, he says: "Every tree has its enemy, few have an advocate" (*Letters*, 321 #241). By the end, the supine Frodo is like a plant and Sam's service to the Shire and Frodo never falters. There is an irritating side to Sam, his smugness, says Tolkien, but what saves him is "a reverence for things nobler than" himself. "Imagine Sam without his education by Bilbo and his fascination with things Elvish!" (*Letters*, 329 #246). Sam is also schooled by Frodo, but he is, at the same time, cocksure and it prevents him "from fully understanding the master that he loved, and from following him in his gradual education to the nobility of service to the unlovable and of perception of damaged good in the corrupt" (*Letters*, 329 #246).

Though there are austere gardens, the English cottage garden is whimsical. Tolkien describes Bilbo's garden thusly: "The late afternoon was bright and peaceful. The flowers glowed red and golden: snap dragons and sun-flowers, and nasturtiums trailing all over the turf walls and peeping in at the round windows" (*FR*, 25). Hobbits are somewhat childlike. As Shaftesbury points out, gardening is about geometry, but ludic, too:[41] the playful is amplified in the cottage garden. Sam's attention to Bilbo's garden matches Kolnai's beautiful lines: "Children, though compelled to obey, are kings because they are enticed away, enchanted, into the fairyland of idealized mankind, into the innocent sphere of pure mathematics, into the abstract and leisurely world of eternal forms."[42] Elves are not destroyers, but nor do they tend. Elves have something of a tree's aloofness, and on account of their detachment, leave Middle-earth unfulfilled, its potencies left untilled. Contrasting the Elves with men, Tolkien:

> That is they are the descendants of Men that tried to repent and fled Westward from the domination of the Prime Dark Lord, and his false worship, and by contrast with the Elves renewed (and enlarged) their knowledge of the truth and the nature of the World. They thus escaped from 'religion' in the pagan sense, into a pure monotheist world, in which all things and beings and powers that might seem worshipful were not to be worshipped, not even the gods (Valar), being only creatures of the One. (*Letters*, 204 #156)

The Elves have something of a cavalier quality about them. By contrast, Sam fusses over Bilbo's garden—"'How bright your garden looks!' said Gandalf" (*FR*, 25); his service to the vulnerable beauty of the garden prepares him for the greater service to Frodo, the Shire, and to Middle-earth itself.

It would not cross Sam's mind to embalm the light of the trees of Valinor (the Silmarils): not because such an act escapes categorically the capacity of a Hobbit, but because Sam's value preference forbids it. Sam is like Tolkien, who tells us of his own "passionate love of growing things" (*Letters*, 212 #163). Sam is, in fact, a *katechon*, because he hits all the marks of the value hierarchy. He loves herbs for his cooking (pragmatic), he is a gardener, marries Rosie, and has a family (vital), adores the harmony of gardens and the elegance of the Elves (intellectual), and, unlike Merry and Pippin, has

---

41 Lord Shaftesbury, *Characteristics of Men, Manners, Opinions, Times* (Cambridge: Cambridge University Press, 2003), 416–17, n. 25.

42 Kolnai, *The War against the West*, 318.

a sharp awareness of the awesome standing of Gandalf (holy). Sam is a moral and political exemplar because gardens relate to place, home, beauty, time, life, obedience, and service. Seasonal and daily tending to a garden is each day to commit afresh to solidarity and balance. Gardening—a story composed in a design of value tones— links geography and history, geometry and harmony. What is the difference between Bilbo's gardens and Fëanor's jewels? Unlike the incorruptible, but corrupting, Silmarils, gardens must be tended. Gardens and gardening make you tenderer. The gardener armed with hoe and shears is a tough-minded protector, controlling, but ultimately, obeying the logic of plants, humbly attuning craft to the seeds of life. Sam is a true knight, for he combines toughness with tenderness. He is a figure, not of glory, but fellowship, giving service to persons, even if the subtle appeal of Stinker escapes him. He is a humble *katechon*. Arwen's Standard of Elendil forces our "attention upwards" (Hume), making us look up at the trees and stars. It heralds a steadfast sovereign affirming the Music of the Ainur and restraining the Gnostic Diabolus. Sam is no king, but he pushes our "attention upwards," too; tending what embodies the sovereign holding back the apocalypse—land, plants, and trees—the value tones. Yet, Sam goes off to war. Flora is strategic—the value tones outline worthy war aims and assist in the fight—but Tolkien's pastoralism is not blind to the terrible blood price civilization oftentimes requires. Once Frodo has looked into the Mirror of Galadriel, Galadriel reveals to him that she is a *katechon* and, as well, she shows the sacrifice demanded of her by her obedience to the gods. Cautioning Frodo:

> "Do not be afraid! But do not think that only by singing amid the trees, nor even by the slender arrows of elven-bows, is this land of Lothlórien maintained and defended against its Enemy. I say to you, Frodo, that even as I speak to you, I perceive the Dark Lord and know his mind, or all of his mind that concerns the Elves. And he gropes ever to see me and my thought. But sill the door is closed!" She lifted up her white arms, and spread out her hands towards the East in a gesture of rejection and denial. Eärendil, the Evening Star, most beloved of the

Elves, shone clear above. So bright was it that the figure of the Elven-lady cast a dim shadow on the ground. Its rays glanced upon a ring about her finger; it glittered like polished gold overlaid with silver light, and a white stone in it twinkled as if the Even-star had come down to rest upon her hand. Frodo gazed at the ring with awe; for suddenly it seemed to him that he understood. (*FR*, 355)

The argument that Tolkien is a philosopher of war closes with Concluding Remarks and a discussion of Nienna, Arwen, and the sorrow of war.

Concluding Remarks

For as lightning cometh out of the east, and appeareth even into the west: so shall the coming of the Son of man be. (Matt. 24:27)

Christopher Tolkien says about his dad's belief: "Before he could prepare a new and final *Silmarillion* he must satisfy the requirements of a coherent theological and metaphysical system" and "he had become absorbed in analytic speculation concerning its underlying postulates."[43] Tolkien pondered his art's architecture:

> LOTR is of course a fundamentally religious and Catholic work; unconsciously so at first, but consciously in the revision. That is why I have not put in, or have cut out, practically all references to anything like "religion," to cults or practices, in the imaginary world. For the religious element is absorbed into the story and the symbolism. (*Letters*, 172 #142)

---

43 J. R. R. Tolkien, *Morgoth's Ring*, xi.

Meredith Veldman comments that *LotR* is "an intensely religious work,"[44] and I have shown in detail just how thoroughgoing is the Catholic philosophical and theological structure of *LotR*. Specifically, I set out to show Tolkien is a Catholic Tory, and how this politics contributes to his philosophy of war.[45]

"The light of the drawing of the swords of the Noldor was like a fire in a field of reeds."[46] Tolkien's works are peppered with such aesthetic battle images. In his own aesthetic investigations, Giorgio Agamben has proposed a new field of study, the choreography of power.[47] What interests him is that, for example, when Hitler addressed the Reichstag to announce the declaration of war against Poland, "Hitler had discarded his customary brown Party jacket for a field-gray uniform blouse resembling that of an officer in the Waffen SS."[48] Tolkien studies might take up Agamben's proposal.

Here is a literal example of choreography toppling a crown. When Beren and Lúthien make their attempt upon Melkor's crown,

---

44 Veldman, *Fantasy, the Bomb, and the Greening of Britain*, 84.

45 It follows that I cannot agree with Veldman's claim that Tolkien is an Edwardian author: "Middle-earth and Narnia are both clearly the creations of British men who came of age before the First World War. Like Kenneth Grahame's *The Wind in the Willows*, the books provide a fascinating glimpse into the world of the Edwardian upper-middle class" (Veldman, *Fantasy, the Bomb, and the Greening of Britain*, 112–13). It is worth remembering that, before 1914, Britain's last great war dated to Napoleon, yet Tolkien's lore is steeped in war, indeed, in absolute war (for this concept, see Clausewitz's *On War*, 583–84). The colonial wars Britain fought during the nineteenth century had nothing like the stakes Tolkien depicts. It is an important point that Tolkien's wars are not medieval. Clausewitz observes that the history of war shows that medieval wars "were waged relatively quickly." History makes clear that the aim of such wars was to punish, not subdue: "When his cattle had been driven off and his castles burned, one could go home." There was a structural political reason for this, thinks Clausewitz. "Peoples themselves were in the scale" only with the advent of cohesive states. Tolkien entered the war with the "conscripted levies" which, as David Jones puts it, "knocked the bottom out of the intimate, continuing, domestic life of small contingents of men" (Jones, *In Parenthesis*, ix). Tolkien's lore depicts existential war. The threat of slavery eradicating the Shire looms over *LotR*. Sauron is annihilated—the fate of Saruman, too (*RK*, 997)—and the Ents and Huorns annihilate Saruman's army when they cut of its possibility of retreat at Helm's Deep. *The Silmarillion* includes comparable annihilations. My argument throughout has been that Tolkien's art is a political contention about WW1, its Gnostic origin and aftermath. For Clausewitz, see *On War*, 583, 587. I thus think Croft is right to point to Letter 73 from 1944, in which Tolkien explains that he "hammered out" the basics of the legendarium during WW1 (Croft, *War and the Works of J. R. R. Tolkien*, 29).

46 J. R. R. Tolkien, *The Tale of the Children of Húrin*, 56.

47 Agamben, *The Kingdom and the Glory*, 168–71, 194.

48 George Stein, *The Waffen SS: Hitler's Elite Guard at War, 1939–1945* (New York: Cornell University Press, 1966), 26.

the assault is in the form of a dance. Melkor "leered horribly" at Lúthien, but soon his gaze was captive:

> Round the hall she fared, swift as a swallow, noiseless as a bat, magically beautiful as only Tinúviel ever was ... and even as she danced she sang in a voice very low and wonderful a song which Gwendeling had taught her long ago, a song that the youths and maidens sang beneath the cypresses of the gardens of Lórien ... nor has any voice or sight of such beauty ever again been seen there [Angamandi] ... Then did Melkor fall forward drowsed, and sank at last in utter sleep down from his chair upon the floor, and his iron crown rolled away.[49]

In view of this book's goals, and on account of passages like this, I argued that aesthetics is basic to Tolkien's account of war; that, for him (and Plato!), war is the problem of how we rightly decorate ourselves. In one sense, Tolkien had to thread his way between the Whig philosophy of history and those of the revolutionary movements that marked his period, fascism and communism. In another sense, however, his was not a threading operation but blunt blocking, an attempt to kneecap the appeal of the triad. War is hard-wired into the Enlightenment, argues Tolkien, because its philosophies of history all trade on vanity.[50] In this sense, the Enlightenment is no different—save in means and scope[51]—from any other period of history. History is a lamentable chronicle of unmoored adornment riding roughshod over human dignity. Tolkien's postliberalism is an exposé: all history is a false promise (*Letters*, 333 #247), including the liberatory philosophies of the Enlightenment.[52]

---

49 J. R. R. Tolkien, *Beren and Lúthien*, 75–76.

50 I have proposed that Tolkien is a Catholic writer doing what Agamben believes the Church needs to do: "it is necessary for it to find again the eschatological experience of its historical action—of all historical action—as a drama in which the decisive conflict is always underway" (Agamben, *The Mystery of Evil*, 37).

51 I wonder whether Mearsheimer's historical analysis of great power security competition and war, starting from the Napoleonic age onwards, is influenced by Smith's philosophy of history. The wars he considers are all after the great historical shift to commercial civilization—animated by vanity—that generated the wealth and population key to Mearsheimer's idea of latent power. Commerce gave the means for war and the accounting data—the evidence—that makes possible his famed analysis.

52 Reissuing her acclaimed volume, *Splintered Light* (1982), in 2002, Verlyn Flieger comments that, in the twenty-year interval, she came to better appreciate the significance of Tolkien. When

Chapter I showed that Tolkien's characterizations of slowness and patience are a riposte to the cult of speed in the Futurism art movement: its modernism glorified the Machine and helped pre-cipitate the political movement of fascism. As his books, letters, and drawings attest, the problem of the Machine was a preoccupation of Tolkien's, and to counter its Gnostic rush to a post-human apoc-alypticism[53] he opposed a sacral "cosmogonical drama." Just compare Umberto Boccioni's 1913 sculpture, *Unique Forms of Continuity in Space* with Tolkien's drawings of Hobbiton: the soft repeating pat-terns of flora, not metal; settled pastures, not movement; the inher-itance of past generations, not the future; and established order, a portrait of serenity, not militancy. Boccioni's sculpture makes evident that fascism is an amped up politics rushing at remaking: Tolkien's lore ends with the Last Battle, an apocalypse with gods leading the line, but it is an apocalypse awaited patiently and with sorrow. Hence, Legolas, imagining a rebuilt Minas Tirith, declares: "'They need more gardens,' said Legolas. 'The houses are dead, and there is too little that grows and is glad. If Aragorn comes into his own, the people of the Wood shall bring him birds that sing and trees that do not die" (*RK*, 854).

Tolkien's sacral "cosmogonical drama" firmly places human experience in space and time: "we are finite creatures with absolute limitations" (*Letters*, 326 #246). Tolkien raged against an angelism in a film script version of *LotR*: "The main action begins in autumn and passes through winter to a brilliant spring: this is basic to the purpose and tone of the tale. The contraction of time and space in Z [the scriptwriter] destroys that. ... We are not in 'fairy-land,' but in real river-lands in autumn. Goldberry represents the actual seasonal changes in such lands" (*Letters*, 272 #210). Apocalypticism always

---

the book first appeared, less than a decade after Tolkien's death, she had recommended Tolkien as "refreshment and entertainment." In 2002, however, she noted: "Tolkien's work is coming to be recognized as being in step with his time and as reflecting its wars, precarious peacetimes, and increasing anxiety about the stability of modern life" (Flieger, *Splintered Light*, viii). Exactly.

53 Gnosticism seeks "some world-immanent state of affairs blessed by the absence of evil" (Jürgen Gebhardt, "Political Eschatology and Soteriological Nationalism in Nineteenth Century Germany," in *The Promise of History: Essays in Political Philosophy*, 54).

aims to contract space and time to a vanishing point, utopia (the old saw "How many angels can dance on the head of a pin?"). Tolkien's aesthetics of patience parallels Przywara's formulation of Thomistic analogy as a "posture of distance." Both Przywara and Tolkien rely on music as a guide to our metaphysical situation: creation posits intervals, the distances of which are to be obeyed; they give to us measure and orient us in a cosmos. Tolkien makes this vivid in the Ban of the Valar. It was Tolkien's conviction that stories true to human experience must engage the problem of persons chafing under a Ban, such is the grip of vanity upon us. This sets up the tension between Meneldur, King of Númenor, and his son, Aldarion. Meneldur's "chief delight was in the watching of the stars,"[54] but Aldarion delighted in the sea, and he was "prouder than his father and ever more bent on his own will."[55] Aldarion's willfulness both sets up Númenor's naval ability to aid Middle-earth in its early resistance to Sauron and the cataclysmic impertinence of the Akallabêth.

Chapter 2 observed that though the role of plants and trees in war is already found in von Clausewitz, Mackinder made thinking about land and war basic to British geographical studies in Tolkien's lifetime. The impact on Tolkien is evident. About Mirkwood, he says: "It was probably the Primitive Germanic name for the great mountainous forest regions that anciently formed a barrier to the south of the lands of Germanic expansion. In some traditions it became used especially of the boundary between Goths and Huns" (*Letters*, 369 #289). Considering the role geography and botany play in Tolkien's account of war upends how we think about Tolkien's pastoralism. It is not escapism or a counter-narrative to the trauma of industrial war (Fussell), but part of his "cosmogonical drama" that war is strategically a contest over land and its potencies and that these are tactically ever-present to the military mind in operations:

> They went on. But before long the snow was falling fast, filling all the air, and swirling into Frodo's eyes. . . . Gandalf halted.

---

54 J. R. R. Tolkien, *Unfinished Tales* (Ballantine), 181.
55 J. R. R. Tolkien, *Unfinished Tales* (Ballantine), 182.

Snow was thick on his hood and shoulders; it was already ankle-deep about his boots.

"This is what I feared," he said. "What do you say now, Aragorn?"

"That I feared it too," Aragorn answered, "but less than other things. I knew the risk of snow, though it seldom falls heavily so far south, save high up in the mountains. But we are not high yet; we are still far down, where the paths are usually open all winter." (*FR*, 281)

Tolkien's is a geographical legendarium because he wants to balance against apocalyptic philosophies of history that would rid us of our standing in a cosmos.[56] The specter of such is evident in his withering comments about the early film script of *LotR*: "Rivendell was *not* 'a shimmering forest'. This is an unhappy anticipation of Lórien (which it in no way resembled). It could not be seen from Weathertop: it was 200 miles away and hidden in a ravine. I can see no pictorial or story-making gain in needlessly contracting the geography" (*Letters*, 272–73 #210). Gardening and husbandry—engagements with geography—are not alternatives to war, but part of it, and decisive in what people think worthy of fighting over.

It is also no accident that Mackinder was a conservative Member of Parliament. Chapter 3 explored Tolkien's Toryism. His "cosmogonical drama" is a modern postliberal critique of Whiggery and revolutionary mass movements. The Distributists—influenced by twentieth-century papal writings on social philosophy—were fellow travelers with Tolkien through the Shire, so to say. Distributism was not an exclusively English social movement. I argued that the Shire comes closest to Max Scheler's concept of the estate (which also operates as a model for good industrial organization, as in Germany's *mittelstand* companies). The Great War equally shaped German culture, a culture to which Tolkien was very much attached.[57] Tolkien

---

56 "The stage is set for the divine messengers who abandon created reality altogether and concentrate on the Gnosis of the redemptive exodus from the cosmos" (Voegelin, *The Ecumenic Age*, 26).

57 White, *J. R. R. Tolkien*, 185. Tolkien was much attached to his German name and, unlike others, refused to change it to an English one in the Great War (Garth, *Tolkien and the Great War*, 42).

thought of his university work as part of Germanic Studies,[58] and the estate was a German Catholic Tory version of syndicalist anarchism, an interest of Tolkien's well-attested by his *Letters*: "I would arrest anybody who uses the word State" (*Letters*, 63 #52). Again, the hapless scriptwriter comes in for it. Passports, oftentimes used for registration purposes at hotels, were only introduced after WW1. When Frodo arrives at the Prancing Pony in Bree, the script proposed a horrible faux pas: "The landlord does *not* ask Frodo to 'register'! Why should he? There are no police and no government. (Neither do I make him number his rooms.)" (*Letters*, 272 #210). Entwined with the experience and consequences of WW1 is the philosophy of Carl Schmitt. It is, I believe I have shown, beyond question that, in some important ways, Tolkien's body of work parallels Schmitt's philosophy of war.[59] Schmitt's thinking is profound, but also notorious.

I suggested that had Hume been asked whether the Shire was worth fighting over, his answer would be "no." It would be no part of Humean war aims to defend the Shire. Chapter 3 is a pivot: it begins the account of what makes war worthy. On the one hand, I argued that Tolkien parallels Schmitt's new turn in Catholic thinking about war. In this postliberal account, the Shire must be defended because every political community is linked to a place, to land, that fundamentally orders its population to other peoples in the world. The borders of the Shire help constitute a people's value orientation. These values are the same as those of the Distributists: rich land, crops, gardens, craft, property holdings, solidaristic living, all are controls on "the hostile modern spirit" (Scheler). The borders of the Shire are literally a way of looking at the world, and without those borders that way of looking vanishes. As John Mearsheimer points out, in great power security competition land armies are decisive

---

58 Lee, "Tolkien in Oxford," 134.

59 Garth points out that Tolkien opposed international courts to arbitrate wars, instead preferring "traditional hierarchies" to settle the delicate and difficult matters of foreign policy (Garth, *Tolkien and the Great War*, 21), a position expressed by Schmitt, too (Schmitt, *Writings on War*, 187–95).

because territory is decisive.[60] For this reason, I paired Schmitt's idea with Rogation Days as evidence that his manring concept was neither new nor controversial in Catholic practice.[61] Nonetheless, on the other hand, my use of Scheler—Schmitt's older German Catholic contemporary—was designed to recognize the role of axiology in Tolkien's writing. No manring is valid independent of its obedience to the value hierarchy. All subsequent chapters linked the "posture of distance" with the extensive use of hierarchy found in Tolkien's art of war.

A guiding question has been: Why is beauty insufficient in maintaining peace? Why can the Elves not just enjoy their magnificent art and one another? Why, despite their divine favor, were the Númenóreans not contented? Their story of rupturing the cosmic harmony repeats that of the Elves. I argued that Tolkien's lore is one long meditation on beauty, and its problematic twin, vanity, properties of which include discord, disobedience, and a fascination with the glamour of novelty: "owing to the (it seems) inevitable boredom of men with the good: there would be secret societies practicing dark cults" (*Letters*, 419 #338). Chapter 4 employed Kolnai's phenomenology of the "nobility of distance" to explore Tolkien's myth in which God "gave special 'sub-creative' powers to certain of His highest created beings. . . . Of course within limits, and of course subject to certain commands or prohibitions" (*Letters*, 195 #153). These limits secure dignity. Saruman's Uruk-hai reveal that disgust sits the other side of blowing through these limits. Distance is basic to dignity, a good example provided by Aulë's fall. God rebukes Aulë for usurping "the Creator's power" and falsifying divine creation, for the Dwarves "only report to thee thine own thought." God refashions Aulë's work and "'Behold! Thy creatures now live, free from thy will!'" (*Letters*, 287 #212). God builds distance into the relationship between Aulë and the Dwarves, otherwise their relationship would mirror Saruman

---

60 Mearsheimer, *The Tragedy of Great Power Politics*, 83–137.

61 Erik Petersen draws attention to the fifth-century *Pascal Poem* by Sedulius: Christ, "whose name embraces everything in an everlasting enclosure and whose empire has no end" (Petersen, *Theological Tractates*, 145).

and the Uruks. It would repeat the possession of the minds of others that is the signature of the Ring and its false lordship.

Countering the Ring, a good illustration of the "garments of civilization" (Kolnai) is Lúthien's cloak by which she liberates Beren from the clutches of the monstrous cat, Tevildo. Tevildo relishes "daintily roasted" fat mice and sets Beren the task of catching some. Tevildo is toying with Beren, for the mice are quick and fierce, and their numbers carefully managed: "Tevildo harboured them for his own private sport and suffered not their numbers to dwindle."[62] Beren's lot is forlorn, and Lúthien comes to get him away from the grasp of Tevildo. "Now of that cloudy hair Tinúviel wove a robe of misty black soaked with drowsiness more magical far than even that one that her mother had worn and danced in long ago, and therewith she covered her garments of shimmering white, and magic slumbers filled the air about her."[63] The cloak imposes distance between her and those who would apprehend her, a distance that gives her and Beren liberty that their love might flourish: "by reason of the greater magic of her being and because of the spell of wonder and of sleep that fared about her no such dangers assailed her as did Beren before."[64] Chapter 4 furnished many other examples from *LotR*, a structural principle of which is the cloying character of the forces of the Enemy and the restraining of those forces by the knightly Gandalf, Elrond, and Aragorn. That restraint stems from height. Perceptively, Nietzsche puts into the mouth of us modern, self-referential, and self-congratulatory people, the bemused question: "What is a star?" However, absent a vivid sense of height, dignity is not possible. Tolkien's use of modesty, humility, and patience is to affirm the upward gesture of obedience to a transcendent order of value tones. In this obedience there is dignity, for otherwise civilization collapses, folds into itself, and becomes invasive, cloying, and disgusting. This is why the Uruks are brutish. Again, Lúthien illustrates. Dancing amidst

62 J. R. R. Tolkien, *Beren and Lúthien*, 50–51.
63 J. R. R. Tolkien, *Beren and Lúthien*, 56.
64 J. R. R. Tolkien, *Beren and Lúthien*, 57.

the trees, Tinúviel senses she is being watched, and, modestly, "she slipped suddenly down among the white hemlocks and hid herself beneath a very tall flower with many spreading leaves; and here she looked in her white raiment like a spatter of moonlight shimmering through the leaves upon the floor."[65] Camouflaging creates distance between Lúthien and Beren, who appears to be spying on her. Here, compressed, is Tolkien's great theme that dignity rests upon a sympathy with plants and the celestial, an obediential sympathy that is ultimately strategic and decisive for war.

This deferential sympathy holds no allure for the Enemy. At the beginning of the Second Age, Sauron, we are told, was "still beautiful to look at, or could still assume a beautiful visible shape—and was not indeed wholly evil, not unless all 'reformers' who want to hurry up with 'reconstruction' and 'reorganization' are wholly evil, even before pride and the lust to exert their will eat them up." Sauron was "corrupted by the Prime Dark Lord" (*Letters*, 190 #153) and both suffer a comeuppance from the logic of the deadly sins. The deadly sins boomerang on those who indulge them, and Melkor is no different, his vanity making him something of a sucker. Brought before Melkor for dispatching, Beren, to save himself, soothes the "Lord of the World" with these words: "Many a great tale has my father made to me aforetime of thy splendor and glory." Tolkien: "Flattery savoured ever sweet in the nostrils of that Ainu, and for all his unfathomed wisdom many a lie of those whom he despised deceived him, were they clothed sweetly in words of praise."[66] Vanity drives Melkor to refuse obedience to the Music of the Ainur, yet vanity subverts his own designs on lordship: lulled by Beren's sweet words, he allows him to live, giving Beren a chance still to steal the Silmaril from Melkor's hideous crown. Likewise, vanity subverts Sauron. He is vaporized at the end of *LotR*, yet Sauron—with Melkor's ruin—"was given an opportunity of repentance." Vanity gets in the way: "he could not face the humiliation of recantation" (*Letters*, 190 #153). His appetite for

---

65 J. R. R. Tolkien, *Beren and Lúthien*, 42.

66 J. R. R. Tolkien, *Beren and Lúthien*, 49.

perverse adornment solidifies the Allies, and though it is a close-run thing, their vengeance for his persecutions prevails.

Departure from the value tones, therefore, begets self-sabotage. Value tones appeal but are not magic. On occasion, they must be insisted upon by those intent on rightful decoration. Tolkien cleaves to Aquinas's just war theory—strongly enunciated by Théoden.[67] Aquinas's classic concept of war provides Tolkien with a rigorous moral account of the use of force that is universally binding: this elevates Schmitt's modern treatment of war—which can tend towards tribalism (ethnos)—into a high ethos of restraint and sacrifice. Vanity might beget self-sabotage, but its glamorous wiles make matching this high ethos horribly hard (*Letters*, 330 #246). The chapter paralleled the Ring with both Aquinas's account of demonic possession and Scheler's vampirism. Scheler's linking vanity and vampirism captures well the lurid primitivism of the Ring's adornment. The Ring's decoration is dignity's desecration. The Ring annuls all borders, political and psychological. Hence the Ringwraiths: great kings of men, their kingdoms stripped from them by Sauron, who "through their nine rings (which he held) had primary control of their wills." To them, the Ring is "an object of terror in their religious cult, by which they had been conditioned to treat one who wielded it with servility" (*Letters*, 331 #246). An element of the book's argument has been a contribution to the recent and growing interpretation of Tolkien's project as modern.[68] Tolkien was no Luddite. As money came in, he wondered whether he could order a bespoke typewriter with Fëanorian (*Letters*, 344 #257). We saw that passages depicting the Ring at work fit Scheler's moral psychology of vampirism as hypnosis. It seems Tolkien turned to the idea as a useful modern take on the demonic possession wrought by the Ring.

Chapter 6 put passages from *LotR* alongside Scheler's hierarchy of values. The Enemy's primitivism twists and inverts that hierarchy, the order of values connected with the mechanical and liberal arts,

---

67 Cf. Anna Thayer, "A Tolkienian Vision of War," in *The Return of the Ring: Proceedings of the Tolkien Society Conference 2012*, vol. 1, 91.

68 Cf. Garth, *Tolkien and the Great War*, 309–10.

as well as free government. The forces of the West seek to shore up that order, which entails the return of the king. In an analytically rich way, Kolnai shows that privilege is a bearer of values. Fighting for civilization means fighting for establishment: "The progress of the tale ends in what is far more like the reestablishment of an effective Holy Roman Empire with its seat in Rome than anything that would be devised by a 'Nordic.'" (*Letters*, 376 #294). Yet, a puzzle needs explaining. Aragorn is heroic, but the real hero, Tolkien tells us, is Sam. Tolkien favored monarchy because its rites make vivid that establishment is a "looking upwards," hence the decoration on Arwen's battle standard, embellished stars and trees. It's the Standard of Elendil, however, that gives the clue to Sam's importance. Making use of St. Paul's mysterious idea of the *katechon*—"I frankly confess I do not know what he means" (Augustine)[69]—I argued that Sam is Tolkien's hero in *LotR* because gardening is a reverential play of value tones; that play—an *intimate* obedience to the value hierarchy—is a restraining of the appetite of men who, mortal, "must not try to become 'immortal' in the flesh" (*Letters*, 189 #153). Gardens place us on earth, subject to the time-signature of the cosmos: *Awake, O north wind; And come, thou south; Blow upon my garden, That the spices thereof may flow out. Let my beloved come into his garden, And eat his pleasant fruits* (Song of Songs 4:16).

Tolkien saw harrowing things at the Somme, but was not a metaphysical pessimist, like Schopenhauer. As befits a conservative, though, he was sober-minded: "I fear it must be admitted that there are human creatures that seem irredeemable short of a special miracle" (*Letters*, 90 #78). Apocalypticism is a false story of perfectionism: "actually the presence (even if only on the borders) of the terrible is, I believe, what gives the imagined world its verisimilitude. A safe fairy-land is untrue to all worlds" (*Letters*, 24 #17). Tolkien admired the refinement and manners evoked by Jane Austen—though was no real fan of the literature—for they "cloaked or indeed held in check

---

69 From Augustine's *City of God*, as quoted in Agamben, *The Mystery of Evil: Benedict XVI and the End of Days*, 62.

... the everlasting cat, wolf, and dog that lurk at no great depth under our social skin" (*Letters*, 72 #61). Chapter 6 frames Sam's gardening as a *katechon*, holding in check "the everlasting cat," because the "delightful art"[70] is a patient practice in collating value tones.

In closing, I hope you have enjoyed reading this book as much as I have enjoyed writing it. I love Tolkien, and imagine you do, as well. Darryl Jones is less of a fan: "What Tolkien was doing, I think, was reimagining England, an England without modernity, without the Industrial Revolution. He had fought at the Somme, and so had seen exactly what modernity could do. Is it any wonder that he spent the rest of his life in flight from this? I think I understand Tolkien's politics, even while profoundly disagreeing with them."[71] I do not think Darryl Jones does understand. War figures in Tolkien's thinking quite differently than Jones thinks. There is something monumental about Tolkien's range of thought, and war is not firstly personal for Tolkien, a part of his biography. It is of far larger scope, it is cosmic, only adequately addressed as part of a political theology.

Sam's tutor, Tolkien tell us, was Bilbo, and about Bilbo he says: "Bilbo was specially selected by the authority and insight of Gandalf as *abnormal*: he had a good share of hobbit virtues: shrewd sense, generosity, patience and fortitude, and also a strong 'spark' yet unkindled" (*Letters*, 365 #281). Bilbo is tutored by Gandalf, who in turn is tutored by Nienna: "Wisest of the Maiar was Olórion [Gandalf]. He too dwelt in Lórien, but his ways took him often to the house of Nienna, and of her he learned pity and patience" (*S*, 30–31). Behind the hero of *LotR* is Nienna, a *katechon*. Nienna's long line of pupils ends with Sam. Tolkien's stories, he relays, are not about types, "but about the achievements of specially graced and gifted individuals. I would say, if saying such things did not spoil what it tries to make explicit, 'by ordained individuals, inspired and guided by an Emissary to ends beyond their individual education and enlargement.' This is

70 Smith, *The Wealth of Nations*, vol. 1, 169.
71 Jones, "Foreword," in *Tolkien: The Forest and the City*, 6.

clear in *The Lord of the Rings.…*" (*Letters*, 365 #281). The decisive Emissary of *LotR* is Nienna, for she is a counter-image of Melkor.

About Melkor: "He had gone often alone into the void places seeking the Imperishable Flame; for desire grew hot within him to bring into Being things of his own, and it seemed to him that Ilúvatar took no thought for the Void, and he was impatient of its emptiness" (*S*, 16). About Nienna: "Mightier than Estë is Nienna, sister of Fëanturi; she dwells alone.… Her halls are west of West, upon the borders of the world; and she comes seldom to the city of Valimar where all is glad.… The windows of her house look outward from the walls of the world" (*S*, 28). Nienna looks on the Void but exercises restraint. She looks on the Void and waits for the mystery of Eru to be revealed. Patience, linked to *patior*, to suffer, makes her a figure of sorrow. Evil is a privation of being, a void, and Nienna looks on the war provoked by Melkor's vanity and bears its wounds. "She is acquainted with grief, and mourns for every wound that Arda has suffered in the marring of Melkor. So great was her sorrow, as the Music unfolded, that her song turned to lamentation long before its end, and the sound of mourning was woven in the themes of the World before it began. But she does not weep for herself.…" (*S*, 29). Sorrow is an original part of the cosmos because war breaks out before it is fully formed. Nienna laments this marring; she does not try to remake the cosmos unblemished. Nienna is the great model of the "posture of distance," a restraint on vanity, because she looks upon privation constantly and yet is steadfast. Like Melkor, she has enormous power to reshape Arda, but, submitting to the mystery of Eru, her "posture of distance"[72] permits only a discreet "intrusion" into Providence. In his epic battle with the Balrog, her greatest pupil, Olórion, remains steadfast—he obeys the "Rules," as Tolkien puts it, and for this very reason a lament sounds in Lothlórien:

---

72 Agamben: "Rather the term *mystērion* indicates a praxis, an action or a drama in the theatrical sense of the term as well, that is, a set of gestures, acts, words through which a divine action or passion is efficaciously actualized in the world and time for the salvation of those who participate in it" (Agamben, *The Mystery of Evil*, 28).

Mithrandir, Mithrandir sang the Elves, *O Pilgrim Grey!* For so they loved to call him. But if Legolas was with the Company, he would not interpret the songs for them, saying that he had not the skill, and that for him the grief was still too near, a matter for tears and not yet for song. (*FR*, 350)

Tolkien did not run from modernity; he sought its correction. Like Nienna, he looked at the void and modernity's apocalyptic rush to fill it. Submitting to God's mystery, which includes the mystery of evil, did not make him resentful, but sorrowful. About wounds he knew plenty—more than most of us could bear to know—and he lamented war.[73] Tolkien saw war as a matter of aesthetics—its hideous arrogance striving against the gladness of dignity's settled order. His art proposed a restraint, a check on the breaking of the ban, not a cancellation or rolling back of historical change. I suspect Darryl Jones is unnerved by apocalyptic politics as much as Tolkien, and may well agree with him more than he knows.

Tory postliberalism is a criticism of counterfeit apocalypticism and, instead of the faux, it waits on orthodox apocalypticism. In the one, the cosmos is upended by the Gnostic Sage, the amped activism of human mentalism, but the other submits to mystery, Gandalf's *sacrificium intellectus* (Voegelin). Of *The Silmarillion*, Tolkien says it ends with a last battle, "with a vision of the end of the world," which owes "more to the Norse vision of Ragnarök than to anything else,

---

73 Given Tolkien's interest in the earth sciences and maps, I think Matthew Dickerson's reading of Tolkien an angelism. Dickerson admits to being stung by a departmental colleague querying his interest in an author who glamorized war. For this reason, I think, he downplays the full scope of war, including its nitty-gritty, in Tolkien in favor of Apocalypticism: "It is not ultimately a war over land or territory, but a war over the hearts of the Children of Ilúvatar. It is, as we saw in the confrontation between Gandalf and the Balrog, a war between Heaven and Hell, between the Secret Fire (the realm of Anor) and the realm of Udûn" (Matthew Dickerson, *Following Gandalf: Epic Battles and Moral Victory in* The Lord of the Rings [Ada, MI: Brazos, 2004], 229). It is certainly right that, for Tolkien, war is cosmic, but it is cosmic in the full sense, right down to the fens and snowdrifts. As Garbowski points out, it is part of the story that its time-signature is set to traveling at the pace of ponies and the tiredness of the Company, made all the worse by the difficulties of terrain and unfamiliar and eerie places (Garbowski, *Recovery and Transcendence for the Contemporary Mythmaker: The Spiritual Dimension in the Works of J. R. R. Tolkien*, 98–99). It is the pace of the infantryman. The problem with Dickerson's line is that he also seems to understate the physicality of the Biblical idea of Apocalyptic evil, which is well explained by John Treloar, SJ, "Tolkien and the Christian Concepts of Evil: Apocalypse and Privation," *Mythlore* 15, no. 2 (1988): 57–58. For a juster appreciation of the physicality of evil in the Christian apocalyptic tradition, see McCarthy's *Blood Meridian*.

though it is not much like it" (*Letters*, 149 #131). In the para-writings of Tolkien's lore, at the end of days, Arda becomes unbroken and the recovered Silmarils are used to resurrect the Two Trees.[74] *The Silmarillion* is very like how Tolkien characterizes his favorite poetry. Of the poetry of the Lancashire Catholic, Francis Thompson: "One must begin with the elfin and delicate and progress to the profound: listen first to the violin and the flute, and then learn to harken to the organ of being's harmony."[75]

There is no end of days in *LotR*. True, with Sauron defeated, Mirkwood becomes Greenwood the Great (*Letters*, 420 #339), but Aragorn's reign begins with "much fighting" (*Letters*, 324 #245). Furthermore, the love story of Arwen and Aragorn repeats the patience of the lives of Nienna and Gandalf. Aragorn, a Dúnedain, is a descendant of the Faithful, a remnant of those Númenóreans who escaped extinction in an apocalypse: the Faithful were spared because they had already suffered persecution for the sake of the gods. In a bleak fracturing, the Númenóreans, inspired by Sauron, turned from God and began to worship Melkor. In their worship, they made human sacrifices of the Faithful. They then compounded these two fractures—against God and their brethren—by a third, launching an amphibious invasion of Valinor, home of the immortal Valar. They did so because impatient for immortality. At the end, Aragorn reverses the trajectory of Númenor: "I am the last of the Númenóreans" (*RK*, 1037). Aragorn means to part this life in the old style of the Númenóreans, with voluntary resignation to death. Arwen pleads with him to tarry longer: "And for all her wisdom and lineage she could not forbear to plead with him to stay yet for a while." Aragorn replies: "'Lady Undómiel,' said Aragorn, 'the hour is indeed hard, yet it was made even in that day when we met under the white birches in the garden of Elrond where none now walk.'" Recalling trees and gardens, Aragorn recommends obedience. Arwen complains about the Doom of Men, but Aragorn, repeating almost

---

74 J. R. R. Tolkien, *The Lost Road and Other Writings*, 333.

75 Garth, *Tolkien and the Great War*, 261.

the words Tolkien uses to describe Gandalf passing the test of obedience, recommends being steadfast and hopeful: "But let us not be overthrown at the final test, who of old renounced the Shadow of the Ring. In sorrow we must go, but not in despair. Behold! We are not bound for ever to the circles of the world, and beyond them is more than memory. Farewell!" (*RK*, 1038). Sorrow is the lot of Arwen: "But Arwen became as a mortal woman, and yet it was not her lot to die until all that she had gained was lost" (*RK*, 1037). Rule, obedience, sorrow, patience, are all here, and there is something else: war and beauty, too. As Aragorn falls into the sleep of the dead:

> Then a great beauty was revealed in him, so that all who after came there looked on him in wonder; for they saw that the grace of his youth, and the valour of his manhood, and the wisdom and majesty of his age were blended together. And long there he lay, an image of the splendour of the Kings of Men in glory undimmed before the breaking of the world. (*RK*, 1038)

Aragorn's obedience to the Ban of Eru is itself an apocalypse: a revelation of monarchical cosmic order "before the breaking of the world."

This revelation is intimated by Arwen's battle standard and, more forcefully, by the grave of a different king. The great Rohan king, Helm, who preserved the Rohirrim in Helm's Deep at a moment of crisis, is laid in a barrow: "Ever after the white *simbelmynë* grew there most thickly, so that the mound seemed to be snow-clad" (*RK*, 1041). Przywara remarks that great Christian art merely garlands the spiritual insight of popular and clumsy religious folk art. Great art should not be misunderstood; it cannot adequately approximate God. The art that understands the scope of the distance between our dignity and God's dignity is found in "the way in which village children decorate a rustic shrine with wreathes of wildflowers" (*AE*, 552). The graves of the kings of Rohan—who were never afflicted with the vanity of the far more sophisticated Númenóreans—are bearers of wildflowers. "'Look!' said Gandalf. 'How fair are the bright eyes in the grass! Evermind they are called, *simbelmynë* in this land of Men, for they blossom in all the seasons of the year, and grow where dead men rest. Behold! We are come to the great barrows where the sires of Théoden sleep" (*TT*, 496). Of all of Tolkien's images, it is perhaps the rustic barrows of the sires of Théoden that most compensates for modernity's fracturing fascination with apocalypticism. The graves of the warrior monarchs of the Rohirrim graced by natural gardens convey a people's settled order in harmony with the imperatives of a cosmos exceeding their ken. *In his days shall the righteous flourish; and abundance of peace so long as the moon endureth* (Ps. 72:7).

Bibliography

Adorno, Theodor. *Philosophy of Modern Music*. London: Continuum, 2004.

Agamben, Giorgio. *The Kingdom and the Glory*. Stanford, CA: Stanford University Press, 2011.

———. *The Mystery of Evil: Benedict XVI and the End of Days*. Stanford, CA: Stanford University Press, 2017.

Akers, Matthew. "Distributism in the Shire." *St. Austin Review* (January-February, 2010).

Alfaiz, Nora. "The Preservation of National Unity." In *Baptism of Fire: The Birth of the Modern British Fantastic in World War I*, edited by Janet Brennan Croft, 80–91. Altadena, CA: Mythopoeic Press, 2015.

Aquinas, Thomas. *On Evil*. Oxford: Oxford University Press, 2003.

———. *Summa theologica*. Turin: Marietti, 1900.

———. *Treatise on Law*. Washington, DC: Regnery, 2001.

Arendt, Hannah. *The Human Condition*. Chicago: The University of Chicago Press, 1958.

Armitage, David. "The Elephant and the Whale: Empires of Land and Sea." *Journal for Maritime Research* 9, no. 1 (2007): 23–36.

Artsen, Jan. "Beauty in the Middle Ages: A Forgotten Transcendental?" Lecture delivered at Catholic University of Leuven (1990): https://ecommons.cornell.edu/bitstream/handle/1813/56590/MPAT_1__1159539705_68_97_pdf.pdf?sequence=1&isAllowed=y.

Ashley Cooper, Anthony (Lord Shaftesbury). *Characteristics of Men, Manners, Opinions, Times*. Cambridge: Cambridge University Press, 2003.

Atkins, Jay. "On Tolkien's Presentation of Distributism through the Shire." *Mallorn* 58 (2017): 23–25.

Balibar, Étienne. "Marxism and War." *Radical Philosophy* 160 (March/April 2010): 9–17. https://www.radicalphilosophy.com/wp-content/files_mf/rp160_article1_marxismwar_balibar.pdf.

Barfield, Owen. *Poetic Diction.* New York: Faber and Faber, 1952.

———. *Saving the Appearances: A Study in Idolatry.* New York: Faber & Faber, 1957.

Basney, Lionel. "Myth, History, and Time in *The Lord of the Rings.*" In *Understanding The Lord of the Rings,* edited by Rose A. Zimbardo & Neil D. Isaacs, 183–94. Boston: Houghton Mifflin, 2004.

Bendersky, Joseph. *Carl Schmitt, Theorist for the Reich.* Princeton, NJ: Princeton University Press, 1983.

———. "Carl Schmitt's Path to Nuremberg: A Sixty-Year Reassessment." *Telos: A Quarterly Journal of Politics, Philosophy, Critical Theory, Culture, and the Arts* 139 (2007): 6–34.

Benedict XVI. *Caritas in Veritate* [Encyclical Letter on Charity in Truth]. The Holy See. June 29, 2009.

———. *Regensburg Address.* Lecture given in the Aula Magna of the University of Regensburg, Germany, September 15, 2006.

Benjamin, Walter. *Arcades Project.* Cambridge, MA: Harvard University Press, 2002.

———. "The Work of Art in the Age of Mechanical Reproduction." In *Illuminations,* edited by Hannah Arendt, translated by Harry Zohn from the 1935 essay. New York: Schocken Books, 1969. Massachusetts Institute of Technology. Accessed March 17, 2024. https://web.mit.edu/allanmc/www/benjamin.pdf.

Berghaus, Günter, ed. *International Futurism in Arts and Literature.* Berlin: De Gruyter, 2000.

Bettelheim, Bruno. *The Uses of Enchantment: The Meaning and Importance of Fairy Tales.* New York: Vintage, 1977.

Birzer, Bradley. *J. R. R. Tolkien's Sanctifying Myth.* Wilmington, DE: Intercollegiate Studies Institute, 2009.

Blast 1 (June 20, 1914). https://monoskop.org/images/1/1b/Blast_1.pdf.

Blissett, William. *The Long Conversation: A Memoir of David Jones.* Oxford: Oxford University Press, 1981.

Bloch, Ernest. "A Philosophical View of the Detective Novel." *Discourse* 2 (Summer 1980): 32–51.

Bloom, Harold. *Modern Critical Interpretations: J. R. R. Tolkien's The Lord of the Rings.* New York: Chelsea House Publications, 2000.

Boswell, George. "Tolkien as Littérateur." *The South Central Bulletin* 32, no. 4 (1972): 188–97.

Brogan, Hugh. "Tolkien's Great War." In *Children and Their Books*, edited by Gillian Avery & Julia Briggs, 351–67. Oxford: Oxford University Press, 1990.

Brown, G. R. "Pastoralism and Industrialism in *The Lord of the Rings*." *English Studies in Africa* 19, no. 2 (1976): 83–91.

Bunting, Nancy. "Tolkien's Jungian Views on Language." *Mallorn: The Journal of the Tolkien Society* 57 (Winter 2016): 17–20.

Camacho, Pamina. "Cyclic Cataclysms, Semitic Stereotypes and Religious Reforms: A Classicist's Númenor." In *The Return of the Ring: Proceedings of the Tolkien Society Conference 2012*, vol. 1, edited by Lynn Forest-Hill, 191–206. Edinburgh: Luna Press, 2016.

Camus, Albert. *The Rebel*. New York: Vintage, 2012.

Carpenter, Humphrey. *The Inklings*. Boston: Houghton Mifflin, 1979.

Chaudhary, Ajay, and Raphaële Chappe. "The Supermanagerial *Reich*." Los Angeles Review of Books, November 7, 2016.

Chayka, Kyle. "Welcome to AirSpace: How Silicon Valley Helps Spread the Same Sterile Aesthetic Across the World." *The Verge*, August 3, 2016. Accessed March 17, 2024. https://www.theverge.com/2016/8/3/12325104/airbnb-aesthetic-global-minimalism-startup-gentrification.

Churchill, Winston. *A Roving Commission*. New York: Charles Scribner's Sons, 1930.

Ciabattari, Jane. "Hobbits and Hippies: Tolkien and the Counterculture." *BBC News*, November 19, 2014. https://www.bbc.com/culture/article/20141120-the-hobbits-and-the-hippies.

Cianci, Giovanni. "Futurism and the English Avant-Garde: the Early Pound between Imagism and Vorticism." *Arbeiten Aus Anglistik Und Amerikanistik* 6, no. 1 (1981): 3–39.

Clarke, James. "Tolkien, the Russians and Industrialisation." In *The Return of the Ring: Proceedings of the Tolkien Society Conference 2012*, vol. 2, edited by Lynn Forest-Hill, 111–22. Edinburgh: Luna Press, 2016.

Clausewitz, Carl von. *On War*. Edited by Michael Howard and Peter Paret. Princeton, NJ: Princeton University Press, 1984.

Collins, Robert. "'Ainulindalë': Tolkien's Commitment to an Aesthetic Ontology." *Journal of the Fantastic in the Arts* 11, no. 3 (2000): 257–65.

Cook, George. "Sir Robert Borden, Lloyd George and British Military Policy, 1917–1918." *The Historical Journal* 14, no. 2 (1971): 371–95.

Cooper, Barry. *Paleolithic Politics*. Notre Dame, IN: University of Notre Dame Press, 2019.

Craft, Robert. "The Rite of Spring: Genesis of a Masterpiece." *Perspectives of New Music* 5, no. 1 (1966): 20–36.

Croft, Janet. "The Great War and Tolkien's Memory: An Examination of World War I Themes in *The Hobbit* and *The Lord of the Rings*." *Mythlore* 23, no. 4 (2002): 4–21.

———. "War." In *A Companion to J. R. R. Tolkien*, edited by Stuart D. Lee, 461–72. Hoboken, NJ: Wiley, 2014.

———. *War and the Works of J. R. R. Tolkien*. New York: Praeger, 2004.

Cunningham, Adrian. "Eric Gill and Workers' Control." *New Blackfriars* 63, no. 745/746 (1982): 304–11.

Cunningham, Michael. "In the Shadow of the Tree: A Study of the Motif of the White Tree in the Context of JRR Tolkien's Middle-Earth." *Mallorn* 44 (2006): 3–8.

Curry, Patrick. *Deep Roots in a Time of Frost*. Zollikofen, Bern: Walking Tree Publishers, 2014.

———. *Defending Middle-earth: Tolkien, Myth and Modernity*. London: St. Martin's Press, 1997.

Curzon, George. *Frontiers: The Romanes Lecture*. Oxford: Clarendon Press, 1908.

Dagnino, Jorge. "The Myth of the New Man in Italian Fascist Ideology." *Fascism* 5, no. 2 (2016): 130–48.

d'Arcy, Martin. *The Mind and Heart of Love: A Study in Eros and Agape*. New York: Faber and Faber, 1945.

Dawson, Christopher. "Essay on War." Catholic Culture. 2024. https://www.catholicculture.org/culture/library/view.cfm?recnum=6369.

———. *Progress and Religion*. London: Sheed & Ward, 1936.

Deutscher, Isaac. "Marxism and the New Left." From tape-recorded discussion, 1967. Marxists Internet Archive. n.d. https://www.marxists.org/archive/deutscher/1967/marxism-newleft.htm.

de Vitoria, Francisco. *On Homicide*. Milwaukee, WI: Marquette University Press, 1997.

Dickerson, Matthew. *Following Gandalf: Epic Battles and Moral Victory in* The Lord of the Rings. Ada, MI: Brazos, 2004.

———. "Water, Ecology, and Spirituality in Tolkien's Middle-earth." In *Light Beyond All Shadow*, edited by Paul E. Kerry and Sandra Miesel, 15–32. Madison, NJ: Fairleigh Dickinson University Press, 2011.

Disraeli, Benjamin. *Whigs and Whiggism*. London: John Murray, 1913.

Edney, Matthew. "British military education, mapmaking, and military 'map-mindedness' in the later Enlightenment." *The Cartographic Journal* 31 (1994): 14–20.

Eksteins, Modris. *Rites of Spring: The Great War and the Birth of the Modern Age.* New York: Anchor Books, 1990.

Eliot, T. S. "London Letter." Published in *The Dial* magazine, October 1921. The World. n.d. https://theworld.com/~raparker/exploring/tseliot/works/london-letters/london-letter-1921-10.html.

Ellison, John. "Tolkien's Art." *Mallorn* 30 (1993): 21–28.

Engberg-Pedersen, Anders. *Empire of Chance: The Napoleonic Wars and the Disorder of Things.* Cambridge, MA: Harvard University Press, 2015.

———. *Martial Aesthetics: How War Became an Art Form.* Redwood City, CA: Stanford University Press, 2023.

Evans, Robley. "Tolkien's World-Creation: Degenerative Recurrence." *Mythlore* 14, no.1 (1987): 5–8, 47.

Ferguson, Adam. *An Essay on the History of Civil Society.* Edited by Fania Oz-Salzberger. Cambridge: Cambridge University Press, 1995.

Ferguson, Niall. "How the World Misunderstood Tolkien, the Ultra-Tory." *Daily Telegraph*, December 3, 2021.

Flieger, Verlyn. "Do the Atlantis story and abandon Eriol-Saga." *Tolkien Studies* 1 (2004): 43–68.

———. *Interrupted Music: The Making of Tolkien's Mythology.* Kent, OH: Kent State University Press, 2005: 43–68.

———. "Jewels, Stone, Ring and the Making of Meaning" In *Tolkien in the New Century*, edited by John Wm. Houghton et al., 65–77. Jefferson, NC: McFarland & Co., 2014.

———. *A Question of Time: J. R. R. Tolkien's Road to* Faërie. Kent, OH: Kent State University Press, 1997.

———. *Splintered Light: Logos and Language in Tolkien's World.* Kent, OH: The Kent State University Press, 2002.

———. *There Would Always Be a Fairy Tale: Essays on Tolkien's Middle-earth.* Kent, OH: The Kent State University Press, 2017.

Francis. *Evangelii Gaudium* [Apostolic Exhortation on The Joy of the Gospel]. The Holy See. November 24, 2013.

———. *Laudato Si'* [Encyclical Letter on Care for our Common Home]. The Holy See. May 24, 2015.

Friedman, Barton. "Tolkien and David Jones: The Great War and the War of the Ring." *CLIO: A Journal of Literature, History, and the Philosophy of History* 11, no. 2 (1982): 115–36.

Frye, Northrop. *Spiritus Mundi: Essays on Literature, Myth, and Society.* Bloomington, IN: Indiana University Press, 1976.

Fukuyama, Francis. *The End of History and the Last Man*. New York: Free Press, 2006.

Furedi, Frank. *First World War—Still No End in Sight*. London: Bloomsbury, 2014.

Fussell, Paul. *The Great War and Modern Memory*. Oxford: Oxford University Press, 1975.

Garbowski, Christopher. *Recovery and Transcendence for the Contemporary Mythmaker: The Spiritual Dimension in the Works of J. R. R. Tolkien*. Zollikofen, Bern: Walking Tree Publications, 2004.

Garth, John. "Revenants and Angels: Tolkien, Machen, and Mons." In *"Something Has Gone Crack": New Perspectives on J. R. R. Tolkien in the Great War*, edited by Janet Brennan Croft and Annika Röttinger, 177–202. Zollikofen, Bern: Walking Tree Publications, 2004.

Garth, John. "Sam Gamgee and Tolkien's Batmen." Blog post, February 13, 2014. John Garth. https://johngarth.wordpress.com/2014/02/13/sam-gamgee-and-tolkiens-batmen/.

———. *Tolkien and the Great War: The Threshold of Middle-earth*. Boston: Houghton Mifflin, 2003.

———. *The Worlds of J. R. R. Tolkien*. Princeton, NJ: Princeton University Press, 2020.

Gebhardt, Jürgen. "Editor's Introduction." In *The Collected Works of Eric Voegelin*, vol. 25, *History of Political Ideas*, vol. VII: *The New Order and Last Orientation*, 1–34. Columbia: University of Missouri Press, 1999.

———. "Political Eschatology and Soteriological Nationalism in Nineteenth Century Germany." In *The Promise of History: Essays in Political Philosophy*, edited by Athanasios Moulakis, 51–68. Berlin: De Gruyter, 1985.

Gentile, Emilio. "The Conquest of Modernity: From Modernist Nationalism to Fascism." *Modernism/modernity* 1, no. 3 (1994): 55–87.

———. *The Origins of Fascist Ideology, 1918–1925*. New York: Enigma Books, 2005.

———. "The Reign of the Man Whose Roots Are Cut: Dehumanism and Anti-Christianity in the Futurist Revolution." In *Italian Futurism 1909–1944*, edited by Vivien Greene et al., 170–71. New York: Guggenheim Museum Publications, 2016.

Gill, Eric. "Eric Gill on Designing War Graves (1919)." Drawing Matter. 2024. https://drawingmatter.org/eric-gill-on-designing-war-graves-1919/.

———. *A Holy Tradition of Working*. Herndon, VA: Lindisfarne Press, 1983.

———. *Work & Property*. London: J. M. Dent, 1937.

Glover, W. B. "The Christian Character of Tolkien's Invented World." *Mythlore* 3, no. 2 (1975): 3–8.

Golynets, Sergei. *Ivan Bilibin.* Leningrad: Aurora Art Publishers, 1981.

Gooch, John. *The Plans of War: The General Staff and British Military Strategy, c. 1900–1916.* London: Routledge, 2017.

GoodKnight, Glen. "A Comparison of Cosmological Geography in the works of J. R. R. Tolkien, C. S. Lewis, and Charles Williams." *Mythlore* 1, no. 3 (1969): 18–22.

Gorman, Siobhan. "How Team of Geeks Cracked Spy Trade." *Wall Street Journal,* September 4, 2009.

Griffin, Roger. *Modernism and Fascism.* London: Palgrave, 2007.

Guardini, Romano. *The Church and the Catholic and The Spirit of the Liturgy.* New York: Sheed & Ward, 1940.

Habermas, Jürgen. "What Does Socialism Mean Today? The Rectifying Revolution and the Need for New Thinking on the Left." *New Left Review* 1/183 (1990): 7–18.

Hall, Molly. "Narrating the Missed Encounter with the Loss of a World." In *"Something Has Gone Crack": New Perspectives on J. R. R. Tolkien in the Great War,* edited by Janet Brennan Croft and Annika Röttinger, 239–61. Zollikofen, Bern: Walking Tree Publications, 2004.

Hammond, Wayne, and Christina Scull. *J. R. R. Tolkien, Artist and Illustrator.* Boston: Houghton Mifflin, 1995.

Henderson Staudt, Kathleen. *At the Turn of a Civilization: David Jones and Modern Poetics.* Ann Arbor: The University of Michigan Press, 1994.

Hiley, Margaret. "Stolen Language, Cosmic Models: Myth and Mythology in Tolkien." *Modern Fiction Studies* 50, no. 4 (2004): 838–60.

Hinz, Manfred. "The Future and Catastrophe: The Concept of History in Italian Futurism." In *The Promise of History: Essays in Political Philosophy,* edited by Athanasios Moulakis, 172–204. Berlin: De Gruyter, 1986.

Hoiem, Elizabeth. "World Creation as Colonization: British Imperialism in 'Aldarion and Erendis.'" *Tolkien Studies* 2 (2005): 75–92.

Holden Reid, Brian. "The British Way in Warfare: Liddell Hart's Idea and Its Legacy." *RUSI Journal* 156, no. 6 (2012): 70–76.

Holland, Tom. *Pax: War and Peace in Rome's Golden Age.* New York: Basic Books, 2023.

Holmes, John. "'Inside a Song': Tolkien's Phonaesthetics." In *Middle-earth Minstrel: Essays on Music in Tolkien,* edited by Bradford Lee Eden, 26–46. Jefferson, NC: McFarland & Co., 2010.

Homans, George. *English Villagers of the Thirteenth Century.* London: Russell & Russell, 1960.

Hoskins, W. G. *The Midland Peasant*. New York: St. Martin's Press, 1957.

Howard, Michael. *The British Way in Warfare: A Reappraisal*. Neale Lecture in English History, vol. 5. London: Jonathan Cape, 1974.

Huizinga, Johan. *Homo Ludens*. Boston: The Beacon Press, 1955.

Hume, David. *Essays: Moral, Political, and Literary*. Indianapolis: Liberty Fund, 1987.

———. *An Inquiry concerning the Principles of Morals*. Oxford: Oxford University Press, 2004.

———. *A Treatise of Human Nature*. Oxford: Oxford University Press, 2011.

Huttar, Charles. "Hell and The City: Tolkien and the Traditions of Western Literature." In *A Tolkien Compass*, edited by Jared Lobdell, 126–55. Chicago: Open Court, 2003.

Hynes, Gerard. "'Beneath the Earth's Dark Keel': Tolkien and Geology." *Tolkien Studies* 9 (2012): 21–36.

ISI Archive. "Christopher Dawson on Conservatism (1932)." Intercollegiate Studies Institute. October 8, 2014. https://isi.org/intercollegiate-review/christopher-dawson-on-conservatism-1932/.

Irving Mitchell, Philip. "'Legend and History Have Met and Fused': The Interlocution of Anthropology, Historiography, and Incarnation in J. R. R. Tolkien's 'On Fairy-stories.'" *Tolkien Studies* 8 (2011): 1–21.

Jackson, Aaron. "Authoring the Century: J. R. R. Tolkien, the Great War and Modernism." *English* 59, no. 224 (2010): 44–69.

Jones, Darryl. "Foreword." In *Tolkien: The Forest and the City*, edited by Helen Conrad-O'Briain and Gerard Hynes, 5–6. Dublin: Four Courts Press, 2013.

Jones, David. "Art in Relation to War." In *The Dying Gaul and Other Writings*, edited by Harman Grisewood, 123–66. New York: Faber & Faber, 1978.

———. *In Parenthesis*. New York: New York Review Books, 2003.

———. "Notes on the 1930s." In *The Dying Gaul and Other Writings*, 41–50.

Josephson-Storm, Jason. *The Myth of Disenchantment*. Chicago: University of Chicago Press, 2017.

Judd, Walter, and Graham Judd. *Flora of Middle-earth: Plants of J. R. R. Tolkien's Legendarium*. Oxford: Oxford University Press, 2017.

Kane, Douglas. *Arda Reconstructed*. Bethlehem, PA: Lehigh University Press, 2009.

———. "Law and Arda." *Tolkien Studies* 9 (2012): 37–57.

Kaplan, Robert D. *Adriatic: A Concert of Civilizations and the End of the Modern Age*. New York: Random House, 2022.

Kennedy, Elizabeth. *Constitutional Failure: Carl Schmitt in Weimar*. Durham, NC: Duke University Press, 2004.

Kennedy, Paul. *Strategy and Diplomacy 1870–1945*. London: George Allen & Unwin, 1983.

Kilby, Clyde. *Tolkien & The Silmarillion*. Wheaton, IL: Harold Shaw, 1976.

Kolnai, Aurel. "Are There degrees of Ethical Universality?" In *Exploring the World of Human Practice: Readings in and about the Philosophy of Aurel Kolnai*, edited by Zoltán Balázs and Francis Dunlop, 83–93. Budapest: CEU Press, 2004.

Kolnai, Aurel. *Ethics, Value, and Reality*. New Brunswick, NJ: Transaction, 2008.

———. *On Disgust*. Chicago: Open Court, 2004.

———. *Politics, Values, & National Socialism*. New Brunswick, NJ: Transaction, 2013.

———. *Privilege and Liberty and Other Essays in Political Philosophy*. Lanham, MD: Lexington, 1999.

———. *The War against the West*. London: Viking Press, 1938.

Lacan, Jacques. *Écrits*, translated by Bruce Fink. New York: W. W. Norton, 2006.

Lacoste, Yves. "Geography, Geopolitics, and Geographical Reasoning." *Hérodote* 146, no. 3 (2012): 14–44.

Larsen, Kristine. "Medieval Organicism or Modern Feminist Science? Bombadil, Elves, and Mother Nature." In *Tolkien and Alterity*, edited by Christopher Vaccaro and Yvette Kisor, 95–108. London: Palgrave, 2017.

Lee, Stuart. "'Tolkien in Oxford' (BBC, 1968): A Reconstruction." *Tolkien Studies* 15 (2018): 115–76.

Lee Eden, Bradford. "The 'Music of the Spheres': Relationships between Tolkien's *The Silmarillion* and Medieval Cosmological and Religious Theory." In *Tolkien the Medievalist*, edited by Jane Chance, 183–93. London: Routledge, 2003.

———. "Strains of Elvish Song and Voices: Victorian Medievalism, Music, and Tolkien." In *Middle-earth Minstrel: Essays on Music in Tolkien*, edited by Bradford Lee Eden, 85–101. Jefferson, NC: McFarland & Co., 2010.

Leibniz, G. W. *Political Writings*. Edited by Patrick Riley. Cambridge: Cambridge University Press, 1996.

Leveque, James. "Futurism's First War: Apocalyptic Space in F. T. Marinetti's Writings from Tripoli." *Romance Notes* 55, no. 3 (2015): 425–37.

Liddell Hart, B. H. *The British Way in Warfare*. London: Penguin, 1942.

———. *Strategy: The Indirect Approach*. New York: Faber & Faber, 1954.

Lista, Giovanni. "Futurist Music." In *Italian Futurism 1909–1944*, edited by Vivien Greene et al., 116–19. New York: Guggenheim Museum Publications, 2016.

Lloyd, Paul. "The Role of Warfare and Strategy in *Lord of the Rings.*" *Mythlore* 3, no. 3 (1976): 3–7.

Lothian, James. *The Making and Unmaking of the English Catholic Intellectual Community, 1910–1950.* Notre Dame: University of Notre Dame Press, 2009.

MacCauley, Brea. "A Cross-cultural Perspective on Upper Paleolithic Hand Images with Missing Phalanges." *Journal of Paleolithic Archaeology* 1, no. 4 (2018): 314–33.

Mackinder, Halford. "The Geographical Pivot of History." *The Geographical Journal* 170, no. 4 (December 2004).

———. *The World War and After.* London: George Philip & Son, 1924.

MacMillan, Margaret. *War: How Conflict Shaped Us.* New York: Random House, 2020.

Malice, Michael, ed. *The Anarchist Handbook.* N. p.: Amazon, 2021.

Manent, Pierre. *A World beyond Politics?* Princeton, NJ: Princeton University Press, 2006.

Marchiò, Roberto. "The Vortex in the Machine: Futurism in England." In *International Futurism in Arts and Literature,* edited by Günter Berghaus, 100–121. Berlin: De Gruyter, 2012.

Marinetti, Filippo. "Let's Murder the Moonlight." In *Futurism: An Anthology,* edited by Lawrence Rainey et al., 54–61. New Haven, CT: Yale, 2009.

———. "The New Religion—Morality of Speed." In *Futurism: An Anthology,* edited by Lawrence Rainey et al., 94–96. New Haven: Yale, 2009.

McAleer, Graham James. "Camus and the Crisis of the West." *Law & Liberty,* August 18, 2023.

———. "Catholic Ideas of War: Why Did Carl Schmitt Reject Natural Law?" *Touro Law Journal* 30, no. 1 (2014): 65–76.

———. *Ecstatic Morality and Sexual Politics.* New York: Fordham University Press, 2005.

———. *Erich Przywara and Postmodern Natural Law.* Notre Dame: University of Notre Dame Press, 2019.

———. "Nazi Sexual Politics: Aurel Kolnai and the Threat of Reprimitivism." In *Aurel Kolnai's The War Against the West Reconsidered,* edited by Wolfgang Bialas, 155–66. London: Routledge, 2019.

———. *To Kill Another: Homicide and Natural Law.* London: Routledge, 2012.

———. "Witness for the Self: *Miranda v. Arizona's* Political Theology." *Touro Law Review* 36, no. 4 (2021): 1079–95.

McAleer, Graham James, and Alexander S. Rosenthal-Pubul. *The Wisdom of Our Ancestors: Conservative Humanism and the Western Tradition*. Notre Dame, IN: University of Notre Dame Press, 2023.

McCarthy, Cormac. *Blood Meridian*. New York: Vintage, 1985.

McIntosh, Jonathan. *The Flame Imperishable: Tolkien, St. Thomas, and the Metaphysics of Faerie*. Brooklyn, NY: Angelico Press, 2017.

McNabb, Vincent. *The Church and the Land*. Norfolk, VA: IHS Press, 2003.

———. *Nazareth or Social Chaos*. Norfolk, VA: IHS Press, 2010.

Mearsheimer, John. *Liddell Hart and the Weight of History*. Ithaca, NY: Cornell University Press, 1988.

———. *The Tragedy of Great Power Politics*. New York: W. W. Norton, 2014.

Mehring, Reinhard. *Carl Schmitt: A Biography*. Cambridge: Polity, 2014.

Miller, William. *An Eye for an Eye*. Cambridge: Cambridge University Press, 2007.

Mitchell, Philip Irving. "Conceptions of the Pastoral in *The Fellowship of the Ring*." In *Approaches to Teaching Tolkien's* The Lord of the Rings *and Other Writings*, edited by Leslie A. Donovan, 108–13. New York: The Modern Language Association of America, 2015.

———. *The Shared Witness of C. S. Lewis and Austin Farrer*. Kent, OH: The Kent State University Press, 2021.

Morgan, Joseph. "Nature, Weber, and a Revision of the French Sublime." *Síneri Revista de Musicología* 15 (2014): 1–34.

Morris, Ian. *Geography is Destiny. Britain and the World: A 10,000-Year History*. New York: Farrar, Straus and Giroux, 2022.

———. *War! What Is It Good For?* New York: Farrar, Straus and Giroux, 2014.

Mortimer, Patchen. "Tolkien and Modernism." *Tolkien Studies* 2 (2005): 113–29.

Naveh, Reuven. "The Ainulindale and Tolkien's Approach to Modernity." In *The Return of the Ring: Proceedings of the Tolkien Society Conference 2012*, vol. 2, edited by Lynn Forest-Hill, 29–52. Edinburgh: Luna Press, 2016.

Nemo, Philippe. *What Is the West?* Pittsburgh: Duquesne University Press, 2005.

North, Michael. *The Political Aesthetic of Yeats, Eliot, and Pound*. Cambridge: Cambridge University Press, 1991.

Nyíri, J. C. "Wittgenstein's Later Work in Relation to Conservatism." In *Wittgenstein and His Times*, edited by Brian McGuiness, 44–68. Chicago: University of Chicago Press, 1982.

Ordway, Holly. *Tolkien's Modern Reading: Middle-earth Beyond the Middle Ages*. Washington, DC: Word on Fire Academic, 2021.

Organ, Michael. "Tolkien's Japonisme: Prints, Dragons, and a Great Wave." *Tolkien Studies* 10 (2013): 105–22.

Panzera, Lisa. "Celestial Futurism and the 'Parasurreal.'" In *Italian Futurism 1909–1944*, edited by Vivien Greene et al., 326–29. New York: Guggenheim Museum Publications, 2016.

Pascal, Blaise. *Pensées*. New York: Penguin, 1995.

Pearce, Joseph. *Frodo's Journey: Discover the Hidden Meaning of the Lord of the Rings*. N.p.: St. Benedict's Press, 2015.

Pepler, Douglas. *The Devil's Devices*, with illustration by Eric Gill. London: The Hampshire House Workshops, 1915.

Petersen, Erik. *Theological Tractates*. Stanford, CA: Stanford University Press, 2011.

Petraeus, David H., et al. *The U.S. Army/Marine Corps Counterinsurgency Field Manual*. Chicago: University of Chicago Press, 2007.

Phelpstead, Carl. "Tolkien, David Jones, and the God Nodens." Academia. 2013. https://www.academia.edu/21037405/Tolkien_David_Jones_and_the_God_Nodens.

Pius XI. *Divini Redemptoris* [Encyclical Letter on Atheistic Communism]. The Holy See. March 19, 1937.

Polk, Nicholas. "The Holy Fellowship: Holiness in *The Lord of the Rings*." *Mallorn: The Journal of the Tolkien Society* 57 (2016): 29–31.

Postrel, Virginia. *Fabric of Civilization*. New York: Basic Books, 2020.

Potts, Michael. "'Evening-Lands': Spenglerian Tropes in *Lord of the Rings*." *Tolkien Studies* 13 (2016): 149–68.

Price, Neil. *Children of Ash and Elm: A History of the Vikings*. New York: Basic Books, 2020.

Prince of Wales, HRH. *Harmony: A New Way of Looking at Our World*. London: HarperCollins, 2010.

———. *Highgrove: An English Country Garden* New York: Rizzoli, 2015.

———. "An Introduction from His Royal Highness the Prince of Wales." Sacred Web Conference, Myer Horowitz Theatre, University of Alberta, Edmonton, Alberta. September 23 and 24, 2006. http://www.sacredweb.com/conference06/conference_introduction.html.

Przywara, Erich. *Analogia Entis*. Grand Rapids, MI: Eerdmans, 2014.

Ratzinger, Joseph. *Christianity and the Crisis of Cultures*. San Francisco: Ignatius, 2006.

———. *Truth and Tolerance*. San Francisco: Ignatius, 2003.

———. *Values in a Time of Upheaval*. New York: Crossroad, 2006.

Ross, Steven. "Blue Water Strategy Revisited." *Naval War College Review* 30, no. 4 (1978): 35–47.

Rossbach, Stefan. *Gnostic Wars: The Cold War in the Context of a History of Western Spirituality*. Edinburgh: Edinburgh University Press, 1999.

Ruskin, John. *Unto This Last and Other Writings*. London: Penguin, 1985.

Sayer, George. "Recollections of J. R. R. Tolkien." In *Tolkien: A Celebration*, edited by Joseph Pearce, 1–16. San Francisco: Ignatius, 2001.

Scheler, Max. *Eternal in Man*. New Brunswick, NJ: Transaction, 2010.

———. *Formalism in Ethics and a Non-Formal Ethics of Value*. Evanston, IL: Northwestern University Press, 1973.

———. *Nature of Sympathy*. New Brunswick, NJ: Transaction, 2008.

Schmitt, Carl. *The Concept of the Political*. Chicago: University of Chicago Press, 2007.

———. *Land and Sea*. Candor, NY: Telos Press, 2015.

———. *The Nomos of the Earth*. Candor, NY: Telos Press, 2003.

———. *Political Romanticism*. New Brunswick, NJ: Transaction, 2011.

———. *Tyranny of Values*. Candor, NY: Telos Press, 2018.

———. *Writings on War*. Cambridge: Polity, 2011.

Schürer, Norbet. "The Shape of Water in J. R. R. Tolkien's *The Lord of the Rings*." *Mythlore* 40, no. 1 (2021): 21–41.

Scruton, Roger. *England: An Elegy*. London: Chatto & Windus, 2000.

———. "Why I Became a Conservative." *The New Criterion*, February 2003.

Seymour, Jessica. "Nature and Beauty in the Hearts of Dwarves." In *Representations of Nature in Middle-Earth*, edited by Martin Simonson, 27–49. Zollikofen, Bern: Walking Tree Publishers, 2015.

Shippey, Thomas. *J. R. R. Tolkien: Author of the Century*. Boston: Houghton Mifflin, 2000.

———. "Tolkien as a Post-War Writer." *Mythlore* 21, no. 2 (1996): 84–93.

———, and John Bourne. "A Steep Learning Curve: Tolkien and the British Army on the Somme." In *"Something Has Gone Crack": New Perspectives on J. R. R. Tolkien in the Great War*, edited by Janet Brennan Croft and Annika Röttinger, 3–25. Zollikofen, Bern: Walking Trees Publishers, 2019.

Smith, Adam. *An Inquiry into the Nature and Causes of the Wealth of Nations*. Indianapolis: Liberty Fund, 1982.

———. *Lectures on Jurisprudence*. Indianapolis: Liberty Fund, 1982.

———. *The Theory of Moral Sentiments*. Indianapolis: Liberty Fund, 1994.

Smith, Murray. "Legal Bother: Law and Related Matters in *The Hobbit*." In *The Return of the Ring: Proceedings of the Tolkien Society Conference 2012*, vol. 2, edited by Lynn Forest-Hill, 123–42. Edinburgh: Luna Press, 2016.

Smith, Ross. "Fitting Sense to Sound: Linguistic Aesthetics and Phonosemantics in the Work of J. R. R. Tolkien." *Tolkien Studies* 3 (2006): 1–20.

Staudt, Henderson. *At the Turn of a Civilization: David Jones and Modern Poetics*. Ann Arbor: The University of Michigan Press, 1994.

Stein, George. *The Waffen SS: Hitler's Elite Guard at War, 1939–1945*. Ithaca, NY: Cornell University Press, 1966.

Stevenson, Shandi. "Beyond the Circles of this World: The Great War, Time, History, and Eternity in the Fantasy of J. R. R. Tolkien and C. S. Lewis." In *Baptism of Fire: The Birth of the Modern British Fantastic in World War I*, edited by Janet Brennan Croft, 110–30. Altadena, CA: Mythopoeic Press, 2015.

Stuart, Joseph T. *Christopher Dawson: A Cultural Mind in the Age of the Great War*. Washington, DC: The Catholic University of America Press, 2022.

Suárez, Francisco. *On Real Relation: Disputatio Metaphysica XLVII*. Milwaukee, WI: Marquette University Press, 2006.

Thayer, Anna. "A Tolkienian Vision of War." In *The Return of the Ring: Proceedings of the Tolkien Society Conference 2012*, vol. 1, edited by Lynn Forest-Hill, 85–97. Edinburgh: Luna Press, 2016.

Thompson, Susan. "Futurism, Fascism, and Mino Somenzi's Journals of the 1930s: *Futurismo*, *Sant'Elia*, and *Artecrazia*." In *Italian Futurism 1909–1944: Reconstructing the Universe*, edited by Vivien Greene, 256–59. New York: Guggenheim Museum, 2014.

Tolkien, J. R. R. *Beren and Lúthien*. Boston: Houghton Mifflin, 2018.

———. *The Fellowship of the Ring*. Boston: Houghton Mifflin, 1994.

———. *The Hobbit*. London: HarperCollins, 1996.

———. *The Letters of J. R. R. Tolkien*. Boston: Houghton Mifflin, 2000.

———. *The Letters of J. R. R. Tolkien: Revised and Expanded Edition*. Edited by Humphrey Carpenter and Christopher Tolkien. New York: HarperCollins, 2023.

———. *The Lost Road and Other Writings*. Edited by Christopher Tolkien. Boston: Houghton Mifflin, 1987.

———. *Morgoth's Ring: The Later Silmarillion*. Edited by Christopher Tolkien. Boston: Houghton Mifflin, 1993.

———. "Mythopoeia." Accessed March 17, 2024. http://vrici.lojban.org/~cowan/mythopoeia.html.

——. *The Nature of Middle-earth*. Edited by Carl Hostetter. Boston: Houghton Mifflin, 2021.

——. *The Peoples of Middle-earth*. Edited by Christopher Tolkien. Boston: Houghton Mifflin, 1996.

——. *Pictures by J. R. R. Tolkien*. New York: HarperCollins, 2021.

——. *The Return of the King*. Boston: Houghton Mifflin, 1994.

——. *The Silmarillion*. Boston: Houghton Mifflin, 2001.

——. *The Tale of the Children of Húrin*. Boston: Houghton Mifflin, 2007.

——. "Tolkien on Fairy Stories." Calvary Georgetown Divide (website). October 2018. https://coolcalvary.files.wordpress.com/2018/10/on-fairy-stories1.pdf.

——. *Tolkien on Fairy Stories*. Edited by Verlyn Flieger and Douglas A. Anderson. New York: HarperCollins, 2008.

——. *The Two Towers*. Boston: Houghton Mifflin, 1994.

——. *Unfinished Tales*. New York: Ballantine, 1980.

Tolkien, John, and Priscilla Tolkien. *The Tolkien Family Album*. Boston: Houghton Mifflin, 1992.

Tönnies, Ferdinand. *Community and Civil Society*. Cambridge: Cambridge University Press, 2001.

Treloar, John. "Tolkien and the Christian Concepts of Evil: Apocalypse and Privation." *Mythlore* 15, no. 2 (1988): 24–31.

Ward, Elizabeth. *David Jones Myth Maker*. Manchester: Manchester University Press, 1983.

Wees, William. "Ezra Pound as a Vorticist." *Wisconsin Studies in Contemporary Literature* 6, no. 1 (1965): 56–72.

White, Michael. *J. R. R. Tolkien*. Indianapolis: Alpha, 2002.

Williams, Raymond. *Culture and Society: 1780–1950*. New York: Columbia University Press, 1983.

Witt, Jonathan, and Jay Richards. *The Hobbit Party*. San Francisco: Ignatius, 2014.

Wood, Ralph. "Tolkien and Postmodernism." In *Tolkien among the Moderns*, edited by Ralph C. Wood, 247–77. Notre Dame, IN: University of Notre Dame Press, 2015.

Veldman, Meredith. *Fantasy, the Bomb, and the Greening of Britain: Romantic Protest, 1945–1980*. Cambridge: Cambridge University Press, 1994.

Vernon, Richard. "Auguste Comte and the Withering-Away of the State." *Journal of the History of Ideas* 45, no. 4 (1984): 549–66.

Voegelin, Eric. *Anamnesis*. Notre Dame, IN: University of Notre Dame Press, 1978.

———. "Christianity's Decisive Difference." A letter to Alfred Shutz, January 1, 1953. *Voegelin View* (January 1, 2015).

———. *The Collected Works of Eric Voegelin*. Vol. 12, Published Essays: 1966–1985. Baton Rouge: Louisiana State University Press, 1990.

———. *The Collected Works of Eric Voegelin*. Vol. 17, *The Ecumenic Age, Vol. IV: Order and History*. Baton Rouge: Louisiana State University Press, 1990.

———. *The Collected Works of Eric Voegelin*. Vol. 22, *History of Political Ideas, Volume IV: Renaissance and Reformation*. Columbia: University of Missouri Press, 1998.

———. *The Collected Works of Eric Voegelin*. Vol. 28, *What Is History? and Other Late Unpublished Writings*, edited by Paul Caringella and Thomas A. Hollweck. Baton Rouge: Louisiana State University Press, 1990.

———. *The Collected Works of Eric Voegelin*. Vol. 30, *Selected Correspondence 1950–1984*. Columbia: University of Missouri Press, 2007.

———. *The Collected Works of Eric Voegelin*. Vol. 33, *The Drama of Humanity and other Miscellaneous Papers, 1939–1985*. Columbia: University of Missouri Press, 2004.

———. "Industrial Society in Search of Reason." In *World Technology and Human Destiny*, edited by Raymond Aron et al., 31–46, 169–73, 214–15, 221–28, 230–33. Ann Arbor: University of Michigan Press, 1963.

———. *The New Science of Politics*. Chicago: The University of Chicago Press, 1966.

———. "Nietzsche, the Crisis and the War." *The Journal of Politics* 6, no. 2 (1944): 177–212.

———. *Order and History*. Vol. I, *Israel and Revelation*. Baton Rouge: Louisiana State University Press, 2001.

———. *Science, Politics and Gnosticism*. Wilmington, DE: Intercollegiate Studies Institute, 2004.

Ware, Gemma, and Daniel Merino. "Keep buildings cool as it gets hotter by resurrecting traditional architectural techniques—podcast." The Conversation. September 15, 2022. https://theconversation.com/keep-buildings-cool-as-it-gets-hotter-by-resurrecting-traditional-architectural-techniques-podcast-190384.

Wilkin, Peter. *Tory Anarchism*. Faringdon, Oxfordshire: Libri, 2010.

Williams, Hamish. "Tolkien's Thalassocracy and Ancient Greek Seafaring." *Tolkien Studies* 17 (2020): 137–62.

Williamson, Samuel. *The Politics of Grand Strategy: Britain and France Prepare for War, 1904–1914*. Cambridge, MA: Harvard University Press, 1969.

Wojtyła, Karol. *Person and Community*. New York: Peter Lang, 1993.

Vaninskaya, Anna. "Tolkien: A Man of His Time?" In *Tolkien and Modernity*, vol. 1, edited by Frank Weinreich and Thomas Honegger, 1–30. Zollikofen, Bern: Walking Tree Publishers, 2006.

Zaleski, Philip, and Carol Zaleski. *The Fellowship: The Literary Lives of the Inklings*. New York: Farrar, Straus and Giroux, 2015.

Žižek, Slavoy. "Ukraine's Tale of Two Colonizations." Project Syndicate. August 30, 2022. https://www.project-syndicate.org/commentary/ukraine-russian-occupation-or-western-neoliberal-colonization-by-slavoj-zizek-2022-08.

Index

Also from
The Catholic University of America Press

The Fantasy of J. R. R. Tolkien:
Mythopoeia and the Recovery of Creation
by Robert J. Dobie; Foreword by Bradley J. Birzer

Catholic Modernism and the Irish "Avant-Garde":
The Achievement of Brian Coffey, Denis Devlin,
and Thomas MacGreevy
by James Matthew Wilson

Acts of Faith and Imagination:
Theological Patterns in Catholic Fiction
by Brent Little; Foreword by Mark Bosco, SJ

Shakespeare and the Idea of Western Civilization
by R. V. Young

Christian Humanism in Shakespeare:
A Study in Religion and Literature
by Lee Oser

Justice after War:
Jus Post Bellum *in the 21st Century*
by David Chiwon Kwon; Foreword by Kenneth R. Himes, OFM

Just War:
Principles and Cases, second edition
by Richard J. Regan

The Third Spring:
G.K. Chesterton, Graham Greene,
Christopher Dawson, and David Jones
by Adam Schwartz

Faithful Fictions:
The Catholic Novel in British Literature, second edition
by Thomas Woodman